THE 60-MINUTE BREAD BOOK
and other fast-yeast recipes you can make in ½ the usual time

THE 60-MINUTE BREAD BOOK

and other fast-yeast recipes you can make in ½ the usual time

◆   ◆   ◆

NANCY BAGGETT

Illustrated by Linda Tunney

◆

G. P. PUTNAM'S SONS
NEW YORK

To Roc, for steadfast support and love along the way, and
in memory of my mother, who taught me to bake bread when I was seven.

Heartfelt thanks go to the following:
To illustrator Linda Tunney for working so tirelessly and for drawing such beautiful bread. To the Kansas Wheat Commission for information and permission to adapt two of its recipes, Super-Nutritious Bran Bread and Hard Rolls. To Sally Churgai and Gary Hunt, who helped develop and test a number of recipes, and Kathy Ward, who tested and retested endlessly without complaint. To all my workshop friends, who sampled breads, made helpful suggestions and dispensed encouragement, as needed. And most of all, to Linda Hayes for helping and caring every step of the way.

G. P. Putnam's Sons
Publishers Since 1838
200 Madison Avenue
New York, NY 10016

Library of Congress Cataloging in Publication Data

Baggett, Nancy, date. The 60-minute bread book and other fast-yeast recipes you can make in ½ the usual time.

Includes index. 1. Bread. I. Title. II. Title: Sixty-minute bread book and other fast-yeast recipes you can make in ½ the usual time.
TX769.B17 1985   641.8'15   84-24756   ISBN 0-399-13020-9

Printed in the United States of America
2   3   4   5   6   7   8   9   10

❖ CONTENTS ❖

   White Casserole Bread / English Muffin Loaves / Dilly Cottage
   Cheese Pull-Apart Loaves / Easy Garlic Baguettes / Buttermilk-
   Wheat Mini-Loaves / Honey-Butter Bread / Easiest-Ever
   Raisin Bread / Rosemary Casserole Bread / Wheat-Bran Cas-
   serole Breads / Rye and Corn Casserole Bread / Cheese
   and Chives Mini-Loaves / Sesame Bread Sticks / Rye Bread
   Sticks / Crispy Parmesan Flatbread Wedges (or Crispy Nacho
   Flatbread Wedges) / Jiffy Pizzas / Poppy Seed White Rolls /
   Jiffy Rye Finger Rolls / Sour Cream and Onion Rolls / Ched-
   dar Mini-Puffies (or Swiss Cheese Mini-Puffies) / Savory No-
   Knead Rye Puffs / No-Knead Caramel Sticky Buns / Jiffy
   Pecan Sticky Buns / 60-Minute Cinnamon Pinwheels / Iced
   Lemon-Spice Puffies / Apricot Streusel Puffs / Fried Apple-
   Spice Puffs / Toasted Almond Coffee Cakes / Orange Crumb-
   Nut Coffee Cake / Sour Cream and Apple Kuchen / Easy Cin-
   namon Streusel Coffee Cakes / Sour Cherry Crumb Kuchen
   (or Blueberry Crumb Kuchen)

*90-minute-or-less recipes

*90-minute-or-less recipes

*90-minute-or-less recipes

◆ INTRODUCTION ◆

*I*f you love fragrant, fresh-from-the-oven breads, but always wished yeast baking took less time, wish no more! Bread making doesn't have to be the slow, complicated process it once was. Now, thanks to the application of modern technology to the baker's craft, you can turn out a wonderful assortment of buttery rolls, plump loaves, coffee cakes, and sweet buns faster and easier than ever before. In fact, breads that used to require two or three hours or more to complete can now be prepared in one-half to one-third the time—without sacrificing old-fashioned goodness or great taste.

Imagine, for example, the pleasure of sitting down with a plate of bubbly-hot Jiffy Pecan Sticky Buns or Iced Lemon-Spice Puffies—that were mixed up and baked in under an hour! Picture the satisfaction of serving up crusty, warm slabs of oven-fresh Italian bread, or tender, butter-laden Country Fair Butter and Egg Rolls, or slices of wholesome Oats and Honey Loaves that were prepared in less than an hour and a half.

If all this sounds too good to be true, it isn't! The secret is in the new fast-acting yeast, which rises twice as quickly as the conventional type, and a host of modern preparation techniques that simplify and streamline the bread-baking task. For the first time, these two remarkable technological advances are teamed up. The exciting end result is this cookbook: a collection of specially developed recipes for making the fastest and easiest breads ever!

In case you've never used the new, fast-acting yeast now on the

11

market, it's a natural leavening agent and microscopic plant organism, just like the older variety. However, the new strain is a "super" plant developed by genetic engineers for faster, more vigorous growth. It raises dough an amazing 50 percent more quickly than conventional yeast and also makes bread "spring up" more in the oven. Two brands now on the market are RapidRise, a Fleischmann's product, and Quick-Rise, introduced by Red Star.

Just what are some of the special time-saving techniques used in this book along with the "super" yeast? One method involves combining the yeast particles with dry ingredients, then adding warmer-than-normal liquids, which gets the leavening agent off to an extra-fast start. Another involves quickly (but thoroughly) "kneading" dough, using an electric mixer, food processor or blender instead of by hand. This means traditional kneading periods can be entirely omitted in some cases and dramatically reduced in others—while still yielding fine-textured bread.

Yet another time-saver is substituting economical dry milk powder and water for fresh milk. Fresh milk must be scalded to destroy yeast-retarding enzymes, then cooled again before being added to bread doughs. Powdered milk eliminates the need for this step. In some recipes, the bread-making process is shortened by integrating the last stages of rising into the beginning of the baking period, by skipping one rising period altogether, or by taking advantage of the extra "oven spring" and heat tolerance of the new fast-acting yeast, letting the bread finish rising while baking.

Not only does this book contain recipes specifically developed to streamline bread baking, but it's especially convenient to use. For instance, each recipe begins by noting the total time required from start to finish, and concludes with a breakdown of preparation time (including kneading), and rising and baking time. This lets you know at a glance about how long to allow for completing the bread, as well as about how much actual preparation and waiting are involved.

There are many added convenience features. For the cook in a hurry, Part I, 60-Minute Breads, groups together all the ultrafast yeast breads, plus a handy selection of quick breads. And, to make it easy to locate the other quick-to-make recipes in the book, all the 90-minute-or-less breads are starred in the recipe list provided in the contents.

In addition, for the individual with special time constraints and scheduling problems, there's a Make-Ahead, Bake-Ahead Breads chapter that features recipes that can be whipped up and held in the refrigerator for a time before baking, as well as partially baked breads that are frozen, then thawed and briefly popped into the oven before serving. There are also separate chapters on no-knead batter breads; traditional breads; healthful, whole-grain recipes; party and specialty breads; festive sweet breads; and even a collection of recipes designed for quick mixing in the food processor.

When time is available, nothing is more gratifying than the unhurried, traditional method of yeast baking. However, it's no longer necessary to forgo the wonderful flavor of homemade bread just because you don't have all day to make it. With this book, it's easy to turn out some No-Knead Caramel Sticky Buns, festive Apricot-filled Twist Loaves, hearty Toasty Oat and Cornmeal Bread, or any of the other delicious breads and pastries included here, even though you have only an hour, or at most two, to spare. At last, the pleasures of the ancient craft of bread making and the incomparable fresh baked goods that result are accessible to everyone.

◆ BEGINNING WITH THE BASICS ◆

*B*read baking has always been a magical craft. For centuries cooks have been turning the simplest of ingredients—flour, water, yeast, salt, and sometimes sugar—into one of the world's most irresistible, soul-satisfying foods: warm, crusty, aromatic bread.

Up until recently, however, this miraculous transformation of raw materials into wonderful food did require a considerable investment in elbow grease and time. But now, happily, all that has changed. Take a few streamlined techniques; add some new, fast-rising yeast, and a modern appliance or two; and presto! Bread magic can be worked quickly and with ease.

That's what the recipes in this book are all about. They team up an exciting set of technological advances so that—finally—all those people who love fresh, wholesome bread are able to simply and quickly make it at home. If you count yourself among them, this special collection of delicious recipes is for you.

Following are the basics on how to use the recipes to best advantage. So, although you're probably eager to get started working your own bread magic, it's a good idea to read through this chapter first.

ABOUT THE RECIPES

As you look through the chapters, you may notice that the recipes differ somewhat from those in older cookbooks. And they are markedly different from the "receipts" our grandmothers used. This is because bread baking has changed quite a bit since our grandmothers' (and even our mothers') day.

15

For example, the old-fashioned method of dissolving yeast in warm water and waiting a few minutes (proofing) before combining it with other ingredients is never employed in *The 60-Minute Bread Book*. Instead, the yeast is stirred directly into a portion of the dry ingredients, then immediately mixed with hot liquids.

Of course, the older, "conventional" method previous generations of cooks used still works. But modern technology makes it possible to do things a faster and easier way. Specifically, the quicker, dry-mix method can be substituted because present-day commercial yeast comes in such fine, easily dissolvable particles and is so reliable that proofing is no longer necessary. (I have baked hundreds upon hundreds of loaves of bread with the new fast-acting dry yeast and have never had a package fail.)

Kneading is another basic procedure that has been modified and streamlined in this volume. In every single recipe, part or all of the kneading (or gluten-developing process) is completed by machine—either a mixer, food processor or a blender. These appliances make quick work of a bread-preparation task that once could only be completed with a lot of physical effort. And all these kitchen machines "knead" just as thoroughly and effectively as human hands—even experienced ones like Grandmother's!

To assure you of good results with the new techniques, recipe directions are always detailed and explicit. For example, they specify a temperature range for liquid ingredients and tell you how long and at what temperature doughs should be set aside to rest or rise. This ensures that the yeast organisms are in just the right environment—warm enough so that they grow vigorously and raise the bread but not so hot that they are killed. Detailed instructions also allow enough time—but no extra—for rising and other preparation stages. By following all directions carefully you will be assured, not only of a successful product, but of preparing it the simplest, most efficient way.

THE NEW YEAST

There are two brands of fast-acting yeast on the market—RapidRise from Fleischmann's and Quick-Rise yeast from Red Star. Some additional recipe modifications reflect the fact that although these two products taste like regular yeast, they do have certain characteristics of their own.

First, of course, the new yeast does work a lot faster, and as a result, rising times in some recipes may seem incredibly short.

"Super" yeast has some other less obvious unique traits as well. For example, it likes a slightly warmer growing climate than the old strain. This means that doughs can now be mixed up and allowed to rise in a warmer spot without developing a strong yeasty taste.

In addition, the fast-acting yeast also tolerates higher temperatures and lives longer once bread is put in to bake. Consequently, in most recipes, dough no longer needs to double in bulk prior to baking, because a good deal of additional rising, or "oven spring," will occur in the oven before the yeast is killed off. (One sign of this added oven spring is an occasional slight cracking along the top sides of finished loaves.)

EQUIPMENT NEEDED

The large majority of recipes in this book are designed to be prepared with an electric mixer. Additionally, a few call for the use of a blender. And one chapter is devoted to food-processor breads.

Electric-mixer recipes have been carefully developed to work with almost any machine. A heavy-duty model isn't necessary. (To make sure, a number of the recipes were tested using an inexpensive, lightweight mixer.) It isn't even essential to have a stand model, although the latter does make the job faster because you can get on with other tasks while it operates.

Likewise, food-processor and blender recipes are designed to work with a wide range of standard machines. You don't need a heavy-duty or fancy model for the job.

Another piece of equipment needed is a candy or cooking/deep-frying thermometer. It is possible to prepare recipes in this book without one, but this is not recommended. Gauging the temperature of ingredients is important in yeast baking and a thermometer is the only completely reliable way. (To "guesstimate" temperature when a thermometer is unavailable, note that at 125° to 130° water feels fairly hot to the touch but not scalding to most people.)

Additionally, it's helpful but not essential to have a kitchen timer. It's the best way to remind yourself at the end of rising and baking periods.

PANS AND PAN SIZES

The pans and pan sizes called for in each recipe indicate what was used in its testing. However, there is a surprisingly varied assortment of bread pans and baking sheets on the market, and for most recipes several different dimensions will work just as well. "Standard" medium-sized "cookie" sheets (baking sheets) range from 15

× 10 inches, to 14 × 10 inches, to 15¼ × 10¼ inches, for example, and these can be used more or less interchangeably.

Likewise, with loaf and casserole breads, your container doesn't have to have the precise dimensions given so long as it holds about the same amount. This is why volume requirements, such as 1 quart, 2 quart, etc., are always indicated along with pan sizes. Use them as a guide when dimensions don't match up. (It's easy to check volume by seeing how many cups of water a container holds.)

To complicate the question of pan dimensions, "standard" ovens come in several sizes, too. As a result, in a few instances you may find that even though a recipe calls for several pans of bread to be baked at once, they won't fit together on the same rack. In this case, place the pans, staggered, on two separate racks; then swap positions halfway through to ensure even baking.

TIME ESTIMATIONS

A unique convenience feature of *The 60-Minute Bread Book* is that it indicates about how much time recipes will take from start to finish and breaks down individual preparation, and rising/baking times. (If you take the trouble to do a little math, you will often discover that the total Start-to-Finish time provided at the head of each recipe is less than the total of the individual time segments given at the bottom. This is because in many cases some preparation is taking place simultaneously with rising or baking.)

Keep in mind that all time estimates are approximate, to be used only as a general guide. They can't take into account time taken by interruptions—and most home cooks have plenty of these. Nor do they count minutes wasted searching for misplaced ingredients or equipment. Other unpredictable factors include varying methods of preparing certain ingredients: Are the nuts in a recipe chopped by hand, with a food processor, or purchased ready to use, for example?

However, the figures given are based on the average length of time several different testers in different kitchens required. As a rule, if you are a very well-organized, speedy worker, you will take less time than that indicated. If you're very methodical, or tired, or a beginning baker, you'll take a little more.

Baking times, too, may vary a bit from stove to stove. However, if your breads consistently take more or less time than recipes in the book specify, try checking thermostat accuracy with an oven thermometer. Many ovens are consistently off by 25° to 50°. Another more unusual possibility is that your timer is inaccurate. I've had one that regularly sounded after 23 minutes had passed even though it was set to 30!

ACHIEVING THE "HOTHOUSE" ENVIRONMENT

A great many of the recipes in this book include the instruction to "set dough aside in a very warm spot (80° to 90°) to rise." Assuming that you're not baking on a hot summer day, there are several ways to provide this optimum environment for the yeast in your bread. If you have a gas stove, set the bread bowl near, but not directly over, the pilot light. Another possibility is to place it near a heat vent or radiator. Or, if the house is quite cold and drafty, turn the oven on to low and let it warm up for about a minute; then turn it off and put the dough inside to rise. Still another approach is to wrap the bowl with a thick towel and place it on a heating pad turned to the lowest setting.

INGREDIENTS

The emphasis in this book is on readily obtainable ingredients, since they make the recipes most convenient to use. All of the white breads can be successfully prepared with all-purpose white or un-bleached flour. The all-purpose brands of whole-wheat flour and medium rye flour normally stocked in supermarkets will yield good results in recipes that call for these. (Of course, if you have access to very fresh flours ground by a local miller, your breads will be better still!)

Here is a quick explanation of these and other types of flours and grain products frequently called for in this book:

All-purpose white flour—A combination of hard and soft wheat flours from which the darker parts (the bran and germ) of kernels have been removed. The flour is bleached for added whiteness.

Unbleached flour—Also an all-purpose wheat flour from which the dark bran and germ portions have been removed. The flour is nearly as white as all-purpose white flour, even though it is not bleached.

Pastry flour—A low-gluten white wheat flour. It is best suited for making nonyeast (quick) breads, in which gluten development causes toughness.

Whole-wheat flour—Flour resulting when all (or occasionally most) of the wheat kernel is ground. See the introduction to the chapter on whole-grain breads for information on the healthfulness of whole-wheat flour.

Medium rye flour—All-purpose rye flour. The sort usually stocked in supermarkets. It is generally ground medium-fine and is neither too light nor too dark. At least some of the bran and germ are usually removed. Sacks that are ungraded and simply labeled "Rye Flour" are also likely to be medium rye.

Dark rye flour—Rye flour that tends to be darker, slightly coarser and stronger in flavor than medium rye. Depending on the miller, the dark type may or may not be a whole-grain flour.

Cornmeal—Meal ground from either white or yellow corn. Most supermarket brands are "degerminated," meaning the germ has been removed. If whole-grain or "undergerminated" cornmeal is available, choose this instead; it offers nutritional benefits without affecting either the taste or texture of the final product.

Rolled oats—The same oats used to make oatmeal for breakfast. Usually some of the bran and germ are removed before the kernels are processed through, and pressed flat by, huge rollers. Unless otherwise indicated, quick-cooking and old-fashioned rolled oats may be used interchangeably.

In most recipes calling for solid shortening, either butter or margarine may be used. When butter is clearly preferred, this is indicated by placing the alternative in parentheses. All eggs called for are assumed to be graded "large" and honey is assumed to be ordinary clover honey found on grocery-store shelves.

Most recipes containing milk call for instant nonfat dry milk powder and water rather than the fresh form. Not only is powdered milk more economical and lower in fat, but it's easier to keep on hand; and it's more convenient for bread baking because, unlike fresh milk, it doesn't have to be scalded first to destroy yeast-retarding enzymes.

BREAD-MAKING TIPS

Here are some specific tips to ensure bread-making success with *The 60-Minute Bread Book.* Even if you're a veteran baker, it's a good idea to look over the suggestions. And if you're new to the baker's craft, they will go far in helping you avoid problems and turn out delicious bread every time you try.

• Start by making sure your yeast is fresh. Check the manufacturer's expiration date stamped on the outside of the packets. "Expired" yeast may no longer be active enough to produce a light, flavorful bread, and may not rise in the time specified by the recipe.

• Unless directed otherwise in a recipe, be sure *all* ingredients are at room temperature when you begin. Although this is recommended in most volumes on yeast baking, it is especially important for the recipes in *The 60-Minute Bread Book.* If ingredients are colder than normal, yeast growth will be inhibited and breads won't rise as much as they should in the allotted time.

• To bring refrigerated eggs to room temperature quickly and easily, place in a cup of warm water when you begin recipe preparations. After a minute, drain off warm water and replace with hot. The eggs will be at room temperature by the time they are to be added to the dough.

• If at all possible, use a candy or cooking thermometer to check the temperature of liquid ingredients. This simple gauge is the only way to be *sure* temperatures are within the required range and is the single best insurance against things going wrong. (An inexpensive, no-frills thermometer is perfectly adequate for preparing the recipes in this book.)

• Flour should always be measured unsifted; omit sifting unless directed in the recipe. To measure correctly, lightly scoop or spoon flour into measuring cup; do not pack down.

• Because different batches of flour have different moisture contents, the exact quantity needed for a dough will also vary from batch to batch. However, unless a recipe specifically directs otherwise, when you're unsure of the amount it's better to "underflour" rather than add too much. In many cases (but not all), overflouring yields a dry loaf.

• Follow carefully all beating, food-processing or blending times specified in recipes. These times determine just how much gluten is developed, so skimping or overprocessing can negatively affect the texture and "riseability" of the bread. (Gluten is a protein abundant in wheat flour, and the beating, whirling or kneading action stretches it into a network of elastic strands. This network traps gas produced by the yeast and expands, or inflates, much like a balloon.)

• If a recipe calls for some hand kneading and you've never done it before, keep in mind that imperfect technique won't ruin a bread! Here's how to proceed: Shape the dough mass and any loose particles clinging to the bowl into a smooth ball. Grasp the far side of the dough. Pull up and fold toward you, then press down and roll outward again with the heels of the hands. Turn ball slightly so a different section can be kneaded and repeat the process. Continue, adding a bit more flour as necessary, until dough is the texture described in the recipe. (Sometimes you're given a choice of kneading in the mixing bowl or on a lightly floured surface. Kneading in the bowl

21

is suggested because it means less fuss and faster cleanup. However, if you find it awkward, just do what's comfortable for you.)

• "Punch down" dough by pushing a fist into the center of the mass, then folding the edges inward until all excess air has been pressed from the ball. The dough will be reduced to its original size.

• There are two basic ways to shape dough into loaves and, unless specific directions are given, either may be used. The fastest method is to simply shape the dough into an oval slightly shorter than the pan length, smoothing and tucking any excess underneath the loaf. Alternately, roll or press out dough to a rectangle slightly shorter than the bread pan and about twice as wide. Then, from one of the longer sides, tightly roll up jelly-roll style, and place seam side down in pan.

• When recipes include directions for glazing the tops of loaves with water, milk or various liquid mixtures prior to baking, these may usually be applied with a paper towel if a pastry brush is unavailable. Plain water, cornstarch mixed with water and egg white are applied to add crispness to the crust. Milk lends a slight shininess and softness. And whole egg or egg yolk beaten with water promotes deep browning and lends a sheen.

• Always bake bread on oven rack placed in the middle of the oven unless other directions are provided. Otherwise, the tops or bottoms of loaves may dry out or burn.

• To prevent sogginess, carefully follow directions on removing finished breads from their pans. Some very tender or hard-to-handle loaves, particularly batter breads, need to cool in the pan for a few minutes, but most should be removed and transferred to racks promptly.

• *Part I* •

60-MINUTE BREADS

◆ 60-MINUTE YEAST BREADS ◆

*T*his chapter emphasizes breads you can make *extra* fast. It features a large collection of yeast breads that are perfect when you've got hungry people clamoring for some home-baked bread—right now!

All the recipes in the following section offer the previously un-heard-of opportunity to mix up, bake and serve good, fresh yeast bread in about 60 minutes or less. This incredible breakthrough is brought about by combining shortcut preparation techniques, fast rising times (thanks to the new quick-acting yeast) and brief baking periods. The collection features an appealing range of tasty rolls, coffee cakes, yeast pastries, small casserole breads and little loaves. (No large loaves are included because they take too long to bake.) For example, you can choose from among mouth-watering 60-Minute Cinnamon Pinwheels, zesty Cheese and Chives Mini-Loaves, Poppy Seed White Rolls, Toasted Almond Coffee Cakes and many more!

Keep in mind that most of the 60-minute yeast breads are specifi-cally designed to be enjoyed still warm from the oven. Since prepara-tions are streamlined, many recipes are for no-knead, batter-type breads. And virtually all feature a single rising period instead of the traditional two. This means that the finished breads, while delicious when fresh, tend to have less "staying power" and will become stale and crumbly a little sooner than those in other chapters. (You proba-bly won't have any leftovers to worry about anyway, but just in case, they can usually be frozen for later use.)

While the ultrafast recipes have been conveniently grouped in this chapter, there are many other extremely quick (and delicious) ones in the book. You can locate these easily by checking the recipe lists in the contents; the 90-minute-or-less breads are marked with a star. And of course, *all* the yeast breads in *The 60-Minute Bread Book* are extra fast compared to those prepared the old-fashioned conventional way!

• *White Casserole Bread* •

Start to Finish: About 1 hour

A tender, fluffy casserole bread that's a perfect accompaniment to simple meals. Served warm from the oven with lots of butter, it's delicious. For an added touch, garnish the top with sesame seeds.

> 2½ *cups all-purpose white or unbleached flour*
> 2½ *tablespoons granulated sugar*
> 1 *tablespoon fast-rising dry yeast (about 1½ packets)*
> ¾ *teaspoon salt*
> ½ *cup water*
> ⅓ *cup plain yogurt (regular or lowfat)*
> ¼ *cup butter or margarine, cut into 3 or 4 pieces*
> 1 *egg, at room temperature*
> ½ *tablespoon sesame seeds (optional)*

Stir together 1 cup flour, the sugar, yeast and salt in a large mixer bowl. Combine water, yogurt and butter in a small saucepan, and heat until butter melts and mixture reaches 125° to 130°. With mixer on low speed, beat liquid mixture into dry ingredients until blended. Raise speed to high and beat for 2½ minutes. Add egg, and beat with mixer on medium speed for 30 seconds longer. Vigorously stir in remaining 1½ cups flour to make a stiff, rubbery batter. Generously grease a 1-quart casserole. Dust casserole with flour; tip back and forth until bottom and sides are completely coated and then tap out any excess. Preheat oven to 250°.

Spoon batter into casserole. Smooth and spread batter out to casserole edges with well-greased knife. If desired, sprinkle top with sesame seeds; pat seeds down into batter slightly with back of a spoon. Cut a ¼-inch-deep X in batter surface with a sharp, well-greased knife. Set casserole in a larger bowl. Carefully fill bowl with enough hot water (120° to 130°) to come ⅔ of the way up sides of casserole. Lay a sheet of wax paper over casserole. Let batter rise for 14 to 15 minutes, then remove wax paper and place casserole in oven. Immediately raise thermostat to 425°. Bake loaf for 28 to 32 minutes, or until light brown on top and slightly springy to the touch. Transfer casserole to rack and let stand for 2 to 3 minutes; then immediately remove loaf and cool on rack at least 5 minutes longer before serving. Bread is best served warm from the oven, cut into thick wedges. Makes 1 small casserole loaf.

Approximate Preparation Time: 15 minutes   *Rising/Baking Time:* 45 minutes

• *English Muffin Loaves* •

Start to Finish: About 1 hour

Incredibly easy, incredibly good! Convenient, toastable slices with the taste of English muffins.

4¼ cups all-purpose white or unbleached flour
2 packets fast-rising dry yeast
¼ cup instant nonfat dry milk
1 tablespoon granulated sugar
1¼ teaspoons salt
2 cups hot water (125° to 130°)
Generous pinch baking soda
Cornmeal for dusting pans and sprinkling over loaves

Stir together 2 cups flour, the yeast, milk powder, sugar and salt in a large mixer bowl. With mixer on low speed, beat water into dry ingredients. Raise speed to high and beat for 3 minutes. Vigorously stir in baking soda and remaining 2¼ cups flour to yield a stiff batter.

Generously grease two 7⅞ × 3⅞ × 2½-inch aluminum foil (or similar 1-quart) loaf pans. Sprinkle pans with cornmeal, and tip back and forth until bottoms and sides are completely coated. Divide batter between pans. Spread out batter, using a knife to smooth surface. Lightly sprinkle loaf tops with cornmeal. Place pans in a larger pan. Carefully fill larger pan with enough hot water (120° to 130°) to come

28

⅔ of the way up sides of bread pans. Lay a sheet of wax paper over pans and let loaves rise for 20 minutes. Preheat oven to 425°.

Remove wax paper and place bread pans in oven. Bake loaves for 23 to 27 minutes, or until tinged with brown and springy to the touch. Immediately remove loaves from pans and let cool on racks. Cut into slices and serve well toasted, along with butter. Freeze loaves for later use, if desired. Makes 2 small loaves.

Approximate Preparation Time: 15 minutes   *Rising/Baking Time:* 45 minutes

◆ *Dilly Cottage Cheese* ◆
Pull-Apart Loaves

Start to Finish: About 1 hour

Delicious, easy and attractive loaves that pull apart into handy slices. Cottage cheese makes this bread moist and tender, and herbs add a subtle, savory taste. Some of the kneading in this recipe is completed with a blender.

> 3¼ to 3¾ cups all-purpose white or unbleached flour
> 1 tablespoon fast-rising dry yeast (about 1½ packets)
> 1 teaspoon granulated sugar
> 1 teaspoon salt
> ¾ cup water
> ½ cup large- or small-curd cottage cheese (preferably lowfat)
> 2 tablespoons vegetable oil
> 1 egg, at room temperature and separated
> 1 tablespoon dried dill weed
> 1 tablespoon dried chopped chives
> ½ teaspoon dill seed for garnishing loaves (optional)

Stir together ¾ cup flour, the yeast, sugar and salt in a large measuring cup. Combine water, cottage cheese and oil in a small saucepan and heat to 125° to 130°. Put cottage cheese mixture in blender container. With blender on low speed, gradually add dry ingredients. Blend for 15 seconds. Add egg white and blend for 15 seconds longer. (Reserve egg yolk for preparing a wash to brush over loaves.) Transfer blended mixture to a medium-sized bowl. Vigorously stir in dill weed and chives, then 2 cups more flour, or enough to yield a smooth, kneadable dough. Working in the bowl, quickly and vigorously knead in enough more flour, to yield a smooth and fairly firm dough. Thoroughly grease a 17½ × 11½-inch (or similar large) baking sheet and set aside.

Divide dough in half. With well-greased hands, shape one half into a smooth, evenly thick log about 10½ inches long. Transfer log to baking sheet, laying it on a diagonal. With a well-greased kitchen knife, mark the dough crosswise into about ten 1-inch strips. Then cut almost completely through dough to pan bottom to form slices; be careful not to dislodge them from the loaf during cutting. Repeat shaping and cutting process with other half of dough. Cover loaves lightly with plastic wrap. Set aside in a very warm spot (80° to 90°) for 15 minutes. Preheat oven to 425°. Beat reserved egg yolk with 1 tablespoon water and set aside.

Using a pastry brush or paper towel, brush loaves with egg yolk-water mixture. Sprinkle tops with dill seed, if desired. Bake loaves for 15 to 18 minutes, or until tops are nicely browned and firm to the touch. Transfer to racks for 4 to 5 minutes; then serve immediately, with butter if desired. Loaves may also be frozen, then thawed and reheated before serving. Makes 2 medium-sized loaves.

Approximate Preparation Time: 27 minutes   *Rising/Baking Time:* 32 minutes

◆ Easy Garlic Baguettes ◆

Start to Finish: About 1 hour

These crispy garlic baguettes can be whipped up in a hurry. They go well with hearty soups, stews and Italian food.

> *3½ to 4 cups all-purpose white or unbleached flour*
> *2 packets fast-rising dry yeast*
> *2 tablespoons granulated sugar*
> *1¼ teaspoons salt*
> *1 cup hot water (125° to 130°)*
> *1 tablespoon vegetable oil*
> *Cornmeal for sprinkling on baking sheet*
> *1 egg white beaten with ½ tablespoon water for brushing over loaves*
> *Garlic salt for sprinkling over loaves*

Stir together 1¼ cups flour, the yeast, sugar and salt in large mixer bowl. With mixer on low speed, beat hot water and oil into dry ingredients until blended. Raise speed to high and beat for 3½ minutes. Vigorously stir in 1¾ cups more flour until blended. Working in the bowl, quickly and vigorously knead in enough more flour to yield a very firm but not dry dough. Cover bowl with plastic wrap and set aside in a very warm spot (80° to 90°) for 5 minutes. Meanwhile, lightly grease a 17½ × 15-inch (or similar very large) baking sheet, or two smaller baking sheets. Sprinkle generously with cornmeal and set aside.

Punch down dough and divide in fourths. Shape portions into 7- to 8-inch-long logs. Gently stretch and roll logs back and forth with fingertips on a clean (unfloured) surface until about 13 inches long. Transfer baguettes to baking sheet, spacing as far apart as possible. Brush tops of baguettes with warm water, using a pastry brush or paper towel. Set aside, uncovered, in a very warm spot (80° to 90°) for 20 minutes. Preheat oven to 450°. Put a shallow pan of hot water on oven floor.

Brush tops and sides of baguettes with beaten egg white-water mixture. Sprinkle tops with garlic salt. Cut five or six ¼-inch-deep random diagonal slashes in each loaf, using a very sharp knife. Bake

31

loaves for 5 minutes. Lightly spray or sprinkle loaves with water. Continue baking for 9 to 13 minutes longer, or until tops are nicely browned and bottoms sound hollow when tapped. Transfer loaves to racks and let cool for 5 minutes before serving. To serve, break (don't cut) baguettes into portion-sized lengths and spread with butter, if desired. Loaves should be used promptly or frozen for later use. Makes 4 small baguettes.

Approximate Preparation Time: 20 minutes   *Rising/Baking Time:* 40 minutes

• *Buttermilk-Wheat Mini-Loaves* •

Start to Finish: About 52 minutes

Bake up these quick little loaves and add some whole-grain goodness *and* good taste to your meal. Even folks who prefer white bread usually like these.

2½ cups all-purpose white or unbleached flour
⅓ cup light or dark brown sugar, packed
1 tablespoon fast-rising dry yeast (about 1½ packets)
¾ teaspoon salt
1¼ cups commercial buttermilk
¼ cup water
¼ cup butter or margarine, cut into 3 or 4 pieces
1 egg, at room temperature
1 cup whole-wheat flour

Stir together 1¼ cups white flour, the brown sugar, yeast and salt in a large mixer bowl. Combine buttermilk, water and butter in a small saucepan, and heat until butter melts and mixture reaches 125° to 130°. With mixer on low speed, beat liquid mixture into flour-yeast mixture until blended. Raise speed to high and beat for 2½ minutes. Add egg and beat with mixer on medium speed for 30 seconds. Vig-

32

orously stir in whole-wheat flour and remaining 1¼ cups white flour to make a stiff, rubbery batter. Generously grease three 5¹¹⁄₁₆ × 3¼ × 2-inch aluminum foil (or similar) mini-loaf pans and set aside. Preheat oven to 250°.

Spoon batter into pans, dividing it equally among them. Smooth and spread batter out to pan edges using well-greased knife. Set pans in a larger pan. Carefully fill larger pan with enough hot water (120° to 130°) to come ⅔ of the way up sides of mini-loaf pans. Let loaves rise, uncovered, for 10 minutes.

Place loaves in oven; immediately raise thermostat to 425°. Bake loaves for 23 to 27 minutes, or until light brown on top and slightly springy to the touch. Transfer pans to racks and let stand for 2 to 3 minutes; then immediately remove loaves from pans and cool on racks at least 3 to 4 minutes longer before serving. Bread is best served warm from the oven, with butter. Loaves may also be frozen and reheated at serving time, if desired. Makes 3 mini-loaves.

Approximate Preparation Time: 17 minutes   *Rising/Baking Time:* 35 minutes

• *Honey-Butter Bread* •

Start to Finish: About 1 hour

Kids are especially fond of this sweet, honey-flavored bread. It's good served for breakfast or as a snack.

2⅓ cups all-purpose white or unbleached flour
1 tablespoon fast-rising dry yeast (about 1½ packets)
¾ teaspoon salt
1¼ cups water
3 tablespoons vegetable oil
3 tablespoons honey
1 egg, at room temperature
¾ cup whole-wheat flour
HONEY BUTTER
⅔ cup confectioners' sugar (sifted if lumpy)
½ tablespoon butter, softened
2 tablespoons honey

Stir together 1⅓ cups white flour, the yeast and salt in a large mixer bowl. In a small saucepan, combine water, oil and 3 table-spoons honey. Stirring until honey dissolves, heat to 125° to 130°. With mixer on low speed, beat liquid into flour-yeast mixture until blended. Raise mixer speed to high and beat for 3 minutes. Add egg and beat for 30 seconds longer. Vigorously stir in whole-wheat flour and remaining 1 cup white flour to yield a stiff batter. Generously grease a 1¼- to 1½-quart casserole or soufflé dish. Spoon batter into casserole. Smooth and spread batter out to edges using well-greased knife. Set casserole in a larger bowl. Carefully fill larger bowl with enough hot water (120° to 130°) to come ⅔ of the way up sides of casserole. Lay a sheet of wax paper over casserole. Let batter rise for 10 minutes. Preheat oven to 250°.

Place casserole, uncovered, in preheated oven; immediately raise thermostat to 400°. Bake loaf for 27 to 32 minutes, or until light brown on top and slightly springy to the touch. Transfer casserole to rack and let stand for 8 to 10 minutes. Meanwhile, prepare Honey Butter as follows: Stir together confectioners' sugar, butter and 2 tablespoons honey until well blended and smooth. Remove loaf from pan and place on rack over a sheet of wax paper to catch drips; spread honey butter over loaf while bread is still slightly warm, but not hot. Let stand briefly; then cut into thick crosswise slices or wedges and serve. Makes 1 small casserole loaf.

Approximate Preparation Time: 23 minutes   *Rising/Baking Time:* 40 minutes

◆ *Easiest-Ever Raisin Bread* ◆

Start to Finish: About 1 hour 2 minutes

A no-knead, one-rise raisin bread that may well be the easiest ever made. It's light and tasty.

> *5 cups all-purpose white or unbleached flour, approximately*
> *2 packets fast-rising dry yeast*
> *Generous ½ cup granulated sugar*
> *¼ cup instant nonfat dry milk*
> *1½ teaspoons ground cinnamon*
> *1 teaspoon salt*
> *2 cups water*
> *⅓ cup vegetable oil*
> *1 egg, at room temperature*
> *1¼ cup seedless raisins*

Stir together 2¼ cups flour, the yeast, sugar, milk powder, cinnamon and salt in a large mixer bowl. Heat water and oil in a small saucepan to 125° to 130°. With mixer on low speed, beat liquid into dry ingredients until blended. Raise speed to high and beat for 2½ minutes. Add egg and beat 30 seconds longer. Vigorously stir in raisins and 2⅔ cups more flour to make a stiff batter. Generously grease three 7⅞ × 3⅞ × 2½-inch (or similar 1-quart) aluminum foil loaf pans. Divide batter among pans; it will be very rubbery. Smooth and spread batter out to pan edges with a greased knife. Turn oven

35

on to low heat for 1 minute; then turn off again. Put pans, uncovered, in warm oven. Let loaves rise for 15 minutes.

Turn oven on to 400° and bake loaves for 24 to 28 minutes, or until tops are slightly springy to the touch and tinged with brown. Remove pans from oven and let stand for 5 minutes. Remove loaves from pans and place on racks. Cool at least 2 to 3 minutes longer before serving. Bread is good warm and served with butter, or toasted. Freeze loaves if you are not planning to use them right away. Makes 3 small loaves.

Approximate Preparation Time: 20 minutes   *Rising/Baking Time:* 42 minutes

NOTE: If desired, Easiest-Ever Raisin Bread may be baked in two generously greased 8½ × 4¼ × 2½-inch (or similar 1½-quart) loaf pans instead). In this case, increase baking time to 30 to 34 minutes. This will yield 2 medium-sized loaves.

• *Rosemary Casserole Bread* •

Start to Finish: About 56 minutes

This easy yet delicious herb bread is perfect for serving with Italian food. The loaf is high, fluffy and very aromatic.

A blender is used to complete the kneading process in just 30 seconds.

> 2⅔ *cups all-purpose white or unbleached flour*
> ¼ *cup instant nonfat dry milk*
> 2 *tablespoons granulated sugar*
> 1 *packet fast-rising dry yeast*
> 1 *teaspoon salt*
> 1 *cup hot water (125° to 130°)*
> 2 *tablespoons olive oil*
> 1 *teaspoon dried rosemary leaves*
> 2 *tablespoons grated Parmesan cheese*

Stir together 1 cup flour, the milk powder, sugar, yeast and salt in a large measuring cup. Combine water and oil in a blender container. With blender on low speed, add flour-yeast mixture to water and oil, and blend for 20 seconds. Add rosemary leaves and blend on low speed for 10 seconds longer. Pour blended mixture into a medium-sized bowl. Vigorously stir in remaining 1⅔ cups flour; batter will be stiff. Generously grease a 1½-quart casserole. Dust casserole with ½ tablespoon Parmesan cheese; tip back and forth until bottom and sides are completely coated. Spoon batter into casserole. Smooth and spread batter out to casserole edges using a well-greased knife. Sprinkle remaining Parmesan over batter; pat cheese down slightly with fingertips. Cover casserole with plastic wrap. Turn oven on low for 1 minute; then turn off again. Set casserole in warm oven for 15 minutes.

Remove plastic wrap from casserole. Immediately set oven thermostat to 375°. Bake loaf for 24 to 28 minutes, or until nicely browned and slightly springy to the touch. Transfer casserole to rack and let stand for 7 to 10 minutes; then remove loaf and cool on rack a few minutes longer. Bread is best served still warm from the oven. Cut crosswise into thick slices or wedges. Makes 1 small casserole loaf.

Approximate Preparation Time: 15 minutes   *Rising/Baking Time:* 41 minutes

• *Wheat-Bran Casserole Breads* •

Start to Finish: About 1 hour

Use a blender to make up these robust, wholesome little casserole breads fast. These tender, high-fiber loaves complement any
simple lunch or supper. Serve them right from the oven, as they don't
keep well.

> 1 cup raisin bran or bran flakes cereal
> ¼ cup hot tap water
> 2¼ cups all-purpose white or unbleached flour
> 1 tablespoon fast-rising dry yeast (about 1½ packets)
> 1 tablespoon granulated sugar
> ¾ teaspoon salt
> 1¼ cups water
> ¼ cup molasses, preferably dark
> 3 tablespoons vegetable oil
> 1 egg, at room temperature
> 1 cup, plus 1 tablespoon whole-wheat flour
> Milk for brushing over tops of loaves

Combine bran cereal and ¼ cup hot tap water in a small bowl.
Stir until flakes are moistened; then set aside to soften. Stir together 1
cup white flour, the yeast, sugar and salt in a large cup. Combine 1¼
cups water, the molasses and oil in a small saucepan. Stirring until
molasses dissolves, heat until mixture reaches 125° to 130°. Put liquid
mixture in blender container. With blender on medium speed, add
flour-yeast mixture and whirl for 20 seconds. Add egg and blend for
10 seconds longer.

Pour blended mixture into deep, medium-sized bowl. With a
large spoon, vigorously stir in reserved softened bran cereal, 1 cup
whole-wheat flour and remaining 1¼ cups white flour to make a fairly
stiff batter. Generously grease two 1-quart flat-bottomed round casseroles or soufflé dishes. Dust casseroles with 1 tablespoon whole-
wheat flour, tipping back and forth until evenly coated. Divide batter
between casseroles. Smooth out tops with a greased knife. Set casseroles in a larger bowl. Carefully add enough hot water (120° to 130°)
to bowl to come ⅔ of the way up sides of casseroles. Lay sheets of

wax paper over tops of casseroles, and let batter rise for 10 minutes. Remove wax paper, and let batter rise for 7 to 8 minutes longer.

Place casseroles in cold oven and immediately turn thermostat to 400°. Bake for 20 minutes. Remove casseroles from oven and generously brush bread tops with milk, using pastry brush or paper towel. Return casseroles to oven and bake 7 to 9 minutes longer, or until breads are nicely browned and slightly springy to the touch. Transfer casseroles to racks and let stand for 5 minutes before removing loaves. Loaves are best cut into wedges and served warm with butter, although they may be frozen for later use and reheated, if desired. Makes 2 small casserole loaves.

Approximate Preparation Time: 15 minutes   *Rising/Baking Time:* 46 minutes

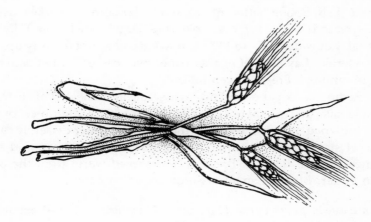

• Rye and Corn Casserole Bread •

Start to Finish: About 1 hour

The interesting combination of rye flour and cornmeal lends a delightfully savory flavor to this hearty casserole loaf.

> 1¾ cups all-purpose white or unbleached flour
> 1 tablespoon fast-rising dry yeast (about 1½ packets)
> 2 tablespoons light or dark brown sugar, packed
> 1½ teaspoons caraway seeds
> ¾ teaspoon salt
> 1 cup commercial buttermilk
> ¼ cup water
> 3 tablespoons butter or margarine, cut into 3 or 4 pieces
> 1 egg, at room temperature
> ¼ cup yellow or white cornmeal
> ¾ cup medium or dark rye flour

Stir together 1 cup white flour, the yeast, brown sugar, caraway seeds and salt in a large mixer bowl. Combine buttermilk, water and butter in a small saucepan, and heat until butter melts and mixture reaches 125° to 130°. With mixer on low speed, beat liquid into flour-yeast mixture until blended. Raise speed to high and beat for 2½ minutes. Add egg and cornmeal and beat with mixer on medium speed for 30 seconds longer. Vigorously stir in rye flour until well blended. Then, stir in ¾ cup more white flour to yield a fairly stiff, rubbery batter. Generously grease a 1¼- to 1½-quart casserole or soufflé dish. Spoon batter into casserole. Smooth out surface using a well-greased knife. Set casserole in a larger bowl. Carefully add enough hot water (120° to 130°) to bowl to come ⅔ of the way up sides of casserole. Lay a sheet of wax paper over casserole. Let batter rise for 15 minutes. Preheat oven to 250°.

Remove wax paper and place casserole in preheated oven; immediately raise thermostat to 425°. Bake loaf for 28 to 32 minutes, or until well browned on top and firm to the touch. Transfer casserole to rack and let stand for 8 to 10 minutes; remove loaf from pan and serve immediately, if desired. Bread is best served warm from the oven, with butter. Makes 1 small casserole loaf.

Approximate Preparation Time: 19 minutes   *Rising/Baking Time:* 45 minutes

• *Cheese and Chives Mini-Loaves* •

Start to Finish: About 54 minutes

Pretty, cheese-and-chives-topped little loaves with zesty flavor. These require only one rising and no kneading. Mix them up fast, using a blender, and serve along with brunch or supper. The loaves have a very soft, delicate texture and become crumbly when stale, so plan on serving them right away, or freeze for later use.

> 2½ cups all-purpose white or unbleached flour
> 1 packet fast-rising dry yeast
> 1 tablespoon granulated sugar
> ½ teaspoon salt
> 1 cup water
> ⅓ cup coarsely chopped or cubed longhorn or mild Cheddar cheese
>   (about 2 ounces)
> 2 tablespoons vegetable oil
> ½ teaspoon dry mustard
> 1 egg, at room temperature
> 2½ teaspoons dried chopped chives
> ¼ cup grated or shredded longhorn or mild Cheddar cheese for gar-
>   nishing tops of loaves (about 1 ounce)

Stir together ¾ cup flour, the yeast, sugar, and salt in a large cup. Combine water, ⅓ cup cheese, the oil and mustard in a small saucepan. Heat to 125° to 130°. Cheese does not have to melt completely. Transfer mixture to blender container. Blend on low speed for 10 seconds. Increase speed to medium and add flour-yeast mixture. Blend on medium speed for 20 seconds. Add egg and blend for 10 seconds longer.

Pour blended mixture into medium-sized bowl. Stir in 2 teaspoons chives. (Reserve remaining ½ teaspoon for garnishing loaves.) With a large spoon, vigorously stir in remaining 1¾ cups flour until batter is well blended. Generously grease three 5¹¹⁄₁₆ × 3¼ × 2-inch aluminum foil mini-loaf pans (or similar mini-pans). Divide batter among pans. (The quantity of batter may seem too small for three pans, but bread will rise a great deal.) Smooth out surface of batter using a greased knife. Set pans in a larger pan. Carefully add enough hot water (120° to 130°) to larger pan to come ⅔ of the way up sides of bread pans. Let batter rise, uncovered, for 17 to 18 minutes. Preheat oven to 400°.

Sprinkle loaves with reserved chives and ¼ cup grated cheese. Bake for 18 to 23 minutes, or until tops are slightly springy to the touch and nicely browned. Transfer pans from oven to racks and let stand for 5 minutes before removing loaves. Loaves are best served still warm from the oven, although they may be frozen for later use and reheated, if desired. Makes 3 mini-loaves.

Approximate Preparation Time: 15 minutes   *Rising/Baking Time:* 38 minutes

• *Sesame Bread Sticks* •

Start to Finish: About 55 minutes

Try these crisp and crunchable bread sticks along with soup and a salad, or as a snack.

1⅓ to 1¾ cups all-purpose white or unbleached flour
1½ tablespoons granulated sugar
1 packet fast-rising dry yeast
¾ teaspoon salt
⅔ cup commercial buttermilk
¼ cup water
½ tablespoon butter or margarine
⅔ cup whole-wheat flour
1½ tablespoons sesame seeds
Additional sesame seeds for sprinkling on baking sheet and bread sticks
1 egg beaten with 1 tablespoon water for brushing over sticks
¼ teaspoon coarse salt (or table salt, if necessary) for sprinkling over sticks

Stir together 1 cup white flour, the sugar, yeast and salt in a large mixer bowl. Combine buttermilk, water and butter in a small saucepan, and heat until butter melts and mixture reaches 125° to 130°. With mixer on low speed, beat liquid into flour-yeast mixture until blended. Raise speed to high and beat for 2½ minutes. With a large spoon, vigorously stir in whole-wheat flour until well blended; batter will still be very wet at this point. Cover bowl with plastic wrap and set aside in a very warm spot (80° to 90°) for 5 minutes. Meanwhile, spread 1½ tablespoons sesame seeds in an ungreased skillet over high heat. Toast seeds, stirring constantly, for 2 minutes, or until skillet is very hot. Reduce heat to medium and, continuing to stir, heat for 1 to 2 minutes, or until seeds are fragrant and just barely tinged with brown. (Be careful not to burn.) Immediately remove pan from heat and transfer seeds to a small bowl; set aside. Preheat oven to 400°. Lightly grease a 17½ × 15-inch (or similar very large) baking sheet. Sprinkle about 1 tablespoon *untoasted* sesame seeds evenly on baking sheet.

Stir toasted sesame seeds into dough. Working in the bowl, stir and then knead in enough more white flour to yield a smooth, malleable and fairly stiff dough. With lightly greased hands, divide dough into eleven or twelve portions the size of golf balls. One at a time, roll portions back and forth with lightly greased hands on a clean work surface to form evenly thick sticks about 11 inches long. Space sticks about ½ inch apart on baking sheet. One or two at a time, brush tops and sides of sticks lightly with egg-water mixture, using a pastry brush or paper towel; immediately sprinkle lightly with sesame seeds, then with salt crystals.

Bake bread sticks for 20 to 24 minutes, or until tops are tinged with brown and sound hollow when tapped. Transfer pan to rack. Loosen sticks from pan with a spatula. Bread sticks may be served still warm from the oven, with butter, or at room temperature. If desired, they may also be frozen and then thawed before serving. Makes 11 to 12 large bread sticks.

Approximate Preparation Time: 27 minutes   *Rising/Baking Time:* 28 minutes

• *Rye Bread Sticks* •

Start to Finish: About 1 hour

Chewy and flavorful, these are good served with salads, soups and stews.

1¼ to 1½ cups all-purpose white or unbleached flour
1 packet fast-rising dry yeast
¾ teaspoon salt
2 tablespoons caraway seeds
½ cup water
⅓ cup plain regular or lowfat yogurt
¼ cup light or dark molasses
2 tablespoons butter or margarine, cut into 2 pieces
1¼ cups medium or dark rye flour
1 egg white beaten with 1 tablespoon water for brushing over bread sticks
¼ teaspoon coarse salt (optional)

Stir together ¾ cup white flour, the yeast, salt and ½ tablespoon caraway seeds in a large mixer bowl. Stir together water, yogurt, molasses and butter, and heat until butter melts and mixture reaches 125° to 130°. With mixer on low speed, beat liquid into flour-yeast mixture until blended. Raise speed to high and beat for 3½ minutes. Vigorously stir in rye flour, using a large spoon. Working in the bowl or on a clean, lightly floured surface, quickly and vigorously knead in enough more white flour to yield a very smooth, malleable dough. Form dough into a ball and return to mixer bowl.

Cover bowl with plastic wrap. Set aside in a very warm spot (80° to 90°) for 15 minutes. Meanwhile, sprinkle 1 tablespoon more caraway seeds evenly on 17½ × 15-inch (or other very large) baking sheet and set aside. Preheat oven to 450°.

Punch down dough. On a very lightly floured work surface, divide dough into twelve equal portions. One at a time, roll dough portions back and forth with lightly greased hands to form evenly thick 11-inch-long sticks. Space sticks about ½ inch apart on baking sheet. Brush tops and sides of sticks lightly with egg white–water mixture, using a pastry brush or paper towel. Sprinkle sticks with remaining ½ tablespoon caraway seeds, and coarse salt, if desired. Set sticks aside, uncovered, in a very warm spot (80° to 90°) for 5 minutes.

Place bread sticks in preheated oven; immediately reduce heat to 425°. Bake for 14 to 17 minutes, or until sticks are brown and sound hollow when tapped. Transfer pan to rack. Loosen sticks from pan with a spatula. Sticks may be served still warm from the oven or at room temperature. Bread sticks may also be frozen and then thawed before serving, if desired. Makes 12 bread sticks.

Approximate Preparation Time: 25 minutes   *Rising/Baking Time:* 35 minutes

Crispy Parmesan Flatbread Wedges

Start to Finish: About 50 minutes

Press the dough for this easy crackerlike bread into a pizza pan, cut into triangles and bake in a hot oven until crunchy-crisp. Flatbread wedges are good served along with lunch or supper, or as a munchable snack.

1½ to 1¾ cups all-purpose white or unbleached flour
1 packet fast-rising dry yeast
1 tablespoon granulated sugar
1 teaspoon dried basil leaves
½ teaspoon celery salt
¼ teaspoon finely crumbled rosemary leaves
⅛ teaspoon onion salt
¾ cup hot water (125° to 130°)
2 teaspoons olive oil or vegetable oil
⅓ cup grated Parmesan cheese
½ cup whole-wheat flour
1 egg beaten with 1 tablespoon water for brushing over dough
¼ teaspoon coarse salt (or substitute table salt, if necessary)

Stir together ¾ cup white flour, the yeast, sugar, basil, celery salt, rosemary leaves and onion salt in a large mixer bowl. With mixer on low speed, beat in water, then oil, until blended. Raise speed to high and beat for 3 minutes. Stir in Parmesan cheese, whole-wheat flour and ½ cup more white flour, using a large spoon. Working in the bowl, quickly and vigorously knead in enough more white flour to yield a firm, smooth dough. Cover bowl with plastic wrap and set aside in a very warm spot (80° to 90°) for 15 minutes. Preheat oven to 475°. Lightly grease a 12-inch-diameter pizza pan.

Punch down dough. Press out dough in an evenly thick layer to pan edges. Brush dough surface with egg-water mixture, using pastry brush or paper towel. Sprinkle coarse salt over dough. Prick dough surface all over with tines of a fork. Cut dough into sixteen wedges, using a pastry wheel, pizza cutter or sharp knife. Place in preheated oven and bake for 15 to 18 minutes, or until wedges are lightly browned and crispy. Remove from pan and cool on racks 3 to 4 minutes. Serve immediately. Makes 16 wedges.

Approximate Preparation Time: 20 minutes   *Rising/Baking Time:* 31 minutes

VARIATION: Crispy Nacho Flatbread Wedges—Follow basic recipe except substitute ¾ teaspoon chili powder for basil and rosemary leaves; substitute scant ½ teaspoon plain table salt for celery salt; substitute ½ cup grated Cheddar cheese for Parmesan; and substitute ½ cup yellow cornmeal for whole-wheat flour.

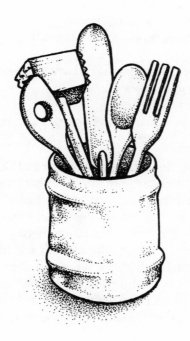

• *Jiffy Pizzas* •

Start to Finish: About 55 minutes

If you want tasty homemade pizza and you want it fast, try this easy recipe. It's whipped up quickly with the aid of a blender. (If desired, you can just make up the dough and then substitute your own favorite pizza sauce recipe and toppings.)

3 to 3⅓ cups all-purpose white or unbleached flour
1 packet fast-rising dry yeast
1 teaspoon granulated sugar
¾ teaspoon salt
1¼ cups hot water (125° to 130°)
1 tablespoon olive oil or vegetable oil
SAUCE
1 8-ounce can tomato sauce
1 6-ounce can tomato paste
2½ teaspoons dried oregano leaves, or Italian seasoning mix
¼ teaspoon onion salt
Generous pinch garlic powder (optional)
Generous pinch hot red pepper flakes (optional)
TOPPINGS
12 to 16 ounces shredded or grated mozzarella cheese
⅓ cup grated Parmesan cheese
2½ to 3 ounces pepperoni slices
Chopped green pepper, onions, mushrooms, black olives, fresh parsley or other toppings to taste

Stir together ¾ cup flour, the yeast, sugar and salt in a large cup. Put water and oil in blender container. With blender on medium speed, add flour-yeast mixture and whirl for 15 seconds. Pour blended mixture into a large bowl. Vigorously stir in 2 cups more flour. Working in the bowl or on a clean, lightly floured surface, knead in enough more flour to yield a smooth and malleable but still moist dough. Cover bowl with plastic wrap. Set dough aside in a very warm place (80° to 90°) for 15 minutes. Meanwhile, generously grease two 12-inch-diameter pizza pans with olive or vegetable oil. Preheat oven to 475°. Stir together tomato sauce, tomato paste, oregano, onion salt, garlic powder and hot pepper flakes in a small bowl until blended. Ready cheeses and desired toppings.

Knead dough briefly. Divide in half. Press each half out into an evenly thick layer on a pan; press all the way to pan rim to form crust edge. Spread dough with sauce, cheeses, pepperoni and other toppings, as desired. Place pizzas in preheated oven and bake for 19 to 22 minutes, or until tops are well browned and bubbly. Cut into wedges and serve. Makes 2 12-inch-diameter pizzas.

Approximate Preparation Time: 23 minutes   *Rising/Baking Time:* 35 minutes

• *Poppy Seed White Rolls* •

Start to Finish: About 58 minutes

Baking is believing! These rolls are not only fast and easy to make but very fluffy and delicious.

(If you don't care for poppy seeds, they may be omitted from the recipe. The plain white rolls are good too.)

> *3 to 3½ cups all-purpose white or unbleached flour*
> *1 packet fast-rising dry yeast*
> *1 tablespoon granulated sugar*
> *¼ cup instant nonfat dry milk*
> *1 tablespoon poppy seeds*
> *½ teaspoon salt*
> *½ cup plain yogurt (regular or lowfat)*
> *½ cup water*
> *3 tablespoons butter or margarine, cut into 2 or 3 pieces*
> *Milk for brushing over tops of rolls*
> *Additional poppy seeds for garnish (optional)*

Stir together 1 cup flour, the yeast, sugar, milk powder, poppy seeds and salt in a large mixer bowl. Stir together yogurt, water and

49

butter in a small saucepan, and heat until butter melts and mixture reaches 125° to 130°. With mixer on low speed, beat liquid into dry ingredients until blended. Raise speed to high and beat for 2½ minutes. Vigorously stir in additional 1¾ cups flour, using a large spoon. Working in the bowl, quickly and vigorously knead in enough more flour to yield a smooth and malleable but not dry dough. Grease a 9- or 10-inch pie plate (or similar-sized baking pan).

With well-greased hands, shape dough into eleven or twelve balls; for best appearance tuck excess dough underneath each roll. Space rolls, slightly separated, in pie plate. Brush rolls with milk, then sprinkle lightly with poppy seeds, if desired. Cover plate with damp towel and set aside in a very warm place (80° to 90°) for 20 minutes. Preheat oven to 425°.

Bake rolls for 10 minutes. Reduce heat to 400° and bake for 6 to 9 minutes longer, or until rolls are springy to the touch and golden brown. Remove rolls from oven and transfer from pan to rack; let stand for 4 to 5 minutes before serving. Poppy Seed White Rolls are best served warm from the oven, with butter. Makes 11 to 12 large rolls.

Approximate Preparation Time: 20 minutes   *Rising/Baking Time:* 37 minutes

• *Jiffy Rye Finger Rolls* •

Start to Finish: About 55 minutes

Enlivened with caraway seeds, these quick rolls are attractive, light and delicious. They disappear rapidly whenever served!

> 2 cups all-purpose white or unbleached flour
> 1 tablespoon fast-rising dry yeast (about 1½ packets)
> ½ teaspoon salt
> ⅔ cup water
> ½ cup plain yogurt (regular or lowfat)
> 2½ tablespoons light molasses
> ½ tablespoon caraway seeds
> ¼ cup vegetable oil
> 1 egg, separated
> 1¼ to 1½ cups medium or dark rye flour
> 1 tablespoon water
> Additional caraway seeds for garnish (optional)

Stir together 1¼ cups white flour, the yeast and salt in a large mixer bowl. Combine ⅔ cup water, the yogurt, molasses, caraway seeds and oil in a small saucepan. Stirring until molasses dissolves, heat to 125° to 130°. With mixer on low speed, beat liquid into flour-yeast mixture until blended. Raise speed to high and beat for 2½ minutes. Add egg yolk and beat for 30 seconds longer. (Reserve egg white to prepare wash to brush over rolls.) Vigorously stir in remaining ¾ cup white flour and 1 cup rye flour, using a large, heavy spoon. Working in the bowl or on a clean, lightly floured surface, knead in enough more rye flour to yield a smooth and malleable but not dry dough. Thoroughly grease a 17½ × 11½-inch (or similar large) baking pan and set aside.

Divide dough in half. With well-greased hands, shape one half into a smooth, evenly thick log about 10 inches long; flatten log slightly to approximately 3½ inches wide. Using a sharp knife, trim off and discard ends of log. Then cut crosswise into ten or eleven even strips. (Each should be approximately 3½ inches long and ⅔ of an inch wide.) Lay strips smooth, not cut, side down (see illustra-

51

tion), about 1 inch apart on baking sheet; flatten slightly to prevent them from falling over onto cut sides. Repeat with second half of dough. Set baking sheet aside, uncovered, in a very warm spot (80° to 90°) for 17 to 18 minutes. Preheat oven to 425°. Beat together reserved egg white and 1 tablespoon water to form wash for rolls. Brush top and sides of each roll with egg white-water mixture, using a pastry brush or paper towel, and sprinkle tops with a few caraway seeds, if desired.

Bake rolls for 12 to 15 minutes, or until tops are light brown and firm to the touch. Transfer rolls to racks for 4 to 5 minutes; then serve immediately, with butter. If preferred, Rye Finger Rolls may also be frozen, then thawed and reheated before serving. Makes 20 to 22 rolls.

Approximate Preparation Time: 23 minutes   *Rising/Baking Time:* 32 minutes

◆ *Sour Cream and Onion Rolls* ◆

Start to Finish: About 1 hour

Sour cream and onions add zest and wonderful flavor in these savory and light pan rolls. They're also simple to prepare.

3 to 3½ cups all-purpose white or unbleached flour
1 packet fast-rising dry yeast
1 tablespoon granulated sugar
¾ teaspoon salt
½ cup commercial sour cream
⅔ cup water
1 tablespoon butter or margarine
1 medium-sized onion, very finely chopped
1 egg beaten with 1 tablespoon water for brushing over rolls

Stir together 1 cup flour, the yeast, sugar and salt in a large mixer bowl. Stir together sour cream and water in a small saucepan, and heat to 125° to 130°. With mixer on low speed, beat liquid into dry ingredients until blended. Raise speed to high and beat for 2½ minutes. Vigorously stir in 1⅓ cups more flour. Working in the bowl, quickly and vigorously knead in enough more flour to yield a smooth and fairly stiff but not dry dough. Grease a 9- or 10-inch pie plate (or similar-sized baking pan).

With well-greased hands, shape dough into eleven or twelve balls; for best appearance tuck excess dough underneath each roll. Space rolls, slightly separated, in pie plate. Cover plate lightly with plastic wrap and set aside in a very warm spot (80° to 90°) for 20 minutes.

Preheat oven to 400°. Combine butter and onion in a small saucepan over medium-high heat. Cook onion, stirring frequently, for 5 to 8 minutes, or until transparent and golden, but not browned. Remove pan from heat and set aside.

Brush rolls with egg-water mixture, using a pastry brush or paper towel. Sprinkle onions over roll tops. Bake for 17 to 21 minutes, or until rolls are golden and onions are tinged with brown. Transfer pan to rack and let stand for 4 to 5 minutes. Serve rolls directly from pan while still warm. Makes 11 to 12 large rolls.

Approximate Preparation Time: 27 minutes   *Rising/Baking Time:* 38 minutes

• Cheddar Mini-Puffies •

Start to Finish: About 47 minutes

Light, puffy morsels, tangy with cheese. These easy treats are especially tasty for brunch or as hors d'oeuvres. For a different but equally tasty treat, also try the Swiss Cheese Mini-Puffies variation provided at the end of the recipe.

1⅔ cups all-purpose white or unbleached flour
1 packet fast-rising dry yeast
¾ teaspoon salt
1 teaspoon granulated sugar
1 cup commercial buttermilk
2½ tablespoons butter or margarine, cut into 2 or 3 pieces
1 cup lightly packed grated sharp Cheddar cheese (about 4 ounces)

Stir together 1⅓ cups white flour, the yeast and salt in a large mixer bowl. In a small saucepan, combine buttermilk and butter and heat until butter melts and mixture reaches 125° to 130°. With mixer on low speed, beat liquid into dry ingredients until blended. Raise speed to high and beat for 2½ minutes longer. Add all but 2 table-spoons cheese, and the remaining ⅓ cup flour. Stir in vigorously with a large spoon; batter will be stiff and rubbery. Generously grease two 12-cup mini-muffin tins (cups about 2 inches in diameter). By generous teaspoonfuls, divide batter among mini-muffin cups. Sprinkle reserved 2 tablespoons cheese over batter. Set puffies aside, un-covered, in a very warm spot (80° to 90°) for 15 minutes. Preheat oven to 425°.

Bake puffies for 13 to 16 minutes, or until lightly browned and slightly springy to the touch. Transfer pans to racks and let stand for 1 to 2 minutes; then run a knife around cups to loosen rolls from pans. Puffies are best served warm, either plain or with butter. They may also be frozen and reheated at serving time, if desired. Makes 24 mini-puffies.

Approximate Preparation Time: 17 minutes   *Rising/Baking Time:* 29 minutes

VARIATION: Swiss Cheese Mini-Puffies—Follow basic recipe except reduce buttermilk to ½ cup and add ⅓ cup water and ⅛ teaspoon ground nutmeg to saucepan along with buttermilk. Also, substitute 1 cup grated or shredded Swiss or Gruyère cheese for Cheddar cheese. Proceed with preparations as directed in basic recipe.

NOTE: If desired, regular-sized muffin tins may be used instead. In this case, divide batter among ten or eleven greased cups and bake for about 16 to 18 minutes.

• *Savory No-Knead Rye Puffs* •

Start to Finish: About 57 minutes

An unusual blend of herbs and spices gives these quick muffin-shaped rolls their intriguing, savory taste.

1½ cups all-purpose white or unbleached flour
1 packet fast-rising dry yeast
1 tablespoon granulated sugar
1 teaspoon caraway seeds
¼ teaspoon ground nutmeg
⅛ teaspoon dried, crumbled sage leaves
1 cup hot water (125° to 130°)
2 tablespoons vegetable oil
1 egg, at room temperature
¾ cup medium or dark rye flour

Stir together 1 cup white flour, the yeast, sugar, caraway seeds, nutmeg and sage in a large mixer bowl. With mixer on low speed, beat hot water, then oil into flour-yeast mixture until blended. Raise speed to high and beat for 2½ minutes. Add egg and beat on medium speed for 30 seconds longer. By hand, quickly and vigorously stir in rye flour and remaining ½ cup white flour; batter will be rubbery. Cover bowl with plastic wrap and set aside in a very warm spot (80° to 90°) for 5 minutes. Meanwhile, generously grease twelve standard-sized muffin-tin cups.

With a spoon, divide batter evenly among the cups. Smooth out batter in cups using a greased knife. Set tin aside, uncovered, in a very warm place (80° to 90°) for 20 minutes. Preheat oven to 400°.

Bake puffs for 14 to 17 minutes, or until tinged with brown and slightly springy to the touch. Run a knife around puffs to loosen from cups and place on racks for 4 to 5 minutes; then serve, along with butter. Makes 12 puffs.

Approximate Preparation Time: 16 minutes   *Rising/Baking Time:* 40 minutes

• *No-Knead Caramel Sticky Buns* •

Start to Finish: About 1 hour

Soft, fluffy, dumplinglike buns bathed in an irresistibly rich caramel sauce. These are so moist and gooey you'll probably want to eat them with a fork.

2⅔ cups all-purpose white or unbleached flour
1 tablespoon fast-rising dry yeast (about 1½ packets)
¼ cup light brown sugar, packed
¾ teaspoon salt
⅔ cup hot water (125° to 130°)
1 tablespoon vegetable oil
1 egg, at room temperature
SAUCE
4 tablespoons butter or margarine, slightly softened
¾ teaspoon all-purpose white or unbleached flour
½ cup light brown sugar, packed
⅔ cup light cream or half-and-half
1 teaspoon vanilla extract
⅓ cup chopped walnuts or pecans

Stir together 1 cup flour, the yeast, ¼ cup brown sugar and the salt in a large mixer bowl. With mixer on low speed, beat hot water and oil into dry ingredients until blended. Raise speed to high and beat for 2 minutes. Add egg and beat for 30 seconds longer. Vigorously stir in 1⅔ cups more flour, using a large spoon; batter will be stiff and rubbery. Set aside.

Grease a 10-inch pie plate or 8 × 8 × 3-inch baking pan with 1 tablespoon butter. Combine remaining 3 tablespoons butter with ¾ teaspoon flour in a small saucepan over medium-high heat. Cook, stirring, until butter melts and mixture is smooth and well blended, about 1 minute. Continuing to stir, add ½ cup brown sugar, then about half the cream to pan. Heat, stirring, for about 1 minute longer, or until sugar dissolves and mixture is well blended. Remove sauce from heat and stir in remaining cream and the vanilla. Pour sauce into greased pan. Sprinkle pan with nuts. By rounded tablespoonfuls, spoon batter over sauce to form about 11 to 13 evenly spaced buns.

Cover pan with plastic wrap and set aside in a very warm spot (80° to 90°) for 15 minutes.

Remove plastic wrap and place buns in a cold oven; immediately set thermostat to 400°. Bake buns for 20 to 23 minutes, or until tinged with brown on top and slightly springy to the touch. Remove pan from oven and immediately invert over serving platter. Spoon any sauce clinging to the pan over buns. Buns are best served warm from the oven. However, they may be frozen and reheated, if desired. Makes about 11 to 13 buns.

Approximate Preparation Time: 23 minutes   *Rising/Baking Time:* 37 minutes

• *Jiffy Pecan Sticky Buns* •

Start to Finish: About 58 minutes

These are so tasty it's hard to believe they're also quick and easy to make.

> *2¾ to 3 cups all-purpose white or unbleached flour*
> *1 tablespoon fast-rising dry yeast (about 1½ packets)*
> *¾ teaspoon salt*
> *¼ teaspoon ground cinnamon*
> *1 cup commercial buttermilk*
> *2 tablespoons water*
> *2 tablespoons butter or margarine, cut into 2 pieces*
> *3 tablespoons light or dark brown sugar, packed*
> SAUCE
> *4 tablespoons butter or margarine, slightly softened*
> *½ cup coarsely chopped pecans*
> *⅔ cup corn syrup, preferably dark*
> *½ cup light or dark brown sugar, packed*

Stir together 1 cup flour, the yeast, salt and cinnamon in a large mixer bowl. Heat buttermilk, water, 2 tablespoons butter and 3 tablespoons brown sugar in a small saucepan until butter melts and mixture reaches 125° to 130°. With mixer on low speed, beat liquid into dry ingredients until blended. Raise speed to high and beat for 2½ minutes. Vigorously stir in 1½ cups more flour, using a large spoon. Working in the bowl or on a clean surface, quickly knead in enough more flour to yield a fairly stiff, malleable dough. Set aside.

Thickly grease two 8- or 9-inch round cake pans with 2 tablespoons softened butter each. Sprinkle ¼ cup pecans evenly into each pan. Drizzle ⅓ cup corn syrup into each pan. Sprinkle ¼ cup brown sugar into each pan.

Divide dough in half. With well-greased hands, shape one half into an evenly thick 8- to 9-inch log. Cut log crosswise into eight or nine slices; if necessary, reshape slices into rough rounds. Place slices, slightly separated, over the mixture of brown sugar and corn syrup in pan. Repeat procedure with second half of dough. Cover pans with a slightly damp cloth and set aside in a very warm spot (80° to 90°) for 20 minutes. Preheat oven to 425°.

Bake buns for 14 to 17 minutes, or until tinged with brown on top and slightly springy to the touch. Remove pans from oven and immediately invert over serving plates. Jiffy Pecan Sticky Buns are best served warm from the oven. However, they may be frozen and reheated, if desired. Makes 16 to 18 buns.

Approximate Preparation Time: 23 minutes   *Rising/Baking Time:* 35 minutes

• *60-Minute Cinnamon Pinwheels* •

Start to Finish: About 1 hour

Delicious cinnamon sweet rolls that make and bake up in a jiffy. For an added touch, drizzle on the optional confectioners'-sugar glaze.

> 2¾ to 3¼ cups all-purpose white or unbleached flour
> 1 tablespoon fast-rising dry yeast (about 1½ packets)
> ¼ cup granulated sugar
> ¼ cup instant nonfat dry milk
> ½ teaspoon salt
> ¼ teaspoon ground cinnamon
> 1 cup water
> 3 tablespoons vegetable oil
> FILLING
> 2½ tablespoons butter or margarine, softened
> 2½ teaspoons ground cinnamon
> ⅓ cup light or dark brown sugar, packed
> ½ cup raisins
> GLAZE (optional)
> ½ cup confectioners' sugar (sifted if lumpy)
> 2 to 3 drops vanilla extract
> 2 to 3 teaspoons water

Stir together 1¼ cups flour, the yeast, granulated sugar, milk powder, salt and ¼ teaspoon cinnamon in a large mixer bowl. Heat water and oil in a small saucepan to 125° to 130°. With mixer on low speed, beat liquid into dry ingredients until blended. Raise speed to high and beat for 2½ minutes. Vigorously stir in 1¼ cups additional flour, using a large spoon. Working on a clean, lightly floured surface, quickly and vigorously knead in enough more flour to yield a smooth, malleable but still slightly moist dough.

Thoroughly grease a 17½ × 11½-inch (or similar large) baking sheet and set aside. On a clean, lightly floured surface, press or roll dough out to form an evenly thick, 10 × 13-inch rectangle. With a knife, spread 2½ tablespoons softened butter evenly over dough. Sprinkle surface with 2½ teaspoons cinnamon, then the brown sugar and raisins. Working from a longer side, tightly roll up dough jelly-roll style. Gently stretch out dough to form an evenly thick 17- to 18-inch log. Cut dough crosswise into seventeen or eighteen pinwheel slices. Space pinwheels about 1 inch apart on baking sheet. Turn on oven to low heat for 1 minute; then turn off again.

Put pinwheels in oven and let rise, uncovered, for 15 minutes; then set thermostat to 375°. Bake pinwheels for 23 to 25 minutes, or until slightly springy to the touch and tinged with brown. If a glaze is desired, prepare as follows while rolls bake: Stir together confectioners' sugar and vanilla; gradually add enough water to yield a smooth, liquefied mixture.

Remove rolls from oven when done and let stand on baking sheet for 1 to 2 minutes; if glaze has been prepared, drizzle over rolls now. Immediately transfer pinwheels to serving platter, using spatula. Cinnamon pinwheels taste best fresh from the oven. However, they may be frozen and reheated, if desired. Makes about 18 pinwheels.

Approximate Preparation Time: 25 minutes   *Rising/Baking Time:* 39 minutes

• *Iced Lemon-Spice Puffies* •

Start to Finish: About 52 minutes

These look like light, puffy muffins and taste a bit like fresh Danish pastries.

> 2½ cups all-purpose white or unbleached flour
> 1 tablespoon fast-rising dry yeast (about 1½ packets)
> ¼ cup granulated sugar
> ¼ cup instant nonfat dry milk
> ⅛ teaspoon ground cinnamon
> ⅛ teaspoon ground nutmeg
> 1 cup water
> ¼ cup butter or margarine, cut into 3 or 4 pieces
> Grated rind of 1 medium-sized, well-washed lemon
> GLAZE
> ¾ cup confectioners' sugar (sifted if lumpy)
> 2½ teaspoons lemon juice
> 2 to 3 drops vanilla extract
> ½ to 1 teaspoon water, approximately

Stir together 1¼ cups flour, the yeast, granulated sugar, milk powder and spices in a large mixer bowl. Heat water and butter in a small saucepan until butter melts and mixture reaches 125° to 130°. With mixer on low speed, beat liquid into dry ingredients. Raise speed to high and beat for 2 minutes. Add grated lemon rind and beat 1 minute longer. Quickly and vigorously stir in 1¼ cups more flour, using a large spoon; batter will be rubbery. Thoroughly grease fifteen or sixteen standard-size muffin-tin cups. With a spoon, divide batter among the muffin cups. (It isn't necessary to smooth out surface of batter.) Set muffin tins aside, uncovered, in a very warm place (80° to 90°) for 17 to 18 minutes. Preheat oven to 400°.

Place puffies in oven; immediately reduce heat to 375° and bake 13 to 16 minutes, or until tops are tinged with brown and slightly springy to the touch. Meanwhile, prepare glaze as follows: Stir together confectioners' sugar, lemon juice and vanilla. Gradually add enough water to yield a smooth and fairly thick yet still spreadable consistency.

62

Run a knife around puffies to loosen from cups, and transfer to racks. Using a knife, quickly swirl a thin layer of glaze over puffies while still hot. Let stand 3 or 4 minutes longer before serving. Puffies are best still warm from the oven, but may be frozen and reheated, if desired. Makes 15 or 16 puffies.

Approximate Preparation Time: 20 minutes   *Rising/Baking Time:* 33 minutes

• *Apricot Streusel Puffs* •

Start to Finish: About 54 minutes

Delicious individual-sized coffee cakes enlivened with chopped apricots and garnished with a sweet streusel topping. These make a special breakfast or brunch treat.

¼ *cup finely chopped dried apricots*
2½ *tablespoons hot tap water*
2¼ *cups all-purpose white or unbleached flour*
1 *tablespoon fast-rising dry yeast (about 1½ packets)*
¼ *cup granulated sugar*
¼ *cup instant nonfat dry milk*
⅛ *teaspoon ground cinnamon*
1 *cup water*
3½ *tablespoons butter or margarine, cut into 2 or 3 pieces*
¾ *teaspoon almond extract*
¼ *teaspoon freshly grated orange rind*
STREUSEL
⅓ *cup all-purpose white or unbleached flour*
¼ *cup granulated sugar*
⅛ *teaspoon freshly grated orange rind*
2 *tablespoons cold butter, cut into 2 pieces*

Combine apricots and hot water in a small bowl, stirring to mix. Set aside. Stir together 1 cup flour, the yeast, ¼ cup sugar, milk powder and cinnamon in a large mixer bowl. Heat 1 cup water and 3½ tablespoons butter in a small saucepan until butter melts and mixture reaches 125° to 130°. With mixer on low speed, beat liquid into dry ingredients until blended. Raise speed to high and beat for 2½ minutes. With a large spoon, vigorously stir in chopped apricots (and any unabsorbed water), almond extract, ¼ teaspoon orange rind and remaining 1¼ cups flour to make a rubbery batter. Generously grease sixteen or seventeen standard-sized muffin-tin cups.

Divide batter evenly among greased muffin cups. (It isn't necessary to smooth out batter surface.) Set tins aside, uncovered, in a very warm place (80° to 90°) for 20 minutes. Preheat oven to 400°. Prepare streusel as follows: Stir together ⅓ cup flour, ¼ cup sugar and ⅛ teaspoon orange rind in a small, deep bowl. With pastry blender, forks or fingertips, work in butter until mixture is crumbly and resembles coarse meal.

Dividing evenly, sprinkle streusel over puffs. Bake puffs for 13 to 16 minutes, or until barely tinged with brown and slightly springy to the touch. Remove from oven and let stand in cups for 2 to 3 minutes. Run a knife around puffs to loosen from cups and place on racks to cool, or serve immediately. Puffs may also be frozen, then thawed and reheated before serving, if desired. Makes 16 or 17 puffs.

Approximate Preparation Time: 22 minutes   *Rising/Baking Time:* 34 minutes

• *Fried Apple-Spice Puffs* •

Start to Finish: About 1 hour

Easy apple-spice fritters that make a great breakfast or coffee-break treat. These offer the taste of homemade doughnuts, but without the fuss or wait.

2¾ *cups all-purpose white or unbleached flour*
1 *tablespoon fast-rising dry yeast (about 1½ packets)*
¼ *cup granulated sugar*
¾ *teaspoon salt*
¼ *teaspoon ground cinnamon*
⅔ *cup hot water (125° to 130°)*
2 *tablespoons vegetable oil*
1 *egg, at room temperature*
½ *cup peeled and very finely chopped tart cooking apple*
¼ *teaspoon freshly grated lemon rind*
Vegetable oil for deep-frying
SUGAR-SPICE MIXTURE
¼ *cup granulated sugar*
½ *teaspoon ground cinnamon*
¼ *teaspoon ground nutmeg*

Stir together 1 cup flour, the yeast, ¼ cup sugar, salt and ¼ teaspoon cinnamon in a large mixer bowl. With mixer on low speed, beat in hot water, then oil, until blended. Raise speed to medium and beat for 30 seconds. Add egg and beat for 30 seconds longer. Stir in apple and lemon rind, then remaining 1¾ cup flour to yield a stiff, rubbery batter. Place bowl in a larger bowl. Carefully add enough hot water (125° to 130°) to larger bowl to come ⅔ of the way up sides of mixer bowl. Lay a sheet of wax paper over mixer bowl. Let stand for 10 minutes.

Vigorously stir down batter. Drain off water from large bowl and replace with more hot water (125° to 130°). Re-cover mixer bowl with wax paper. Set aside for 15 minutes. Meanwhile, ready a large saucepan or pot for deep frying by filling 3 to 3½ inches deep with oil. Set out a rack and top with a layer of paper towels. Combine ¼ cup sugar, ½ teaspoon cinnamon and ¼ teaspoon nutmeg in a medium-sized paper bag and shake to mix. Set aside.

When batter has risen for about 10 minutes, place deep-frying oil over medium-high heat and bring to about 370°. Working lightly so as not to deflate batter, drop by smooth, rounded tablespoonfuls into oil; fry five or six puffs at a time. Turn puffs with a slotted spoon about every 30 seconds to ensure even cooking, and fry for a total of about 2 to 2½ minutes, or until deep golden brown all over. Raise or lower heat as necessary to maintain temperature at about 370°. Transfer puffs to rack lined with paper towels to cool. When all are cooked, place in batches in a paper bag with sugar-spice mixture and shake until thoroughly coated. Puffs are best served while still warm. Makes about 22 to 25 puffs.

Approximate Preparation Time: 20 minutes   *Rising/Frying Time:* 40 minutes

• *Toasted Almond Coffee Cakes* •

Start to Finish: About 1 hour

Delicately flavored, feather light and easy to make, these attractive coffee cakes will disappear fast.

> 2¾ cups all-purpose white or unbleached flour
> 1 packet fast-rising dry yeast
> ¼ cup granulated sugar
> ½ teaspoon salt
> ¼ teaspoon ground cinnamon
> 1 cup water
> 2 tablespoons vegetable oil
> 1 egg, at room temperature
> ¾ teaspoon almond extract
> TOPPING
> ¾ cup slivered, blanched almonds
> 1⅓ cups all-purpose white or unbleached flour
> ⅔ cup granulated sugar
> ½ cup cold butter or margarine

Stir together 1¼ cups flour, the yeast, ¼ cup sugar, salt and cinnamon in a large mixer bowl. Combine water and oil in small saucepan and heat to 125° to 130°. With mixer on low speed, beat liquid into dry ingredients until blended. Raise speed to high and beat for 2½ minutes. Add egg and almond extract, and beat for 30 seconds longer. Vigorously stir in remaining 1½ cups flour to make a fairly stiff batter. Generously grease two 10-inch round or square baking pans (or 9½-inch *deep dish* pie plates). Divide batter between pans; it will be very rubbery. Smooth and spread batter out to pan edges with a greased knife. (Layers will be thin but will rise a great deal.) Cover pans with plastic wrap. Turn oven on to low heat for 1 minute; then turn off again. Put pans in oven and let coffee cakes rise, uncovered, for 20 minutes.

Meanwhile, prepare topping as follows: Spread almonds in ungreased skillet over high heat. Toast almonds, stirring constantly, for 2 minutes. Reduce heat to medium and toast, stirring constantly, for 1 to 1½ minutes longer, or until almonds are fragrant and just barely tinged with brown. Immediately remove pan from heat and continue stirring for 30 seconds longer. Set aside. Stir together 1⅓ cups flour and ⅔ cup sugar in a medium-sized bowl. With pastry blender, forks or fingertips, work in butter until mixture is crumbly and resembles coarse meal. Set aside.

Sprinkle half of flour-sugar topping mixture, then half of toasted almonds over each coffee cake. Return pans to cold oven and immediately set thermostat to 375°. Bake for 23 to 26 minutes, or until coffee cake tops are slightly springy to the touch and barely tinged with brown. Remove pans from oven and let stand for 2 to 3 minutes before serving. Coffee cakes are best served warm from the oven but may be frozen and reheated, if desired. Makes 2 coffee cakes, 6 to 8 servings each.

Approximate Preparation Time: 20 minutes   *Rising/Baking Time:* 44 minutes

◆ *Orange Crumb-Nut Coffee Cake* ◆

Start to Finish: About 56 minutes

Mixed up quickly, using a blender, this easy coffee cake is moist, tender and very tasty.

> 2¼ cups all-purpose white or unbleached flour
> 1 packet fast-rising dry yeast
> ⅓ cup granulated sugar
> ½ teaspoon salt
> ¾ cup water
> ¼ cup vegetable oil
> 1 strip of orange peel 2½ inches long and 1 inch wide (orange part only)
> 1 egg, at room temperature
> ¼ cup chopped walnuts
> CRUMB-NUT TOPPING
> ⅓ cup all-purpose white or unbleached flour
> 3 tablespoons granulated sugar
> ¾ teaspoon freshly grated orange rind
> 2 tablespoons cold butter or margarine
> ¼ cup chopped walnuts

Stir together ½ cup flour, the yeast, ⅓ cup sugar and salt in a large cup. Combine water and oil in small saucepan and heat to 125° to 130°. Put water-oil mixture in a blender container. Cut strip of orange peel into four or five pieces. Add to blender and blend on high speed for 1 minute. Reduce speed to medium and add flour-yeast mixture. Blend on medium speed for 20 seconds. Add egg and ¼ cup more flour, and blend 10 seconds longer.

Pour blended mixture into deep, medium-sized bowl. With a large spoon, vigorously stir in remaining 1½ cups flour and ¼ cup walnuts until batter is well blended. Generously grease a 10-inch round or square baking pan (or 9½-inch *deep dish* pie plate). Spoon batter into pan; smooth out top of batter with a greased knife. Cover pan with plastic wrap. Set aside in a very warm spot (80° to 90°) for 20 minutes. Meanwhile, prepare topping as follows: Stir together ⅓ cup flour, 3 tablespoons sugar and orange rind in a small bowl. With pastry blender, forks or fingertips, work in butter until mixture is crumbly and resembles coarse meal. Stir in ¼ cup walnuts and set aside.

Sprinkle topping evenly over batter. Place coffee cake in cold oven and immediately set thermostat to 400°. Bake for 23 to 26 minutes, or until coffee cake's top is slightly springy to the touch and tinged with brown. Remove pan from oven and let stand for 3 to 4 minutes before serving. Makes 1 coffee cake, 8 or 9 servings.

Approximate Preparation Time: 17 minutes   *Rising/Baking Time:* 44 minutes

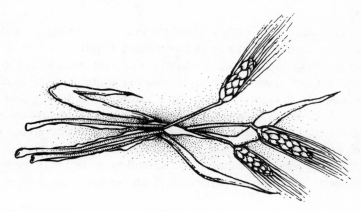

• *Sour Cream and Apple Kuchen* •

Start to Finish: About 1 hour

Moist, tender and creamy-rich, this kuchen can be served for dessert or as a special breakfast treat.

> 2¾ cups all-purpose white or unbleached flour
> 1 tablespoon fast-rising dry yeast (about 1½ packets)
> ¼ cup granulated sugar
> ½ teaspoon salt
> ¼ teaspoon ground cinnamon
> 1 cup water
> 1 tablespoon vegetable oil
> ¼ cup commercial sour cream
> 1 egg, at room temperature
> 1 medium apple, peeled, cored and chopped
> ⅓ cup golden raisins
> SOUR CREAM MIXTURE
> 1 tablespoon sugar
> Generous 1 tablespoon cornstarch
> ¾ cup commercial sour cream
> 1 teaspoon vanilla extract
> SUGAR TOPPING
> ⅔ cup granulated sugar
> 2¼ teaspoons ground cinnamon
> 1 tablespoon cold butter or margarine

Stir together 1¼ cups flour, the yeast, ¼ cup sugar, salt and ¼ teaspoon cinnamon in a large mixer bowl. Combine water, oil and ¼ cup sour cream in small saucepan, and heat to 125° to 130°. With mixer on low speed, beat liquid into dry ingredients until blended. Raise speed to high and beat for 2½ minutes. Add egg and beat 30 seconds longer. Vigorously stir in chopped apple, raisins and remaining 1½ cups flour to make a stiff batter. Generously grease two 10-inch round or square pans (or 9½-inch *deep dish* pie plates). Divide batter between pans. Smooth and spread batter out to pan edges with a greased knife. Cover pans with plastic wrap. Turn oven on to low

72

heat for 1 minute; then turn off again. Put pans in warm oven. Let kuchen rise for 17 to 18 minutes.

Meanwhile, prepare sour cream mixture as follows: Stir together 1 tablespoon sugar and cornstarch in a small bowl until blended. Stir in ¾ cup sour cream and vanilla until smooth and well mixed. Prepare topping as follows: Stir together ⅔ cup sugar and 2¼ teaspoons cinnamon in a small deep bowl until blended. Cut in butter with pastry blender, forks or fingertips until incorporated. Set aside.

Lightly spoon half of sour cream mixture over each kuchen. Working lightly so as not to deflate batter, evenly spread sour cream mixture over batter surface using a knife. Dividing evenly between pans, sprinkle topping mixture over sour cream. Place kuchen in cold oven and immediately set thermostat to 400°. Bake for 24 to 27 minutes, or until tops are slightly springy to the touch and tinged with brown. Remove pans from oven and let stand for 4 to 5 minutes before serving kuchen. Serve while still warm from the oven, or reheated. Makes 2 kuchen, 6 to 8 servings each.

Approximate Preparation Time: 23 minutes   *Rising/Baking Time:* 44 minutes

Easy Cinnamon Streusel Coffee Cakes

Start to Finish: About 1 hour

Enjoy the delicious taste of traditional streusel-topped coffee cakes made the time-saving way. These require only one rising and can be ready for the breakfast or coffee table in under an hour.

4¼ cups all-purpose white or unbleached flour
2 packets fast-rising dry yeast
½ cup granulated sugar
¼ cup instant nonfat dry milk
1 teaspoon salt
1½ teaspoons ground cinnamon
1½ cups water
½ cup butter or margarine, cut into 5 or 6 pieces
1 egg, at room temperature
STREUSEL
1 cup all-purpose white or unbleached flour
½ cup light brown sugar, packed
1¼ teaspoons ground cinnamon
7 tablespoons cold butter or margarine, cut into 6 or 7 pieces

Stir together 2 cups flour, the yeast, granulated sugar, milk powder, salt and 1½ teaspoons cinnamon in a large mixer bowl. Heat water and butter in a small saucepan until butter melts and mixture reaches 125° to 130°. With mixer on low speed, beat liquid into dry ingredients until blended. Raise speed to high and beat for 2 minutes. Add egg and beat 30 seconds longer. Vigorously stir in 2¼ cups more flour to make a stiff batter. Grease two 10-inch round or square baking pans (or 9½-inch *deep dish* pie plates). Divide batter between pans. Smooth and spread batter out to pan edges with a greased knife. Turn oven on to low heat for 1 minute; then turn off again. Put pans, uncovered, in warm oven. Let batter rise for 20 minutes. Meanwhile, prepare streusel topping as follows: Stir together all streusel ingredients, except butter, in a medium-sized bowl. With pastry blender, forks or fingertips, work in 7 tablespoons cold butter until mixture is crumbly and resembles very coarse meal. Set aside.

Sprinkle half of streusel evenly over batter in each pan. Put pans in cold oven and immediately set thermostat to 400°. Bake coffee cakes for 23 to 27 minutes, or until tops are slightly springy to the touch and tinged with brown. Remove pans from oven and let coffee cakes stand for 5 minutes before serving. Coffee cakes may also be frozen and reheated before serving, if desired. Makes 2 coffee cakes, 8 to 9 servings each.

Approximate Preparation Time: 18 minutes   *Rising/Baking Time:* 45 minutes

• *Sour Cherry Crumb Kuchen* •

Start to Finish: About 1 hour

The perfect dessert for a coffee klatch. It's deliciously rich and moist.

For an equally tasty kuchen that can be made using blueberries, see the variation given at the end of this recipe.

> *2¼ cups all-purpose white or unbleached flour*
> *1 packet fast-rising dry yeast*
> *¼ cup granulated sugar*
> *½ teaspoon salt*
> *¾ cup hot water (125° to 130°)*
> *3 tablespoons vegetable oil*
> *Grated rind from half a well-washed, medium-sized lemon*
> FRUIT LAYER
> *2 tablespoons all-purpose white or unbleached flour*
> *¼ cup granulated sugar*
> *½ cup commercial sour cream*
> *½ teaspoon vanilla extract*
> *1 16-ounce can unsweetened, pitted sour (pie) cherries*
> CRUMB TOPPING
> *½ cup all-purpose white or unbleached flour*
> *¼ cup granulated sugar*
> *¼ teaspoon ground cinnamon*
> *2½ tablespoons cold butter*

Stir together 1 cup flour, the yeast, ¼ cup sugar and salt in a large mixer bowl. With mixer on low speed, beat water, then oil, into dry ingredients until blended. Raise mixer speed to high and beat for 3 minutes. Vigorously stir in lemon rind and 1¼ cups more white flour; batter will be fairly stiff and rubbery. Generously grease an 8- or 9-inch-square by *3-inch-deep* baking pan (or 10-inch pie plate). Spoon batter into pan, spreading out to edges with a greased knife. Cover pan with plastic wrap and set aside in a very warm place (80° to 90°) for 15 minutes. Meanwhile, prepare fruit layer as follows: Stir together 2 tablespoons flour and ¼ cup sugar in a small bowl until well blended. Add sour cream and vanilla and continue stirring until smooth. Set cherries aside in a colander to drain thoroughly. Prepare crumb mixture by stirring together ½ cup flour, ¼ cup sugar and cinnamon until well blended. Cut in cold butter with a pastry blender, forks or fingertips until mixture resembles coarse meal.

Working gently so as not to deflate batter, spread sour cream mixture over surface with a knife. Sprinkle cherries over sour cream; then sprinkle crumb mixture evenly over top. Place kuchen in a cold oven; immediately set thermostat to 400°. Bake for 22 to 27 minutes, or until top is lightly browned and bubbly hot. Transfer pan to rack and let cool at least 4 or 5 minutes before serving kuchen. Cut into squares or wedges and serve from pan. Makes 1 kuchen, 8 or 9 servings.

Approximate Preparation Time: 25 minutes   *Rising/Baking Time:* 39 minutes

VARIATION: Blueberry Crumb Kuchen—Prepare as for cherry kuchen except substitute 1½ cups fresh (or frozen thawed and well-drained) blueberries for sour cherries. Also, in the fruit layer reduce sugar from ¼ cup to 2 tablespoons.

◆ 60-MINUTE QUICK BREADS ◆

When "quick" breads got their name, they really were much quicker to prepare than ones leavened with yeast. With the advent of fast-rising yeast and modern baking techniques, however, the distinction between the two types of breads has begun to blur. Simple yeast breads can be whipped up nearly as fast as biscuits and muffins.

Still, quick breads do have a special charm of their own. And they are the only solution when you want homemade bread and happen to be out of yeast. This section contains a tasty variety of muffins, biscuits and quick-bread loaves, all of which are designed for the cook in a hurry. Every one can be prepared in about 60 minutes, and most take only 30 to 40 minutes.

You'll notice that in this section only, the recipes call for all-purpose white or unbleached flour or *pastry flour*. All of the breads will come out fine made with white or unbleached flour, but if you can obtain it, pastry flour is a good choice because it's lower in gluten than the other two. Although gluten is essential in breads raised with yeast, it has no advantages for breads leavened with baking powder and soda. In fact, developing the gluten in these breads tends to make them tough. This is why recipes included here usually warn against overmixing. Gently stir ingredients until well blended, but resist the impulse to give the batter any extra turns for good measure!

• *Strawberry Muffins* •

Start to Finish: About 38 minutes

Yogurt makes these muffins tender. Strawberries make them delicious.

   2⅓ cups all-purpose white or unbleached flour or pastry flour
   ⅓ cup granulated sugar
   2¼ teaspoons baking powder
   ½ teaspoon baking soda
   ¼ teaspoon salt
   ¾ cup fresh (or frozen, thawed and drained) sliced strawberries
   2 tablespoons vegetable oil
   1 egg, lightly beaten
   ⅔ cup plain yogurt, preferably lowfat
   1 teaspoon vanilla extract
   About 1½ tablespoons sugar for sprinkling over muffins

Preheat oven to 400°. Lightly grease fifteen standard-sized muffin-tin cups, or fit with paper liners. Stir together flour, sugar, baking powder, soda and salt in a medium-sized bowl until well mixed. Put strawberries in a small, deep bowl. If slices are large, mash lightly with a fork to break up into small pieces. Stir oil, egg, yogurt and vanilla into strawberries. Add strawberry mixture to dry ingredients; gently stir until thoroughly blended, but do not overmix. Divide batter evenly among prepared cups. Lightly sprinkle muffin tops with sugar.

Bake muffins for 22 to 25 minutes, or until tops are tinged with brown and springy to the touch. Strawberry Muffins are best served warm, although they may be frozen and reheated, if desired. Makes 15 medium-sized muffins.

Approximate Preparation Time: 15 minutes   *Baking Time:* 23 minutes

• *Walnut-Maple Muffins* •

Start to Finish: About 35 minutes

Tasty, walnutty muffins sweetened with maple syrup. These are good with coffee or tea or a glass of milk.

2¼ cups all-purpose white or unbleached flour or pastry flour
¼ cup instant nonfat dry milk
1 tablespoon baking powder
½ teaspoon salt
¼ cup vegetable oil
1 egg, lightly beaten
Generous ⅓ cup maple or maple-flavored syrup
½ cup water
1 teaspoon vanilla extract
½ cup finely chopped walnuts

Preheat oven to 400°. Lightly grease twelve standard-sized muffin-tin cups, or fit with paper liners. Stir together flour, milk powder, baking powder and salt in a medium-sized bowl until well blended. Add all remaining ingredients, except walnuts, to flour mixture. Gently stir until thoroughly blended but not overmixed; batter will be stiff. Gently fold in walnuts. Divide batter evenly among prepared cups.

Bake muffins for 18 to 22 minutes, or until tinged with brown and springy to the touch. Serve warm from the oven. Makes 12 large muffins.

Approximate Preparation Time: 15 minutes   *Baking Time:* 20 minutes

◆ *Apple Crumb Muffins* ◆

Start to Finish: About 45 minutes

Large, high muffins with a contrasting light crumb topping. These look special and taste great!

CRUMB TOPPING
¾ *cup all-purpose white or unbleached flour or pastry flour*
¼ *cup granulated sugar*
¼ *teaspoon ground cinnamon*
⅛ *teaspoon ground nutmeg*
¼ *cup cold butter or margarine*

BATTER
1¼ *cups all-purpose white or unbleached flour or pastry flour*
1 *cup whole-wheat flour*
½ *cup granulated sugar*
1¾ *teaspoons baking powder*
½ *teaspoon baking soda*
½ *teaspoon ground cinnamon*
¼ *teaspoon ground mace*
¼ *teaspoon ground allspice*
¼ *teaspoon salt*
1 *egg*
½ *cup milk*
¼ *cup vegetable oil*
¼ *cup orange juice*
1⅓ *cups peeled and finely chopped tart cooking apple*

Combine all crumb topping ingredients, except butter, in a medium-sized bowl. With pastry blender, forks or fingertips, work in butter until mixture is crumbly. Set topping aside. Preheat oven to 400°. Lightly grease sixteen or seventeen standard-sized muffin-tin cups, or fit with paper liners.

To make batter, stir together white flour, whole-wheat flour, sugar, baking powder, soda, spices and salt in a medium-sized bowl until well mixed. Lightly beat egg in a small, deep bowl. Stir all remaining ingredients, except apple, into beaten egg until blended. Gently stir liquid mixture and apple into dry ingredients until thoroughly blended, but do not overmix. Divide batter evenly among prepared cups. Spoon a heaping teaspoon of crumb mixture over each muffin. Divide any leftover topping among cups.

Bake muffins for 22 to 25 minutes, or until crumb mixture is just tinged with brown and tops are springy to the touch. Apple Crumb Muffins are best served warm. Freeze for later use and then reheat before serving, if desired. Makes 16 to 17 large muffins.

Approximate Preparation Time: 20 minutes   *Baking Time:* 23 minutes

• *Almond Muffins* •

Start to Finish: About 38 minutes

These are tender and delicately flavored muffins with a sprinkling of sliced almonds on top. Serve them along with a meal or with coffee or tea.

> 2 cups all-purpose white or unbleached flour or pastry flour
> Generous ⅓ cup granulated sugar
> ¼ cup instant nonfat dry milk
> 2½ teaspoons baking powder
> ½ teaspoon salt
> ¾ cup water
> 2 eggs
> ½ teaspoon almond extract
> ½ teaspoon vanilla extract
> 3 tablespoons butter, melted
> ½ cup coarsely chopped unblanched sliced almonds

Preheat oven to 425°. Generously grease twelve standard-sized muffin-tin cups, or fit with paper liners. Stir together flour, sugar, milk powder, baking powder and salt in a medium-sized bowl until well blended. With a fork, beat water, eggs and extracts together in a small bowl until smooth. Add liquid mixture and melted butter to dry ingredients and gently stir until batter is blended but not overmixed. (Batter will be fairly runny.) Divide mixture evenly among prepared muffin cups. Top each muffin with a sprinkling of almonds.

Bake muffins for 17 to 21 minutes, or until nicely browned and tops are springy to the touch. Muffins are best served warm from the oven, plain or with butter. They may be frozen for later use, if desired. Makes 12 medium-sized muffins.

Approximate Preparation Time: 17 minutes   *Baking Time:* 19 minutes

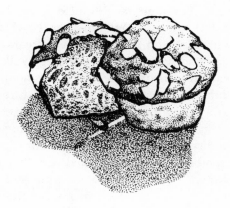

• *Lemon and Blueberry Muffins* •

Start to Finish: About 40 minutes

Light, delicately textured, slightly sweet muffins with a hint of lemon to heighten the blueberry flavor.

2⅔ cups all-purpose white or unbleached flour or pastry flour
⅓ cup instant nonfat dry milk
4 teaspoons baking powder
¾ teaspoon salt
7 tablespoons butter or margarine, at room temperature
¾ cup granulated sugar
1 egg plus 1 egg yolk
1 teaspoon freshly grated lemon rind
½ teaspoon vanilla extract
1 cup warm water
1⅓ cups rinsed fresh (or frozen) unsweetened blueberries
1 tablespoon all-purpose white or unbleached flour or pastry flour

Generously grease fifteen standard-sized muffin-tin cups. Preheat oven to 425°. Stir together 2⅔ cups flour, the milk powder, baking powder and salt in a medium-sized bowl. In a small, deep mixing bowl, with mixer on medium speed, cream butter and sugar until well blended and fluffy. Add egg and egg yolk, lemon rind and vanilla, and beat until mixture is light and smooth. Reduce mixer speed to low and beat in warm water until mixture is well blended.

Pat blueberries dry with paper towels. Stir together berries and 1 tablespoon flour in a small bowl until berries are well coated. Add liquid mixture to dry ingredients and gently stir together until batter is thoroughly blended but not overmixed. Gently fold in blueberries until just distributed. Divide batter among greased muffin cups.

Place muffins in preheated oven; immediately reduce heat to 400°. Bake about 19 to 21 minutes, or until muffin tops are tinged with brown and springy to the touch. Remove tins to racks to cool 2 to 3 minutes. Gently run a knife around muffins to loosen from cups. Muffins are best served warm from the oven, or they may be frozen for later use. Serve plain or with butter. Makes 15 large muffins.

Approximate Preparation Time: 20 minutes   *Baking Time:* 20 minutes

◆ *Banana-Bran Muffins* ◆

Start to Finish: About 38 minutes

Perfect for breakfast or brunch, these muffins are hearty and wholesome, yet light and tender too.

1 cup all-purpose white or unbleached flour or pastry flour
⅔ cup whole-wheat flour
¼ cup instant nonfat dry milk
2½ teaspoons baking powder
½ teaspoon baking soda
½ teaspoon salt
½ cup unprocessed (wheat) bran
½ cup finely chopped walnuts
1 egg, at room temperature, separated
¼ cup butter or margarine, at room temperature
¼ cup light brown sugar, packed
¾ cup mashed ripe, but not overripe, bananas (about 2 medium)
½ cup water

Preheat oven to 425°. Lightly grease twelve standard-sized muffin-tin cups. Stir together white flour, whole-wheat flour, milk powder, baking powder, baking soda, salt, bran and walnuts in a medium-sized bowl until thoroughly blended.

In a small, deep, grease-free mixer bowl, with mixer on medium speed, beat egg white until frothy. Raise speed to high and beat until white stands in firm but not dry peaks. Set aside.

In another mixer bowl, with mixer on medium speed, cream butter and brown sugar until very fluffy and smooth. Add egg yolk and banana pulp, and beat 2 minutes longer, or until almost smooth. Reduce mixer speed to low, and gradually beat in water until well blended.

Add banana mixture and beaten egg white to dry ingredients. Gently fold into dry ingredients until thoroughly incorporated but not overmixed; batter will be slightly stiff. Divide batter evenly among greased muffin cups.

Place muffins in preheated oven; immediately reduce heat to 400°. Bake 18 to 21 minutes, or until tops are tinged with brown and

85

springy to the touch. Remove tin to rack to cool 3 to 4 minutes. Run a knife around muffins to loosen from cups. Serve muffins warm, with lots of butter. Banana-Bran Muffins may also be served at room temperature or frozen for later use, if desired. Makes 12 muffins.

Approximate Preparation Time: 19 minutes   *Baking Time:* 19 minutes

• *Pumpkin Spice Muffins* •

Start to Finish: About 40 minutes

The pleasant, spicy taste of pumpkin pie in muffin form. These easy treats are very moist and flavorful.

> 1¾ *cups all-purpose white or unbleached flour or pastry flour*
> ½ *cup granulated sugar*
> ¼ *cup instant nonfat dry milk*
> 2½ *teaspoons baking powder*
> 1½ *teaspoons ground cinnamon*
> 1 *teaspoon ground allspice*
> ½ *teaspoon ground ginger*
> ¼ *teaspoon salt*
> ½ *cup finely chopped dates*
> ½ *cup finely chopped walnuts (optional)*
> ⅓ *cup water*
> 1 *egg*
> ¼ *cup vegetable oil*
> ⅔ *cup canned pumpkin (not pumpkin pie filling)*
> 1 *teaspoon vanilla extract*

Preheat oven to 375°. Generously grease twelve standard-sized muffin-tin cups, or fit with paper liners. Stir together flour, sugar, milk powder, baking powder, cinnamon, allspice, ginger and salt in a medium-sized bowl until well mixed. Stir in dates, and walnuts (if desired), and set aside.

86

Combine water and egg in a small, deep bowl, and beat with a fork until blended. Add all remaining ingredients and beat until smooth. Add liquid mixture to dry ingredients, and gently stir until batter is well blended but not overmixed. Divide batter evenly among muffin cups; cups will be nearly full.

Bake for 20 to 24 minutes, or until muffins are tinged with brown and tops are springy to the touch. Immediately run a knife around cups to loosen muffins and remove to racks. Serve muffins warm from the oven, or at room temperature. Makes 12 large muffins.

Approximate Preparation Time: 17 minutes   *Baking Time:* 22 minutes

• *Cranberry-Cream Muffins* •

Start to Finish: About 40 minutes

Cranberries and cream team up to lend these fragrant, puffy muffins an appealing smooth-tart taste. The muffins are very pretty, too.

2¼ *cups all-purpose white or unbleached flour or pastry flour*
1 *tablespoon baking powder*
¼ *teaspoon baking soda*
¼ *teaspoon ground cinnamon*
½ *teaspoon salt*
½ *cup granulated sugar*
1 *egg*
1 *cup light cream or half-and-half*
3½ *tablespoons vegetable oil*
½ *teaspoon vanilla extract*
1⅓ *cups fresh or frozen cranberries, sorted, rinsed and well drained*
2 *tablespoons granulated sugar*
1 *tablespoon all-purpose white or unbleached flour or pastry flour*

Preheat oven to 425°. Generously grease twelve standard-sized muffin-tin cups. Stir together 2¼ cups flour, the baking powder, baking soda, cinnamon and salt in a medium-sized bowl until well mixed.

Combine ½ cup sugar and egg in a small, deep mixer bowl. With mixer on medium speed, cream until mixture is very fluffy and light. Reduce mixer speed to low and beat in cream, oil and vanilla until well blended and slightly frothy. Pat cranberries completely dry on paper towels. Coarsely chop cranberries and set aside in a small, deep bowl.

Gently stir cream mixture into dry ingredients until thoroughly blended, but do not overmix. Immediately sprinkle 2 tablespoons sugar and 1 tablespoon flour over cranberries and toss until thoroughly coated. Fold cranberries into batter until just distributed. Divide batter among greased muffin cups.

Bake muffins 19 to 22 minutes, or until tops are nicely browned and springy to the touch; if tops begin to brown too rapidly, reduce heat to 400° for last 5 minutes of baking time. Remove muffin tin to rack to cool 4 to 5 minutes. Gently run a knife around muffins to loosen from cups. Muffins are best when served warm from the oven, although they may be frozen and reheated for later use, if desired. Serve plain, with butter or with slightly softened cream cheese. Makes 12 large muffins.

Approximate Preparation Time: 20 minutes   *Baking Time:* 20 minutes

◆ *Honey-Pecan Muffins* ◆

Start to Finish: About 43 minutes

These moist, tender muffins feature the subtle taste of sweet pecans and golden honey.

¾ cup finely chopped pecans
2 cups all-purpose white or unbleached flour or pastry flour
¼ cup instant nonfat dry milk
1 tablespoon baking powder
⅛ teaspoon baking soda
½ teaspoon salt
¾ cup warm water
¼ cup honey
3 tablespoons butter, at room temperature
2½ tablespoons light brown sugar, packed
1 egg

Preheat oven to 375°. Spread pecans in a pie plate or similar flat baking dish. Toast pecans in oven for 10 minutes, stirring occasionally. Reduce oven temperature to 350°. Grease twelve standard-sized muffin-tin cups. Stir together flour, milk powder, baking powder, baking soda and salt in a medium-sized bowl until well mixed. Add all except 2½ tablespoons toasted pecans to dry ingredients and stir until blended. (Reserve remaining 2½ tablespoons pecans for garnishing muffins.) Combine water and honey in a small bowl, and stir until honey dissolves.

Combine butter and brown sugar in a small, deep mixer bowl. With mixer on medium speed, beat until well blended. Add egg and beat about 2 minutes longer, or until mixture is very light and fluffy. Reduce mixer speed to low and gradually beat in water-honey mixture until blended. Add liquid mixture to dry ingredients. Stir gently until batter is thoroughly blended, but do not overmix. Divide batter evenly among greased muffin cups. Sprinkle with toasted pecans.

Bake muffins about 20 to 23 minutes, or until tops are lightly browned and springy to the touch. Remove tin to rack and let cool 4 to 5 minutes. Gently run a knife around muffins to loosen from cups. Muffins are best served still warm from the oven, with butter. Makes 12 large muffins.

Approximate Preparation Time: 22 minutes   *Baking Time:* 21 minutes

• *Spiced Orange Muffins* •

Start to Finish: About 40 minutes

The combination of zesty orange and a careful blend of spices makes these delicious.

1 cup all-purpose white or unbleached flour or pastry flour
1 cup whole-wheat flour
1½ teaspoons baking powder
¾ teaspoon baking soda
1¼ teaspoons ground mace
1 teaspoon ground cinnamon
½ teaspoon ground ginger
¼ teaspoon salt
⅓ cup cold butter or margarine, cut into 4 or 5 pieces
Half a medium-sized, well-washed, thin-skinned (juice) orange, seeded and coarsely chopped
Scant ¼ cup milk
⅔ cup granulated sugar
2 teaspoons vanilla extract
2 eggs
⅔ cup raisins
⅓ cup finely chopped walnuts

Preheat oven to 375°. Lightly grease fifteen standard-sized muffin-tin cups, or fit with paper liners. Stir together white flour, whole-wheat flour, baking powder, baking soda, spices and salt in a medium-sized bowl until thoroughly mixed. Cut in butter with pastry blender or forks until mixture resembles coarse meal. Place all remaining ingredients, except raisins and walnuts, in blender container or food-processor bowl. Blend on medium speed or process for 30 seconds. Scrape down container sides or processor bowl, and blend or process 1 minute longer, or until mixture is completely pureed and smooth. Pour pureed mixture, then raisins and walnuts, into dry ingredients. Gently stir until thoroughly blended, but not overmixed. Divide mixture evenly among prepared cups.

Bake muffins for 22 to 25 minutes, or until muffins are golden brown and tops are springy to the touch. Serve warm. Muffins may also be frozen and reheated for later use. Makes 15 muffins.

Approximate Preparation Time: 17 minutes   *Baking Time:* 23 minutes

• *Honey and Oats Muffins* •

Start to Finish: About 38 minutes

Try these delicious, yet healthful muffins once, and you'll probably make them over and over again.

> 1 cup old-fashioned or quick-cooking rolled oats
> 1¼ cups commercial buttermilk
> ¼ cup honey
> ¾ cup all-purpose white or unbleached flour or pastry flour
> ¾ cup whole-wheat flour
> ¼ cup light brown sugar, packed
> 1¾ teaspoons baking powder
> ½ teaspoon baking soda
> ½ teaspoon salt
> 1 egg, lightly beaten
> ¼ cup vegetable oil

Preheat oven to 400°. Lightly grease twelve standard-sized
muffin-tin cups, or fit with paper liners. Combine oats, buttermilk
and honey in a small saucepan. Bring to a boil over medium heat,
stirring. Simmer 30 seconds; then set aside to cool.

Stir together white flour, whole-wheat flour, brown sugar, baking powder, baking soda and salt in a medium-sized bowl until thoroughly mixed. Add cooked oats mixture, then egg and oil to dry
ingredients; stir gently until thoroughly blended but not overmixed.
Divide batter evenly among prepared cups.

Place in preheated oven; immediately reduce temperature to
375°. Bake for 21 to 23 minutes, or until muffins are golden brown and
tops are slightly springy to the touch. Serve warm, with butter if
desired. Makes 12 muffins.

Approximate Preparation Time: 16 minutes   *Baking Time:* 22 minutes

• Corn Muffins •

Start to Finish: About 38 minutes

An old standby full of corn goodness and flavor. These will add interest and nutrition to any meal.

2 cups all-purpose white or unbleached flour or pastry flour
1 cup yellow or white cornmeal
¼ cup instant nonfat dry milk
¼ cup granulated sugar
1 tablespoon baking powder
1 teaspoon salt
1 cup water
2 eggs
¼ cup vegetable oil

Preheat oven to 400°. Generously grease eighteen standard-sized muffin-tin cups, or fit with paper liners. Stir together flour, cornmeal, milk powder, sugar, baking powder and salt in a medium-sized bowl until thoroughly mixed. With a fork, beat all remaining ingredients together in a small bowl until smooth. Add liquid mixture to dry ingredients, and gently stir until batter is well blended but not over-mixed. (Batter will be fairly runny.) Divide mixture evenly among prepared muffin cups.

Bake muffins for 23 to 26 minutes, or until tops are tinged with brown and springy to the touch. Corn muffins are best served warm from the oven, with butter if desired. Makes 18 medium-sized muffins.

Approximate Preparation Time: 13 minutes   *Baking Time:* 25 minutes

• *Sunflower Seed Muffins* •

Start to Finish: About 35 minutes

Sunflower seeds give these savory muffins an interesting crunch and distinctive nutty flavor. Incidentally, they also contribute a considerable amount of extra protein.

1 cup roasted sunflower seeds, preferably unsalted
1 cup all-purpose white or unbleached flour or pastry flour
1 cup whole-wheat flour
¼ cup instant nonfat dry milk
2½ teaspoons baking powder
¾ teaspoon salt (if salted sunflower seeds are used, reduce salt to ½
teaspoon)
1 cup water
1 egg
3 tablespoons vegetable oil
1 tablespoon honey

Preheat oven to 425°. Lightly grease twelve standard-sized muffin-tin cups, or fit with paper liners. Place sunflower seeds in a blender container. Blend on medium speed until chopped moderately fine; stop motor once or twice and stir to redistribute seeds if necessary. Combine white flour, whole-wheat flour, milk powder, baking powder, salt and all but 3 tablespoons of chopped sunflower seeds in a medium-sized bowl. Stir until thoroughly mixed. With a fork, beat all remaining ingredients, except reserved sunflower seeds, together in a small bowl until honey dissolves and mixture is smooth. Add liquid mixture to dry ingredients and gently stir until batter is well blended but not overmixed.

Divide batter evenly among muffin cups (they will be full). Sprinkle reserved 3 tablespoons seeds over batter. Place muffins in oven and immediately reduce heat to 400°. Bake 16 to 19 minutes, or until tinged with brown and tops are springy to the touch. Sunflower Seed Muffins do not keep well, so serve still warm from the oven, with butter if desired. Makes 12 large muffins.

Approximate Preparation Time: 17 minutes   *Baking Time:* 18 minutes

• *Easy Yogurt Biscuits* •

Start to Finish: About 30 minutes

Yogurt makes these easy biscuits moist and tender without contributing a "yogurty" taste.

> 2¼ *cups all-purpose white or unbleached flour or pastry flour*
> 2 *teaspoons baking powder*
> ¾ *teaspoon baking soda*
> ¾ *teaspoon salt*
> ⅓ *cup cold butter or margarine*
> *About ⅔ to ¾ cup plain yogurt, preferably lowfat*

Preheat oven to 450°. Stir together flour, baking powder, soda and salt in a medium-sized bowl. Cut butter into dry ingredients with a fork or pastry blender until mixture resembles coarse meal. Add ⅔ cup yogurt to flour mixture and vigorously stir with a fork to blend. If necessary, a bit at a time, stir in enough more yogurt to hold particles together, but do not overmoisten. Mixture will gradually become cohesive and smooth. Working in the bowl, briefly knead dough and form into a smooth ball.

On a clean work surface, press or roll out dough ½ inch thick. Cut out biscuits with 2-inch (or similar) round cutter. Transfer to ungreased 15 × 10-inch (or similar) baking pan or sheet; for soft biscuits, arrange so rounds are touching, for crisper biscuits, space about ½ inch apart. Combine scraps, reroll and cut out additional biscuits. Transfer to baking pan. Place pan in preheated oven; immediately reduce heat to 425°. Bake biscuits for 13 to 15 minutes, or until lightly browned and puffy. Biscuits are at their best served warm from the oven, with butter. Makes about 15 to 16 medium-sized biscuits.

Approximate Preparation Time: 15 minutes   *Baking Time:* 14 minutes

Sweet Irish Soda Bread with Currants

Start to Finish: About 53 minutes

Irish Soda Bread is most often served at room temperature, thinly sliced. This somewhat unusual sweet version is also delicious served still warm from the oven and cut into wedges. It is remarkably quick and easy to prepare.

3 cups all-purpose white or unbleached flour or pastry flour
¼ cup granulated sugar
1¼ teaspoons salt
1¼ teaspoons baking soda
1 cup dried currants
1 to 1¼ cups commercial buttermilk, approximately

Preheat oven to 400°. Grease an 8-inch round cake pan and set aside. Stir together all ingredients except buttermilk in a medium-sized bowl until well blended. Gradually stir in enough buttermilk to yield an almost firm yet still slightly moist dough. Knead dough six or seven times and shape into a round about 7¾ inches in diameter. Place round in greased cake pan. With a greased and floured sharp knife, cut a large X about ½ inch deep in center of dough top.

Bake bread for 35 to 40 minutes, or until top is firm and lightly browned. Remove pan to rack and let stand for 3 or 4 minutes. Lift bread from pan and let stand on rack at least 5 minutes longer before serving. Cut into wedges and serve immediately, with butter, or allow bread to cool and cut crosswise into thin slices. (These may be toasted, if desired.) Makes 1 medium-sized round loaf.

Approximate Preparation Time: 15 minutes   *Baking Time:* 38 minutes

• *Tropical Isle Loaves* •

Start to Finish: About 1 hour 5 minutes

Enlivened with citrus juice and rind, coconut, candied pineapple and nuts, these sweet and fruity loaves make a nice addition to the tea or coffee table. They can also be iced and served as a light dessert.

3¼ *cups all-purpose white or unbleached flour or pastry flour*
1 *tablespoon baking powder*
½ *teaspoon baking soda*
2 *eggs*
1 *cup granulated sugar*
⅓ *cup vegetable oil*
Juice and grated rind 1 large lemon
⅔ *cup orange juice*
½ *teaspoon grated orange rind*
1 *cup finely chopped dried pineapple rings or candied pineapple*
½ *cup shredded coconut*
⅔ *cup finely chopped macadamia or cashew nuts*
1 *tablespoon rum (or water, if preferred)*
GLAZE *(optional)*
½ *cup sifted confectioners' sugar*
2 *to 3 teaspoons lemon juice, approximately*

Preheat oven to 375°. Thoroughly grease two 7⅞ × 3⅞ × 2½-inch aluminum foil (or similar 1-quart) loaf pans. Stir together flour, baking powder and soda in a medium-sized bowl. Combine eggs and sugar in a large mixer bowl. With mixer on medium speed, beat 2½ minutes, or until mixture is very thick and fluffy. Add oil and beat 30 seconds longer. Gradually add dry ingredients, alternating with citrus juices and rinds; beat after each addition until mixture is smooth and well blended. Fold pineapple, coconut, nuts and rum into batter. Spoon batter into pans, smoothing surface and spreading out to edges.

Bake loaves for 41 to 46 minutes, or until tops are golden brown and loaves test done when a toothpick is inserted in thickest part. Remove pans to rack and cool for 10 minutes. Remove loaves from pans and cool on racks. Serve loaves plain or iced with confectioners'-sugar glaze.

To prepare glaze, gradually stir enough lemon juice into confectioners' sugar to yield a smooth, liquefied but not runny glaze. Spread thinly over warm, but not hot, loaves. Let stand until glaze sets. Makes 2 small loaves.

Approximate Preparation Time: 22 minutes   *Baking Time:* 42 minutes

◆ *Molasses Brown Bread* ◆

Start to Finish: About 1 hour 5 minutes

Dark and somewhat coarse textured, this hearty whole-grain bread is moist and richly flavored with molasses. The loaf tastes a bit like classic Boston brown bread, but since it is baked instead of steamed it is much quicker to prepare. It goes with hearty, stick-to-the-ribs fare.

2⅓ *cups whole-wheat flour*
1 *cup medium or dark rye flour*
1¾ *teaspoons baking powder*
1 *teaspoon baking soda*
¾ *teaspoon salt*
⅛ *teaspoon ground mace*
1 *egg*
¼ *cup vegetable oil*
1½ *cups commercial buttermilk*
¾ *cup dark molasses*
⅔ *cup raisins*

Preheat oven to 350°. Generously grease a 9 × 5 × 3-inch (or similar 2-quart) loaf pan and set aside. Stir together whole-wheat flour, rye flour, baking powder, soda, salt and mace in a medium-

97

sized bowl. Combine egg and oil in a small, deep bowl, and beat with a fork until smooth. Stir in buttermilk and molasses until well blended. Gently stir buttermilk mixture and raisins into dry ingredients until thoroughly blended but not overmixed. Spoon batter into pan, carefully smoothing surface and spreading batter out to edges.

Bake bread for 52 to 57 minutes, or until center of loaf top is firm and springy to the touch, and a toothpick inserted in the thickest part comes out clean. Remove pan to rack and cool for 5 minutes. Remove loaf from pan to rack. Bread may be served slightly warm, or at room temperature. It is very good sliced fairly thin with a sharp knife and spread with cream cheese or butter. Makes 1 large loaf.

Approximate Preparation Time: 12 minutes   *Baking Time:* 54 minutes

· *Part II* ·

MORE FAST-YEAST BREADS

◆ TRADITIONAL BREADS ◆

*T*his chapter contains a wide variety of traditional recipes that have been updated for quick mixing and rising. By teaming up modern bread-baking techniques and the new fast-rising yeast, it's now possible to serve such old-fashioned favorites as Farmstead White Bread, crullers, raised doughnuts, rolls and English muffins two to three times faster than in the past. For example, the luscious Cinnamon-Raisin Sweet Rolls in this chapter used to take more than three hours to prepare, but now can be made in about one hour and twenty-five minutes.

Moreover, breads made the updated, new-yeast way are just as delicious as those prepared using conventional methods. The only thing missing is the long wait before the reward!

• *Farmstead White Bread* •

Start to Finish: About 1 hour 40 minutes

Delicately flavored and fine textured, this bread is good for sandwiches or toast.

> 5½ to 6¼ cups all-purpose white or unbleached flour
> 2 packets fast-rising dry yeast
> ⅓ cup instant nonfat dry milk
> ⅓ cup granulated sugar
> 1½ teaspoons salt
> 1¾ cups water
> ¼ cup butter or margarine, cut into 3 or 4 pieces
> 1 egg, at room temperature
> Milk for brushing over tops of loaves

Stir together 1¾ cups flour, the yeast, milk powder, sugar and salt in a large mixer bowl. Combine water and butter in a small saucepan, and heat until butter melts and mixture reaches 125° to 130°. With mixer on low speed, beat liquid into dry ingredients until blended. Raise speed to high and beat for 4½ minutes. Add egg and ½ cup more flour and beat for 1 minute longer. With a large spoon, stir in 2½ more cups flour, or enough to yield a kneadable dough. Turn dough out onto a clean, lightly floured surface and gradually knead in enough more flour to yield a smooth and malleable yet still slightly moist dough. Transfer dough to a clean, well-greased bowl and cover with plastic wrap. Set aside in a very warm place (80° to 90°) for 20 minutes. Meanwhile, generously grease two 9 × 5 × 3-inch (or similar 2-quart) loaf pans and set aside.

Punch down dough. With well-greased hands, divide dough in half. Shape halves into smooth loaves and place in pans. Cover pans with plastic wrap and set aside in a very warm place (80° to 90°) for 20 minutes. Preheat oven to 375°.

Brush tops of loaves with milk. Cut a ¼-inch-deep slash lengthwise down center of loaves. Bake for 34 to 38 minutes, until loaves are nicely browned and sound hollow when tapped on top. Remove loaves from pans and transfer to racks to cool. Serve at room temperature or toasted. Loaves may be frozen for later use, if desired. Makes 2 large loaves.

Approximate Preparation Time: 22 minutes
Rising/Baking Time: 1 hour 15 minutes

• *Italian Bread* •

Start to Finish: About 1 hour 50 minutes

Crusty outside, fine textured inside, this bread is the perfect accompaniment to Italian food.

6¾ to 7½ cups all-purpose white or unbleached flour
2 packets fast-rising dry yeast
1 tablespoon granulated sugar
2½ teaspoons salt
Scant 2½ cups hot water (125° to 130°)
2½ tablespoons olive oil or vegetable oil
1 egg white
Cornmeal for sprinkling on baking sheets
1 egg white beaten with 1 tablespoon water for brushing over loaves

Stir together 2½ cups flour, the yeast, sugar and salt in a large mixer bowl. With mixer on low speed, beat hot water, then oil, into dry ingredients until blended. Raise speed to high and beat for 3½ minutes. Add egg white and beat for 1 minute longer. Vigorously stir in 3 to 3¼ cups flour, or enough more to yield a kneadable dough. Working on a clean, lightly floured surface, vigorously knead in enough more flour to yield a smooth and firm yet not dry dough; kneading should take about 5 to 6 minutes. Cover bowl with a slightly damp towel. Set aside in a very warm spot (80° to 90°) for 15 minutes. Meanwhile, lightly grease two 15 × 10-inch (or similar) baking sheets, or one 17½ × 15-inch sheet. Sprinkle sheets with cornmeal.

Punch down dough and knead 1 minute. Divide dough in half. On a clean, very lightly floured surface, roll or press out one half to a 9 × 13-inch rectangle. Starting from a longer side, tightly roll up jelly-roll style to form a 13-inch log. Transfer to baking sheet, seam side down. Smooth and stretch out as necessary to produce an evenly thick log. Taper ends of log slightly. Repeat process with other half of dough. Lightly cover loaves with damp towels. Set pans aside in a very warm place (80° to 90°) for 25 minutes. Preheat oven to 425°.

Brush loaves with egg white-water mixture, using pastry brush or paper towel. Bake for 39 to 44 minutes, or until tops are nicely browned and loaves sound hollow when tapped on the bottom. Remove from pans and transfer to racks. Serve warm or at room temperature. Freeze loaves for later use, if desired. Makes 2 large loaves.

Approximate Preparation Time: 24 mins.   *Rising/Baking Time:* 1 hour 25 mins.

• *Cuban Bread* •

Start to Finish: About 1 hour 15 minutes

For crusty white hearth loaves that are fast and easy to make, as well as delicious, try this recipe. Unlike many Cuban or French breads, the following version includes a small amount of fat. This addition not only helps the loaves brown, but makes them keep better. The bread is still quite good the second day, and even acceptable the third, although the crust softens a bit.

> *4¼ to 4½ cups all-purpose white or unbleached flour*
> *2 packets fast-rising dry yeast*
> *1 tablespoon granulated sugar*
> *1¾ teaspoons salt*
> *1½ cups hot water (125° to 130°)*
> *1 tablespoon butter or margarine, at room temperature*
> *Cornmeal for sprinkling on baking sheets*

Stir together 1⅓ cups flour, the yeast, sugar and salt in a large mixer bowl. With mixer on low speed, beat water and butter into flour-yeast mixture until blended. Raise speed to high and beat for 3½ minutes. Stir in 2⅓ cups more flour, or enough to yield a kneadable dough. Then working in the bowl, quickly and vigorously knead in enough more flour to yield a firm, very elastic dough. Cover bowl with plastic wrap and set aside in a very warm spot (80° to 90°) for 15 minutes. Meanwhile, sprinkle one 17½ × 15-inch (or similar very large) baking sheet with cornmeal and set aside.

Punch down dough and divide in half. Shape halves into smooth, 9½-inch-long tapered ovals and place on baking sheets. Make three or four ¼-inch-deep random diagonal slashes in loaf tops with a sharp knife. Set loaves aside, uncovered, in a very warm place (80° to 90°) for 10 minutes.

Brush or spray loaves with water. Place in a cold oven; immediately set thermostat to 425°. Place a pan of hot water on oven floor. Several times during baking, brush or spray loaves with water. Bake for 29 to 34 minutes, or until loaf tops are hard and lightly browned and bottoms sound hollow when tapped. Let loaves cool on racks at least 5 minutes and preferably 10 before serving, or cool thoroughly and serve at room temperature. The loaves can be frozen for later use. Makes 2 medium-sized loaves.

Approximate Preparation Time: 20 minutes   *Rising/Baking Time:* 55 minutes

• *Country Cornmeal Hearth Loaves* •

Start to Finish: About 1 hour 10 minutes

Flavorful and fragrant, these hearty corn loaves make a perfect accompaniment for a simple soup or stew. The loaves have an attractive, rough-textured crust. For a delicate corn taste, use white cornmeal; for more pronounced "corniness," use the yellow variety.

> *1 cup white or yellow cornmeal*
> *1 cup boiling water, approximately*
> *4¼ to 4¾ cups all-purpose white or unbleached flour*
> *2 packets fast-rising dry yeast*
> *3 tablespoons granulated sugar*
> *1½ teaspoons salt*
> *1 cup hot water (125° to 130°)*
> *1½ tablespoons butter or margarine*
> *Additional cornmeal for sprinkling on baking sheets and loaves*

Place cornmeal in a medium-sized bowl. Gradually stir in enough boiling water to yield a smooth but not mushy paste. Set aside. Stir together 1¼ cups flour, the yeast, sugar and salt in large mixer bowl. With mixer on low speed, beat 1 cup hot water and butter into dry ingredients until blended. Raise speed to high and beat for 3½ minutes. Vigorously stir in 2 cups more flour and the cornmeal-water mixture until blended. Working in the bowl, quickly and vigorously knead in enough more flour to yield a firm, malleable dough. Cover bowl with plastic wrap and set dough aside in a very warm spot (80° to 90°) for 10 minutes. Meanwhile, lightly grease one 17½ × 15-inch (or similar very large) baking sheet, or two small baking sheets. Sprinkle with cornmeal and set aside.

Punch down dough and divide in half. Shape portions into high round loaves and place on baking sheet. Lightly spray or sprinkle loaves with water; then lightly sprinkle loaves with cornmeal. Using a sharp knife, cut ¼-inch-deep slashes in a starburst pattern (see illustration on page 106) in center of loaf tops. Turn oven on low for 1 minute; then turn off again. Place uncovered loaves in oven for 10 minutes.

With loaves still in the oven, set thermostat to 450°. Place a shallow pan of hot water on oven floor. Lightly spray or sprinkle loaves with water. (Repeat spraying once more midway through baking.) Bake for 30 to 35 minutes, or until loaf tops are tinged with brown and bottoms sound hollow when tapped. Transfer to racks and let cool for 5 minutes before serving. Serve with butter. Bread will hold for a day or so, or can be frozen for later use. Makes 2 medium-sized loaves.

Approximate Preparation Time: 20 minutes   *Rising/Baking Time:* 52 minutes

◆ *Oatmeal Bread* ◆

Start to Finish: About 1 hour 45 minutes

This is my updated version of a very old recipe. It makes a good, basic toasting bread and, when fresh, can be used for sandwiches too.

3 cups quick-cooking or old-fashioned rolled oats
1½ cups hot tap water
5¾ to 6½ cups all-purpose white or unbleached flour
3 packets fast-rising dry yeast
⅓ cup granulated sugar
2½ teaspoons salt
1½ cups water
⅓ cup vegetable oil

Stir together rolled oats and hot tap water in a medium-sized bowl until well blended. Set aside until the consistency of oatmeal.

Stir together 1¾ cups flour, the yeast, sugar and salt in a large mixer bowl. Combine water and oil in a saucepan, and heat to 125° to 130°. With mixer on low speed, beat liquid into dry ingredients until blended. Raise speed to high and beat for 5 minutes. Vigorously stir in reserved oats-water mixture and about 3¼ cups more flour, or enough to yield a kneadable dough. Working in the bowl or on a clean surface, quickly and vigorously knead in enough more flour to yield a smooth and malleable yet still slightly moist dough. Cover bowl with a damp towel. Set aside in a very warm spot (80° to 90°) for 20 minutes. Meanwhile, grease two 9 × 5 × 3-inch (or similar 2-quart) loaf pans.

Punch down dough and divide in half. With well-greased hands, form halves into smooth, evenly shaped loaves and place in pans. Cover pans with damp towels and set aside in a very warm spot (80° to 90°) for 20 minutes. Preheat oven to 400°.

Place pans in preheated oven; immediately reduce thermostat to 375°. Bake loaves for 40 to 45 minutes, or until they are lightly browned and sound hollow when tapped on top. Remove from pans and transfer to rack to cool. Bread may be served slightly warm, or cooled and used for toast. Makes 2 large loaves.

Approximate Preparation Time: 20 minutes
Rising/Baking Time: 1 hour 23 minutes

• *Poppy Seed Twist Loaves* •

Start to Finish: About 1 hour 45 minutes

Large, handsome twists with a rich taste, delicate texture and pleasant crunch of poppy seeds.

>5½ to 6¼ cups all-purpose white or unbleached flour
>2 packets fast-rising dry yeast
>½ cup instant nonfat dry milk
>¼ cup granulated sugar
>1½ teaspoons salt
>1¾ cups water
>¼ cup butter or margarine, cut into 3 or 4 pieces
>1 egg, at room temperature
>¼ cup poppy seeds
>1 egg yolk beaten with 1 tablespoon water for brushing over loaves

Stir together 1¾ cups flour, the yeast, milk powder, sugar and salt in a large mixer bowl. Combine water and butter in a small saucepan, and heat until butter melts and mixture reaches 125° to 130°. With mixer on low speed, beat liquid into dry ingredients until blended. Raise speed to high and beat for 3 minutes. Add egg, all but 1 tablespoon of poppy seeds and ½ cup more flour. Beat for 30 seconds. Stir in 2½ cups more flour, or enough to yield a kneadable dough. Turn dough out on a clean, lightly floured surface and gradually knead in enough more flour to yield a smooth and malleable yet still slightly moist dough. Transfer dough to a clean, well-greased bowl and cover with plastic wrap. Set aside in a very warm spot for 25 minutes. Meanwhile, thoroughly grease one 17½ × 15-inch (or similar-sized) baking sheet, or two smaller baking sheets.

Punch dough down. With well-greased hands, divide dough into four equal parts. Shape each portion into a smooth, 6-inch log. On a lightly greased work surface, roll each log back and forth and gently stretch out to form an evenly thick, 10-inch-long log. (Be careful not to tear dough.) Lay two logs together on baking sheet and entwine back and forth over one another to form an evenly thick twist about 11 inches long. Firmly tuck and smooth ends of twist underneath. Repeat process with remaining two dough logs and form a second twist.

Space twists as far apart as possible on baking sheet. Cover very lightly with plastic wrap and set aside in a very warm spot (80° to 90°) for 20 minutes. Preheat oven to 375°.

Neatly brush egg yolk–water wash over tops and sides of twists. Sprinkle with reserved 1 tablespoon poppy seeds and bake twists for 32 to 37 minutes, until they are golden brown and sound hollow when lightly tapped on top. Transfer twists to racks and let cool for 10 minutes. Serve immediately, or cool thoroughly and freeze for later use. Reheat before serving. Makes 2 large loaves.

Approximate Preparation Time: 23 minutes
Rising/Baking Time: 1 hour 20 minutes

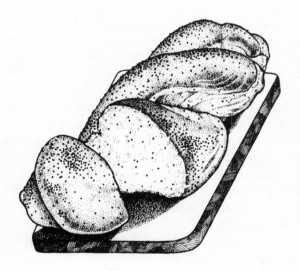

• *Old-fashioned Raisin-Oat Bread* •

Start to Finish: About 1 hour 59 minutes

This is a slightly sweet and homey bread with a pleasantly chewy, dense texture. The loaves give off a wonderful aroma during baking. They make delicious toast.

5¾ to 6½ cups all-purpose white or unbleached flour
2 packets fast-rising dry yeast
1½ teaspoons salt
2 cups water
½ cup honey
2½ tablespoons butter or margarine, cut into 2 pieces
1 cup quick-cooking or old-fashioned rolled oats
1½ cups raisins
Milk for brushing tops of loaves

Stir together 2½ cups flour, the yeast and salt in a large mixer bowl. Combine water, honey and butter in a small saucepan. Stirring until honey dissolves, heat until mixture reaches 125° to 130°. With mixer on low speed, beat liquid into dry ingredients until blended. Raise speed to high and beat for 3½ minutes. Vigorously stir in oats, raisins and 2½ cups more flour, using a large spoon. Working in the bowl or on a clean surface, quickly and vigorously knead in enough more flour to yield a smooth and malleable, yet still slightly sticky, dough.

Cover bowl with a damp towel and set aside in a very warm spot (80° to 90°) for 20 minutes. Meanwhile, grease two 8½ × 4½ × 2½-inch (or similar 1½-quart) loaf pans. Punch down dough and divide in half. With well-greased hands, form halves into smooth, evenly shaped loaves and place in pans. Cover pans with damp towels. Turn oven on low for 1 minute; turn off again. Place pans in warm oven and let dough rise for 25 minutes.

Remove loaves from oven and brush tops with milk. Cut a ⅛-inch-deep slash lengthwise down center of each loaf with a sharp knife. Return to oven. Set temperature to 350°, and bake loaves for 49 to 54 minutes, or until they are lightly browned and sound hollow when tapped on top. Remove from pans and transfer to rack to cool. Bread may be served slightly warm, or cooled and used for toast. Makes 2 medium-sized loaves.

Approximate Preparation Time: 23 minutes
Rising/Baking Time: 1 hour 36 minutes

• *Raisin-Cinnamon Swirl Bread* •

Start to Finish: About 1 hour 40 minutes

A spicy-sweet pinwheel swirl of cinnamon and raisins adorns this classic loaf. Excellent for toast.

4¾ to 5 cups all-purpose white or unbleached flour
2 packets fast-rising dry yeast
½ cup instant nonfat dry milk
Generous ⅓ cup granulated sugar
1¼ teaspoons salt
Scant 1¼ cups water
¼ cup butter or margarine, cut into 3 or 4 pieces
1 egg plus 1 egg yolk, at room temperature
4 teaspoons ground cinnamon
1¼ cups raisins
Milk for brushing over top of loaves (optional)

Stir together 1¼ cups flour, the yeast, milk powder, sugar and salt in a large mixer bowl. Heat water and butter in a small saucepan until butter melts and mixture reaches 125° to 130°. With mixer on low speed, beat liquid into dry ingredients until blended. Raise speed to high and beat 3½ minutes. Add egg and egg yolk and ½ cup more flour, and beat for 1 minute longer. Stir in about 1¾ to 2 cups more flour, or enough to yield a kneadable dough. Working in the bowl, quickly and vigorously knead in enough more flour to yield a smooth, malleable, fairly stiff dough. Grease dough top. Cover bowl with plastic wrap and set aside in a very warm spot (80° to 90°) for 15 minutes. Meanwhile, grease two 8½ × 4½ × 2½-inch (or similar 1½-quart) loaf pans.

Punch down dough and divide in half. On a lightly floured work surface, roll or press out one half into a 7½ × 12-inch, evenly thick rectangle. Sprinkle dough surface evenly with half the cinnamon, then half the raisins. Working from a shorter side of rectangle, tightly roll up dough jelly-roll style to form a plump, 8-inch-long log. Place log seam side down in pan. Repeat process with second half of dough. Cover pans with plastic wrap. Turn oven onto low heat for 1 minute; then turn off again. Place pans in oven and let loaves rise for

111

25 minutes. Brush tops of loaves with milk, if desired. Make a ¼-inch-deep cut lengthwise down center of each loaf with a sharp knife.

Return pans to cold oven; immediately set thermostat to 375°. Bake loaves for 30 to 35 minutes, or until tops are browned and bottoms sound hollow when tapped. Transfer loaves to racks. Serve warm or at room temperature. Makes 2 medium-sized loaves.

Approximate Preparation Time: 26 minutes
Rising/Baking Time: 1 hour 12 minutes

• *Welsh Fruit Bread (Bara Brith)* •

Start to Finish: About 1 hour 40 minutes

There are dozens of recipes for the delicious traditional Welsh tea bread called Bara Brith. Like many similar recipes, this particular one features a technique not often used in American-style breads—the cold butter is cut into the flour instead of being melted and beaten into it. This lends a springiness to the dough and a velvety, almost cakelike texture to the finished loaves.

4 to 4½ cups all-purpose white or unbleached flour
2 packets fast-rising dry yeast
⅓ cup light brown sugar, packed
½ teaspoon ground cinnamon
¼ teaspoon ground nutmeg
⅛ teaspoon ground cloves
1 cup hot water (125° to 130°)
½ cup cold butter (or margarine)
1 egg, at room temperature
⅓ cup instant nonfat dry milk
½ cup raisins
½ cup currants
⅓ cup mixed candied, diced citrus peel
1½ tablespoons strong tea or brandy
About 2 tablespoons honey for glaze (optional)

Stir together 1⅓ cups flour, the yeast, brown sugar and spices in a large mixer bowl. With mixer on low speed, beat hot water into flour mixture until blended. Raise speed to high and beat for 3 minutes. In another bowl combine 2⅓ cups more flour and butter. With two forks or a pastry blender, work butter into flour until mixture resembles coarse meal. Set aside. Add egg and milk powder to flour-yeast mixture, and beat for 30 seconds longer. With a large spoon, stir flour-butter mixture into dough until well blended. Working in the bowl, stir and then knead in enough more flour to yield a very smooth and springy dough. Cover bowl with a slightly damp towel and set aside in a very warm spot (80° to 90°) for 25 minutes. Stir together raisins, currants, candied peel and tea in a small bowl and

113

set aside. Generously grease two 8½ × 4½ × 2½-inch (or similar 1½-quart) loaf pans.

Punch down dough. Press dough out on a very lightly floured surface. Incorporate fruit-peel mixture evenly into dough by sprinkling a tablespoonful or two at a time over surface, then repeatedly rolling up dough and pressing it out again to expose a new surface. Continue until all fruit is incorporated. Divide dough in half. With well-greased hands form halves into smooth, well-shaped loaves. Place in greased pans. Lightly cover pans with a damp towel and set aside in a very warm spot (80° to 90°) for 20 minutes. Preheat oven to 375°.

Bake loaves for 30 to 34 minutes, or until they are nicely browned and sound hollow when tapped on top. Place loaves on racks to cool. Welsh Fruit Bread is traditionally served at tea time, but it goes well with coffee too. It may be served at room temperature or slightly warm. If glaze is desired, brush a tablespoon of honey over loaf top just before serving. The loaves may be frozen for later use, if desired, although the texture will not be quite as fine. Makes 2 medium-sized loaves.

Approximate Preparation Time: 25 minutes
Rising/Baking Time: 1 hour 15 minutes

114

• *Glazed Saffron Cake Bread* •

Start to Finish: About 1 hour 45 minutes

Aromatic and slightly sweet, this fruited bread is reminiscent of traditional saffron breads popular in England. It has a tender, almost cakelike texture, and the finished loaf also looks a bit like a layer cake. The saffron lends a subtle yet distinctive flavor and appealing soft yellow color.

The bread is delicious spread with butter and served still warm from the oven. It is a perfect accompaniment to coffee or tea.

> *Scant ⅛ teaspoon saffron threads*
> *2 tablespoons hot tap water*
> *¼ cup cold butter or margarine, cut into 4 or 5 pieces*
> *3½ to 4¼ cups all-purpose white or unbleached flour*
> *1 packet fast-rising dry yeast*
> *Generous ⅓ cup granulated sugar*
> *¼ cup instant nonfat dry milk*
> *¼ teaspoon ground cinnamon*
> *¼ teaspoon ground nutmeg*
> *½ teaspoon salt*
> *1 cup hot water (125° to 130°)*
> *1 egg yolk, at room temperature*
> *½ cup golden raisins*
> *⅓ cup dried currants (or substitute brown raisins if desired)*
> GLAZE
> *2 tablespoons milk or water*
> *1 tablespoon granulated sugar*
> *2 or 3 drops vanilla extract*

Finely crumble saffron threads between fingers. Combine in a small bowl or cup with 2 tablespoons hot tap water. Stir until well mixed and set saffron aside to soak. In a medium-sized bowl, using pastry blender or two forks, cut the butter into 1 cup flour until mixture resembles coarse meal. Set aside.

Stir together 1 cup more flour, the yeast, sugar, milk powder, spices and salt in large mixer bowl. Stir together saffron liquid and 1 cup hot water. With mixer on low speed, beat saffron-water mixture into dry ingredients until blended. Raise speed to high and beat for 3 minutes. Add egg yolk and beat for 30 seconds longer. Stir in raisins, currants, reserved flour-butter mixture, and about 1 cup more flour until dough is well mixed and stiff enough to knead. Working in the bowl or on a clean surface, quickly and vigorously knead in enough more flour to yield a smooth and manageable but still slightly moist dough. Form dough into a ball and transfer to a large, well-greased bowl. Cover bowl with plastic wrap. Set aside in a very warm spot (80° to 90°) for 20 minutes. Meanwhile, grease an 8- or 9-inch cake pan and set aside.

Punch down dough. Shape into a smooth ball and center in cake pan. Gently flatten ball slightly to almost cover pan bottom. Lay a greased sheet of wax paper over pan and set aside in very warm place (80° to 90°) for 30 minutes. Preheat oven to 375°.

Bake loaf for 35 to 40 minutes, or until top is nicely browned and sounds hollow when tapped. Remove loaf to rack and let stand for 10 minutes before adding glaze.

Meanwhile, prepare glaze as follows: Stir together milk and sugar in a small saucepan. Bring to a boil over medium-high heat and boil for 1 minute, stirring constantly. Remove pan from heat and stir in vanilla. Set aside.

When loaf has cooled to warm, evenly brush top with glaze, using a pastry brush or paper towel. Loaf is best served still warm from the oven. Makes 1 large loaf.

Approximate Preparation Time: 22 minutes
Rising/Baking Time: 1 hour 26 minutes

• *Country Fair Butter and Egg Rolls* •

Start to Finish: About 1 hour 30 minutes

These rich pan rolls are fragrant and delicious, not to mention simple to prepare.

4¾ to 5¼ cups all-purpose white or unbleached flour
2 packets fast-rising dry yeast
Generous ⅓ cup granulated sugar
1¼ teaspoons salt
¾ cup water
⅔ cup butter, cut into 6 or 7 pieces
4 eggs, at room temperature
Additional flour for dusting rolls

Stir together 1½ cups flour, the yeast, sugar and salt in a large mixer bowl. Heat water and butter in a small saucepan until butter melts and mixture reaches 125° to 130°. With mixer on low speed, beat liquid into dry ingredients until blended. Raise speed to high and beat for 1 minute. Add eggs and ½ cup more flour, and beat for 2½ minutes longer. With a large spoon, vigorously stir in 2½ cups more flour until blended. Working in the bowl or on a lightly floured surface, knead in enough more flour to yield a smooth, manageable yet still moist dough. Cover bowl with damp towel and set aside in a very warm spot (80° to 90°) for 15 minutes. Meanwhile, lightly grease three 9-inch (or similar-sized) pie plates or cake pans. Lightly dust plates with flour, tipping back and forth to evenly coat bottoms and sides.

Punch down dough and divide into thirds. Divide each third into nine or ten pieces. Shape each into a smooth ball, tucking excess dough underneath. Dip top of each roll into flour; then place on pie plate. Space balls, evenly separated, nine or ten to a plate. Cover plates loosely with plastic wrap and set aside in a very warm spot (80° to 90°) for 25 minutes. Preheat oven to 400°.

Bake rolls for 19 to 23 minutes, or until puffy and golden brown. Loosen rolls from pans with spatula and transfer to racks. Serve warm and very fresh, with butter. Rolls do not keep well but may be frozen for later use, if desired. Makes 27 to 30 rolls.

Approximate Preparation Time: 27 minutes
Rising/Baking Time: 1 hour 2 minutes

• *White Sponge Rolls* •

Start to Finish: About 1 hour 30 minutes

These are light, delicately flavored white pan rolls. "Sponge" refers to the old-fashioned sponge method of preparation, *not* the texture of the rolls!

> ¼ *cup butter or margarine*
> 4½ *to* 5¼ *cups all-purpose white or unbleached flour*
> 2 *packets fast-rising dry yeast*
> ¼ *cup granulated sugar*
> ¾ *teaspoon salt*
> 1½ *cups hot water (125° to 130°)*
> 1 *egg, at room temperature*

Melt butter and set aside to cool. Thoroughly stir together 1¾ cups flour, the yeast, sugar and salt in a large mixer bowl. With mixer on low speed, beat water into dry ingredients until well blended. Raise speed to high and beat for 2½ minutes. Add egg and reserved melted butter and beat for 30 seconds longer. Cover bowl with damp towel. Set aside in a very warm spot (80° to 90°) for 15 minutes. Meanwhile, grease two 9- or 10-inch (or similar-sized) pie plates or cake pans.

Beat down sponge with a large spoon. Stir in 2 cups more flour, or enough to yield a kneadable dough. Working in the bowl, quickly and vigorously knead in enough more flour to yield a smooth, soft and still slightly sticky dough. Set bowl aside, uncovered, for 5 minutes.

Knead dough briefly. With well-greased hands, shape dough into small walnut-sized balls. Space rolls, almost touching, in pie plates. Cover with slightly damp towel and set aside to rise in a warm spot (80° to 90°) for 20 minutes. Meanwhile, preheat oven to 375°.

Bake rolls for 21 to 25 minutes, or until golden brown on top and slightly springy to the touch. Rolls are best served warm, with butter. They will keep for several days. They may also be frozen and reheated at serving time, if desired. Makes 24 to 27 medium-sized rolls.

Approximate Preparation Time: 25 minutes
Rising/Baking Time: 1 hour 3 minutes

◆ *Scottish White Rolls (Baps)* ◆

Start to Finish: About 1 hour 12 minutes

These wonderfully light, feathery rolls are very popular in the British Isles, particularly in Scotland, where they originated. Although baps feature the most ordinary of ingredients, the preparation method is unusual in that the fat is cut into the flour instead of being melted and beaten into it. This lends the rolls a very pleasing, velvety texture. Baps are excellent with butter or jam or for sandwiches.

> *3¼ to 3½ cups all-purpose white or unbleached flour*
> *1 tablespoon fast-rising dry yeast (about 1½ packets)*
> *1 tablespoon granulated sugar*
> *⅓ cup instant nonfat dry milk*
> *1 teaspoon salt*
> *1 cup hot water (125° to 130°)*
> *¼ cup cold butter or margarine*
> *Additional flour for dusting rolls*

Stir together 1¼ cups flour, the yeast, sugar, milk powder and salt in a large mixer bowl. With mixer on low speed, beat water into flour mixture until blended. Raise speed to high and beat for 2 minutes longer. In another bowl, place 1 cup more flour and the butter. With two forks or a pastry blender, work butter or margarine into flour until mixture resembles very coarse meal. Vigorously stir flour-butter mixture into dough until well blended. Stir in enough more flour to yield a very soft yet springy dough. Cover bowl with a slightly damp towel and set dough aside to rise in a very warm spot (80° to 90°) for 20 minutes. Generously grease two 15 × 11½-inch (or similar-sized) baking sheets and set aside.

Punch down dough. With well-greased hands, divide dough in half. Divide each half into six equal portions. Shape portions into smooth ovals, each about 3 inches long and 1½ inches wide. Space ovals 3 inches apart on baking sheets. Lightly cover with a damp towel. Set rolls aside in a very warm spot (80° to 90°) for 15 minutes. Preheat oven to 400°.

Sprinkle roll tops lightly with flour. Bake rolls for 14 to 16 minutes, or until they are nicely browned and sound hollow when tapped on top. Remove from pans and serve. Makes 12 large rolls.

Approximate Preparation Time: 22 minutes   *Rising/Baking Time:* 50 minutes

119

◆ *Golden Cornmeal Rolls* ◆

Start to Finish: About 1 hour 10 minutes

Aromatic and flavorful, these large, homey rolls are likely to become a favorite. Serve them along with a meal.

1 cup yellow cornmeal
1 to 1¼ cup boiling water, approximately
3½ to 4¼ cups all-purpose white or unbleached flour
2 packets fast-rising dry yeast
¼ cup granulated sugar
¼ cup instant nonfat dry milk
1¼ teaspoons salt
¾ cup water
¼ cup butter or margarine, cut into 3 or 4 pieces

Put cornmeal in a small bowl. Gradually stir in 1 cup boiling water, or enough more to yield a smooth, but not mushy, paste. Set aside. Stir together 1 cup flour, the yeast, sugar, milk powder and salt in a large mixer bowl. Combine ¾ cup water and the butter in a small saucepan and heat until butter melts and mixture reaches 125° to 130°. With mixer on low speed, beat liquid into dry ingredients until blended. Raise speed to high and beat for 3½ minutes. Stir in cornmeal-water mixture and 2¼ cups more flour until blended. Working in the bowl, quickly and vigorously stir, then knead in enough more flour to yield a smooth and fairly stiff yet not dry dough. Cover bowl with a slightly damp towel and set aside in a very warm spot (80° to 90°) for 10 minutes. Generously grease a 17½ × 15-inch baking sheet, or 2 smaller sheets, and set aside.

Punch down dough. Knead briefly with lightly greased hands. Divide dough into thirteen or fourteen pieces and shape into smooth 3½ × 1½-inch ovals. Space ovals as far apart as possible on baking sheet. Make ⅛-inch-deep, lengthwise slashes in rolls with a sharp knife. Cover with a damp towel and set aside in a very warm spot (80° to 90°) for 15 minutes.

Place rolls in a cold oven; immediately set thermostat to 400°. Bake for 18 to 22 minutes, or until tops are nicely browned and rolls sound hollow when tapped on the bottom. Remove from baking sheet and serve. Makes 13 or 14 large rolls.

Approximate Preparation Time: 24 minutes   *Rising/Baking Time:* 44 minutes

120

• *Crusty Seeded Rolls* •

Start to Finish: About 1 hour 20 minutes

These large, crusty rolls are similar to the kaiser rolls delicatessens use for sandwiches. They are very attractive and tasty. Great for sandwiches!

This recipe is adapted from one for hard rolls published by the Kansas Wheat Commission.

> 5 to 5½ cups all-purpose white or unbleached flour
> 2 packets fast-rising dry yeast
> 2 tablespoons granulated sugar
> 2 teaspoons salt
> 1½ cups water
> 3 tablespoons butter or margarine, cut into 2 or 3 pieces
> 1 egg white
> GLAZE AND GARNISH
> 1 teaspoon cornstarch
> ½ cup water
> About 1 tablespoon poppy seeds or sesame seeds for sprinkling over
>   rolls

Stir together 1¾ cups flour, the yeast, sugar and salt in a large mixer bowl. Combine water and butter in a small saucepan, and heat until butter melts and mixture reaches 125° to 130°. With mixer on low speed, beat liquid into dry ingredients until mixed. Raise speed to medium and beat for 3½ minutes. Add egg white and ½ cup more flour, and beat for 30 seconds longer. Stir in 2 to 2¼ cups more flour, or enough to yield a kneadable dough. Working in the bowl or on a clean, lightly floured surface, quickly and vigorously knead in enough more flour to yield a smooth, malleable, fairly stiff dough. Shape dough into a ball and transfer to a large, well-greased bowl. Cover dough with a slightly damp towel and set aside to rise in a very warm spot (80° to 90°) for 10 minutes. Generously grease two 15 × 10-inch baking sheets (or one very large sheet).

Punch down dough. Divide dough in half; then divide each half into seven or eight equal portions. With well-greased hands, shape portions into round balls. Space rolls at least 2½ inches apart, seven or eight to each baking sheet. Lightly cover with damp towels and set aside in a very warm place (80° to 90°) for 20 minutes. Meanwhile, prepare glaze as follows: Put cornstarch in a small saucepan and gradually stir in water until completely blended; bring to a boil over high heat, stirring. Boil 1 to 2 minutes, or until mixture is clear and smooth. Remove from heat and cool until lukewarm. Preheat oven to 450°.

One at a time, brush rolls with water-cornstarch glaze, using a pastry brush or paper towel; then sprinkle lightly with poppy or sesame seeds. With a razor blade or very sharp knife, cut a ½-inch square in the center of each roll (as shown in illustration); work gently so as not to deflate rolls. Then cut a ¼-inch-deep and about 1¼-inch-long slash starting at each corner of square and extending down sides of roll.

Place rolls in preheated oven. Immediately reduce heat to 400°. Bake for 14 to 16 minutes, or until rolls are lightly browned and sound hollow when tapped on top. Remove from pans to racks and cool at least 10 minutes before serving. Rolls may be frozen for later use. Makes 14 to 16 large kaiser-style rolls.

Approximate Preparation Time: 32 minutes   *Rising/Baking Time:* 45 minutes

• *English Muffins* •

Start to Finish: About 1 hour 25 minutes

Homemade always taste better, as this recipe proves. And the muffins look as attractive as ones you buy.

If you don't have a 3-inch cookie cutter, save a tuna-fish can to cut out your muffins. It's the right size and will work fine.

> *2⅔ to 3 cups all-purpose white or unbleached flour*
> *1 tablespoon fast-rising dry yeast (about 1½ packets)*
> *¼ cup instant nonfat dry milk*
> *1 teaspoon granulated sugar*
> *1 teaspoon salt*
> *1 cup hot water (125° to 130°)*
> *1½ tablespoons vegetable oil*
> *Generous pinch baking soda*
> *Cornmeal for sprinkling on baking sheet and muffins*

Stir together 1 cup flour, the yeast, milk powder, sugar and salt in a large mixer bowl. With mixer on low speed, beat water and oil into dry ingredients until blended. Raise speed to high and beat for 3 minutes. With a large spoon, vigorously stir in soda and 1½ cups more flour. Turn dough out onto a clean, very well floured surface and quickly and vigorously knead in enough more flour to yield a smooth and malleable but still slightly moist dough. Form into a ball and let rest for 3 or 4 minutes. Meanwhile, lightly grease a 17½ × 15-inch (or similar very large) baking sheet, or two smaller baking sheets. Sprinkle baking sheet heavily with cornmeal.

Flour work surface once more and roll out dough ⅓ to ½ inch thick. (The ½-inch thickness yields muffins similar in appearance to those sold commercially; the ⅓-inch yields slightly thinner muffins that crisp faster and fit better in many toasters.) Cut out muffins with a 3-inch-diameter cutter. Transfer muffins to baking sheet with spatula, spacing about 1 inch apart. Brush muffin tops with water, using a pastry brush or paper towel. Sprinkle muffin tops with cornmeal. Lightly cover with wax paper and set aside in a very warm spot (80° to 90°) for 35 minutes. About 5 minutes before end of rising period, gradually heat a large ungreased skillet, griddle or fry pan to hot, but not smoking.

In batches of four to six, gently transfer muffins to skillet with spatula; be careful not to deflate when placing in pan. Toast for 3 to 3½ minutes, or until nicely browned on first side. Gently turn over with spatula and toast until browned; then transfer to racks to cool. After toasting each batch, brush out any crumbs or cornmeal from skillet and wipe surface clean with a paper towel. Serve muffins split in half and toasted. Makes 11 to 14 English muffins, depending on thickness.

Approximate Preparation Time: 25 minutes   *Rising/Toasting Time:* 1 hour

VARIATION: Wheat and Raisin English Muffins—Prepare as for regular muffins except substitute 2 tablespoons packed light or dark brown sugar for 1 teaspoon granulated sugar. And add 1 cup whole-wheat flour and ½ cup white flour along with the baking soda, instead of the 1½ cups white flour. Also add ⅓ cup raisins.

◆ *Hot Cross Buns* ◆

Start to Finish: About 1 hour 30 minutes

    3¾ to 4¼ cups all-purpose white or unbleached flour
    2 packets fast-rising dry yeast
    ⅓ cup granulated sugar
    ¼ cup instant nonfat dry milk
    ½ teaspoon ground cinnamon
    ¼ teaspoon ground allspice
    ¼ teaspoon ground ginger
    ¾ teaspoon salt
    ¾ cup water
    ⅓ cup butter or margarine, cut into 4 or 5 pieces
    2 eggs, at room temperature
    ½ cup dried currants
    ¾ teaspoon grated orange rind
    GLAZE (optional)
    ¾ cup confectioners' sugar
    ¼ teaspoon vanilla
    3 to 4½ teaspoons milk or water

Combine 1 cup flour, the yeast, granulated sugar, milk powder, spices and salt in a large mixer bowl. Combine water and butter in small saucepan, and heat until mixture reaches 125° to 130°. With mixer on low speed, beat liquid into dry ingredients until blended. Raise speed to high and beat for 2 minutes. Add eggs and ½ cup more flour, and beat for 1 minute longer. Stir in about 2 cups more flour, or enough to yield a kneadable dough, until well mixed. Turn dough out on a clean, lightly floured surface. Gradually knead in enough more flour to yield a smooth and fairly firm but not dry dough. Shape dough into a ball and transfer to a large well-greased bowl. Grease dough top. Cover bowl with plastic wrap and set aside in a very warm spot (80° to 90°) for 25 minutes. Meanwhile, grease a 17½ × 15-inch (or similar large) baking sheet, or two smaller sheets.

Punch down dough and knead in bowl briefly. Divide dough in half. Divide first half into eleven or twelve equal portions. Shape portions into balls, smoothing and tucking excess dough underneath buns. Place buns at least 1 inch apart on baking sheet; pat down to flatten slightly. Repeat process with second half of dough. Cover buns with slightly damp towel and set aside in a very warm spot (80° to 90°) for 20 minutes. Preheat oven to 375°.

Cut a ¼-inch-deep and about 1½-inch-wide cross in top of rolls, using very sharp knife. Bake buns in preheated 375° oven for 18 to 23 minutes, or until well browned on top and slightly springy to the touch. Transfer to racks to cool. Meanwhile, prepare glaze, if desired. Stir together confectioners' sugar, vanilla and 2½ teaspoons milk. Gradually stir in enough more milk to yield a liquefied, yet still fairly stiff glaze. Drizzle glaze over the crosses on warm, but *not hot*, buns. Serve buns while still warm from the oven. They may also be frozen and reheated at serving time, if desired. Makes about 22 to 24 small buns.

Approximate Preparation Time: 23 minutes
Rising/Baking Time: 1 hour 5 minutes

NOTE: If you are planning to glaze buns and are in a hurry, the traditional slashing may be omitted. In this case, simply pipe or drizzle icing to form a cross over the top of each bun.

• *Cinnamon-Raisin Sweet Rolls* •

Start to Finish: About 1 hour 20 minutes

The perfect breakfast treat. Nobody can resist them!

4½ to 5 cups all-purpose white or unbleached flour
2 packets fast-rising dry yeast
½ cup instant nonfat dry milk
⅓ cup granulated sugar
¾ teaspoon salt
1¼ cups water
⅓ cup butter or margarine, cut into 4 or 5 pieces
1 egg, at room temperature
FILLING
2 tablespoons butter or margarine, softened
¼ cup light brown sugar, packed
1 tablespoon ground cinnamon
⅔ cup seedless raisins
SAUCE
⅔ cup light brown sugar, packed
2½ tablespoons butter or margarine
3 tablespoons dark corn syrup
3 tablespoons water

Stir together 1½ cups flour, the yeast, milk powder, granulated sugar and salt in a large mixer bowl. Heat water and ⅓ cup butter in a small saucepan until butter melts and temperature reaches 125° to 130°. With mixer on low speed, beat liquid into dry ingredients until blended. Raise speed to high and beat for 2½ minutes. Add egg and ¼ cup more flour and beat 30 seconds longer. Stir in additional 2½ to 2¾ cups more flour, or enough to yield a cohesive but still soft, moist dough. Working in the bowl or on a lightly floured board, knead in just enough more flour to yield a manageable, less sticky dough. Shape dough into a ball and transfer to a large greased bowl. Grease dough top. Cover bowl with damp cloth and set aside in a very warm spot (80° to 90°) for 20 minutes. Meanwhile, grease three 8- or 9-inch cake pans or pie plates.

127

Punch dough down. Turn out on a lightly floured work surface and knead briefly. Roll or press out dough to form an evenly thick 18 × 12-inch rectangle. Spread dough surface with 2 tablespoons butter; then sprinkle evenly with ¼ cup brown sugar, cinnamon and raisins. Working from a long side, roll up dough jelly-roll style to form an 18-inch-long log. Stretch out until evenly thick and about 24 inches long. Cut log into about twenty-three or twenty-four evenly thick slices and divide rolls among pans. Cover with damp cloth and set aside in a very warm spot (80° to 90°) for 15 minutes. Preheat oven to 375°.

Bake rolls for 10 minutes. Reduce heat to 350° and bake for 8 to 10 minutes longer, until just barely browned. Meanwhile, prepare sauce as follows: Combine all ingredients in small saucepan over low heat. Cook, stirring, until sugar dissolves and sauce is smooth. Set aside. When rolls are just barely browned, remove from oven and spoon sauce over them. Return rolls to oven for 2 to 3 minutes, or until sauce is bubbling. Sweet rolls are best served while still warm. They may also be frozen and reheated at serving time. Makes about 24 large sweet rolls.

Approximate Preparation Time: 26 minutes　　*Rising/Baking Time:* 54 minutes

• *Orange-Almond Sticky Buns* •

Start to Finish: About 1 hour 15 minutes

The zesty orange sauce and almond pieces make these easy sticky buns tasty indeed. The sauce also gives them a pretty orange-gold sheen.

2½ to 2¾ cups all-purpose white or unbleached flour
1 tablespoon fast-rising dry yeast (about 1½ packets)
¼ cup granulated sugar
⅛ teaspoon ground cinnamon
½ teaspoon salt
Scant 1¼ cups commercial buttermilk
3 tablespoons vegetable oil
1 teaspoon freshly grated orange rind
SAUCE AND GARNISH
⅔ cup granulated sugar
2 tablespoons butter or margarine
¼ cup light corn syrup
¼ cup orange juice
1 tablespoon lemon juice
1 teaspoon freshly grated orange peel
½ cup coarsely chopped slivered almonds

Stir together 1 cup flour, the yeast, ¼ cup sugar, cinnamon and salt in a large mixer bowl. Heat buttermilk and oil in a small saucepan to 125° to 130°. With mixer on low speed, beat liquid into dry ingredients until blended. Raise speed to high and beat for 2 minutes. Add grated orange rind and beat for 1 minute longer. Quickly and vigorously stir in about 1 cup flour, or enough to yield a kneadable dough. Working in the bowl, quickly knead in enough more flour to yield a soft, yet malleable dough. Cover bowl with a slightly damp cloth. Set aside in a very warm spot (80° to 90°) for 10 minutes. Meanwhile, prepare sauce.

Combine all sauce ingredients except almonds in a small saucepan. Stirring constantly, bring to a boil over medium-high heat. Reduce heat and simmer, stirring, for 3 minutes. Set aside. Generously

129

grease two 8- or 9-inch cake pans or pie plates. Sprinkle almonds evenly over pan bottoms. Pour sauce over almonds and set aside to cool slightly.

Knead dough in the bowl briefly. Divide in half. With well-greased hands shape each half into a smooth, evenly thick 9-inch-long log. With a sharp knife, cut each log crosswise into nine or ten buns. Lay buns, just barely separated, over sauce. Cover pans with plastic wrap and set aside in a very warm spot (80° to 90°) for 20 minutes. Preheat oven to 375°.

Bake buns for 19 to 22 minutes, or until lightly browned on top and slightly springy to the touch. Remove pans from oven and immediately invert over serving plates. Serve Orange-Almond Sticky Buns while still hot, or freeze and reheat at serving time. Makes 18 to 20 buns.

Approximate Preparation Time: 28 minutes   *Rising/Baking Time:* 51 minutes

Sweet English Pinwheel Buns
(Chelsea Buns)

Start to Finish: About 1 hour 25 minutes

These sweet, fruit-filled buns were once sold by a highly successful London bakery called the Chelsea Bun House. The bakery no
longer exists, but you can still make its famous product at home!

> 4¼ to 4¾ cups all-purpose white or unbleached flour
> 2 packets fast-rising dry yeast
> ¼ cup granulated sugar
> ⅓ cup instant nonfat dry milk
> ¾ teaspoon freshly grated lemon rind
> ½ teaspoon salt
> 1 cup hot water (125° to 130°)
> 6 tablespoons butter, cut into 5 or 6 pieces
> 2 eggs, at room temperature
> FILLING
> ½ cup golden raisins
> ½ cup dried currants
> ⅓ cup diced, mixed candied fruit peel
> ½ cup light brown sugar, packed
> 3 tablespoons butter, softened
> GLAZE
> ¼ cup granulated sugar
> 1½ tablespoons milk or cream
> ¼ teaspoon vanilla extract

To prepare dough, stir together 1 cup flour, the yeast, sugar,
milk powder, lemon rind and salt in a large mixer bowl. With mixer
on low speed, beat water into dry ingredients until blended. Raise
speed to high and beat for 2½ minutes. In another bowl combine 2½
cups more flour and the butter. With two forks or a pastry blender,
cut butter into flour until mixture resembles very coarse meal. Add
eggs and ½ cup more flour to flour-yeast mixture, and beat on medium speed for 30 seconds longer. Stir the flour-butter mixture into
dough until well blended. Working in the bowl, stir and then knead
in enough more flour to yield a smooth, malleable yet still moist
dough. Cover bowl with a slightly damp towel and set dough aside in

a very warm spot (80° to 90°) for 20 minutes. Meanwhile, generously grease two 17½ × 11-inch (or similar) baking sheets. Stir together raisins, currants and candied peel for filling. Ready remaining filling ingredients and set aside.

Punch down dough. With lightly greased hands, roll or press out dough to an 18 × 12-inch evenly thick rectangle on a very lightly floured work surface. Spread softened butter evenly over dough surface. Sprinkle brown sugar, then fruits evenly over surface. Working from a longer side, tightly roll up dough jelly-roll style. Gently stretch out dough to form an evenly thick, 24-inch-long log. Cut log crosswise into twenty-four buns using a sharp knife. Place half the slices in neat rows, four down and three across, about ½ inch apart on one baking sheet. (This allows buns to spread and take on a character-istic squarish appearance during rising and baking.) Arrange remaining buns on second sheet. Lightly cover buns with damp towel. Set aside in a very warm spot (80° to 90°) for 20 minutes. Preheat oven to 375°.

Bake buns for 13 to 17 minutes, or until tops are lightly browned and slightly springy to the touch. Meanwhile, prepare glaze by com-bining sugar and milk in a small saucepan. Bring to a boil over me-dium heat, stirring. Boil, stirring, for 1½ minutes, or until sugar dissolves and glaze is smooth. Remove from heat and stir in vanilla. Set aside. Remove buns from oven and let stand on sheets for 5 minutes. Meanwhile, brush bun tops with glaze. With spatula, gently separate buns and transfer to racks. Serve immediately, or cool and freeze for later use. Makes 24 large buns.

Approximate Preparation Time: 30 minutes   *Rising/Baking Time:* 54 minutes

• *Crullers* •

Start to Finish: About 1 hour 35 minutes

Use the following dough to prepare tasty cinnamon-sugar sprinkled crullers, or to make old-fashioned glazed doughnuts as outlined in the variation below.

> 3⅔ to 4 cups all-purpose white or unbleached flour
> 2 packets fast-rising dry yeast
> ⅓ cup instant nonfat dry milk
> Generous ⅛ teaspoon ground cinnamon
> Generous ⅛ teaspoon ground mace
> 1 cup plus 2 tablespoons hot water (125° to 130°)
> ¼ cup butter or margarine, at room temperature
> ¼ cup granulated sugar
> ¾ teaspoon salt
> 1 egg, at room temperature
> Vegetable oil for deep-frying
> TOPPING
> ⅔ cup granulated sugar
> 1¼ teaspoons ground cinnamon

Stir together 1 cup flour, the yeast, milk powder and spices in a large mixer bowl. With mixer on low speed, beat hot water into flour-yeast mixture until blended. Raise speed to medium and beat for 1 minute. Set aside. Combine butter, sugar and salt in small mixer bowl. With mixer on medium speed, cream mixture until light colored and fluffy, about 3 minutes. Add creamed mixture and egg to flour-yeast mixture and beat for 30 seconds longer, or until well blended. Stir in 2½ cups more flour, or enough to yield a kneadable dough. Working in the bowl or on a clean, lightly floured surface, knead in enough more flour to yield a smooth and malleable but still moist dough. Cover bowl with damp towel. Set aside in a very warm spot (80° to 90°) for 20 minutes. Meanwhile, thoroughly grease two 15 × 11½-inch (or similar) baking sheets.

Punch dough down. Divide in half with lightly floured hands. Working on a lightly floured surface, roll or press out each half to form an evenly thick 11 × 8-inch rectangle. Cut each rectangle

133

crosswise into twelve or thirteen 8-inch-long and about ¾-inch-wide strips. Fold each strip in half (see illustration) and give the two halves three or four twists to entwine them. Press ends together to prevent them from untwisting. Transfer twists to greased baking sheets, stretching them out to about 9½ to 10 inches long and spacing as far apart from one another as possible. Cover twists with wax paper and set aside in a very warm spot (80° to 90°) for 30 minutes. Ready a kettle or pot for deep-frying by filling about 3 inches deep with oil. Set out a large rack and top with a layer of paper towels. Meanwhile, prepare topping by shaking together sugar and cinnamon in a heavy, medium-sized paper bag.

When twists have risen for about 25 minutes, place kettle over medium-high heat and gradually bring oil to 365° to 370°. In batches of three or four, carefully transfer twists to hot oil and deep-fry for 1 to 1½ minutes on the first side, or until golden brown. Then turn over using tongs and fry until second side is golden, about 1½ minutes

Crullers and Doughnuts

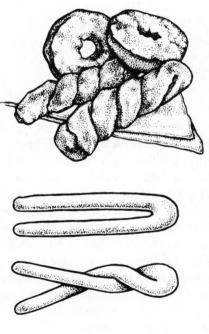

longer. Raise or lower heat as necessary to maintain oil temperature at 365° to 370°. Immediately transfer fried crullers to rack lined with paper towel. When all crullers are cooked, transfer to paper bag in batches and shake in sugar-cinnamon topping until lightly coated. Crullers are best served very fresh. However, they may be frozen for later use and then reheated, if desired. Makes about 24 large crullers.

Approximate Preparation Time: 30 minutes
Rising/Frying Time: 1 hour 10 minutes

VARIATION: Old-fashioned Raised Doughnuts—Prepare dough as directed for crullers except increase cinnamon and mace to ¼ teaspoon each. After dough has rested 20 minutes and been punched down, lay on lightly floured surface and evenly roll or press out approximately ½ inch thick. Cut out doughnuts with doughnut cutter. Separate doughnuts and holes and transfer to greased baking sheets. Cover lightly with wax paper and let rise for 30 minutes. Prepare oil for frying as directed for crullers. Also, during rising, prepare vanilla glaze as follows: Stir together 1½ cups confectioners' sugar (sifted if lumpy) and ½ teaspoon vanilla extract. Gradually add enough water to yield a smooth, fairly runny glaze and set aside. When doughnuts are ready, carefully transfer to oil with spatula; fry in batches of three or four as directed for crullers. When all doughnuts have been fried and drained on paper towels, dip in glaze. Let excess glaze drip back into bowl, and transfer doughnuts to racks set over wax paper for 3 to 4 minutes to allow glaze to set. Serve doughnuts warm and fresh, if possible. Makes about 30 doughnuts and 30 holes.

BATTER BREADS
(NO-KNEAD BREADS)

*B*atter breads are all those yeast breads too moist to be kneaded. Sometimes the dough is almost as thin as cake or quick-bread batter. Other times, the dough is nearly, but not quite, stiff enough to knead. The characteristic softness of the dough means that the gluten must be developed entirely by machine—usually an electric mixer. After resting or rising, the batter is simply spooned into a pan instead of being shaped into a loaf by hand.

This technique results in breads with somewhat coarser or more open texture than those made by other methods. But since it eliminates the "need to knead," the preparation process becomes an extremely easy, fuss-free affair. Batter breads are a boon to the busy cook, not to mention the novice baker.

Traditionally, batter breads require two full rising periods. But the majority of the ones in this chapter are specially designed for two abbreviated risings, or a short resting period and one full rising. As a result, they are much quicker to make than most conventional recipes. (There are a number of even faster one-rise batter breads in the section on 60-minute yeast breads.)

Although batter breads are especially easy to make, for best results, be sure to follow all directions on greasing or "dusting" bread pans and on removing finished loaves from their baking containers carefully. Some batter breads do have a tendency to stick, and these instructions will help you head off such problems. Always grease pans with solid shortening unless otherwise directed.

Buttermilk Mixed-Grains Batter Bread

Start to Finish: About 1 hour 25 minutes

A rough-topped, somewhat chewy bread with a hearty, soul-satisfying flavor and pleasing aroma. This easy loaf is very good served with soup, stews and other homey meals.

1¾ cups all-purpose white or unbleached flour
2 packets fast-rising dry yeast
3 tablespoons granulated sugar
2 teaspoons salt
¼ teaspoon baking soda
1¼ cups commercial buttermilk
¾ cup water
3 tablespoons vegetable oil
2 cups quick-cooking or old-fashioned rolled oats
1 cup medium or dark rye flour
½ cup whole-wheat flour

Stir together 1¾ cups white flour, the yeast, sugar, salt and soda in a large mixer bowl. Combine buttermilk, water and oil in a medium-sized saucepan, and heat to 125° to 130°. With mixer on low speed, beat liquid mixture into flour-yeast mixture until blended. Raise speed to high and beat for 3½ minutes. With a large spoon, vigorously stir in oats, rye flour and whole-wheat flour until well blended; batter will be fairly stiff.

Cover bowl with plastic wrap and set aside in a very warm spot (80° to 90°) for 15 minutes. Meanwhile, generously grease a 9 × 5 × 3-inch (or similar 2-quart) loaf pan.

Stir down batter. Spoon into prepared pan, spreading out to pan edges. Smooth top with a knife. Lay a sheet of wax paper over pan. Set aside in a very warm spot (80° to 90°) for 15 minutes. Preheat oven to 375°.

Remove wax paper and bake loaf for 32 to 36 minutes, or until top is well browned and sounds hollow when tapped. Let stand in pan for 5 minutes. Then transfer loaf to rack to cool at least 5 minutes before serving. This bread is best served still warm from the oven, cut into thick slices and buttered. Makes 1 large loaf.

Approximate Preparation Time: 20 minutes
Rising/Baking Time: 1 hour 4 minutes

100 Percent Whole-Wheat Batter Bread

Start to Finish: About 1 hour 25 minutes

Even those who object to whole wheat often get hooked on this quick and easy bread. Though made entirely of whole-grain flour, it is quite airy and very delicious. If you don't care for raisins, they may be omitted; however, most people find them a nice addition.

2¾ cups whole-wheat flour
2 packets fast-rising dry yeast
1 teaspoon salt
Scant 1¼ cups water
¼ cup light molasses
1 tablespoon vegetable oil
½ cup raisins (optional)
Additional whole-wheat flour for dusting baking dish

Stir together 1¼ cups flour, the yeast and salt in a large mixer bowl. Combine water, molasses and oil in a small saucepan. Stirring until molasses dissolves, heat to 125° to 130°. With mixer on low speed, beat liquid mixture into dry ingredients until blended. Raise speed to medium and beat for 3½ minutes. With a large spoon, stir in remaining 1½ cups flour and the raisins (if desired); batter will be fairly stiff.

Cover bowl with plastic wrap. Set aside in a very warm spot (80° to 90°) for 10 minutes. Meanwhile, generously grease a 1¼- to 1¾- quart soufflé dish or casserole. Dust dish with whole-wheat flour; tip back and forth to evenly coat bottom and sides. Tap out any excess flour and set dish aside.

Stir down batter and spoon into dish. Smooth and spread batter out to edges with back of spoon. Cover dish with plastic wrap. Set aside in a very warm spot (80° to 90°) for 15 minutes.

Place dish, uncovered, in cold oven; immediately set thermostat to 400°. Bake bread for 40 to 44 minutes, or until top is browned and sounds hollow when tapped. Place dish on rack and cool for 5 minutes before removing loaf. Serve bread warm, cut into wedges and buttered. Makes 1 medium-sized loaf.

Approximate Preparation Time: 17 minutes
Rising/Baking Time: 1 hour 7 minutes

• *Oats and Wheat Batter Bread* •

Start to Finish: About 1 hour 47 minutes

This is a high-rising, airy bread enlivened with molasses. It's very good served with a hearty meal.

> *About 2¾ cups all-purpose white or unbleached flour*
> *2 packets fast-rising dry yeast*
> *1 teaspoon salt*
> *2½ cups water*
> *¼ cup butter or margarine, cut into 3 or 4 pieces*
> *Generous ¼ cup light or dark molasses*
> *1 egg, at room temperature*
> *1 cup whole-wheat flour*
> *1 cup quick-cooking or old-fashioned rolled oats*

Stir together 1¼ cups flour, the yeast and salt in a large mixer bowl. Combine water, butter and molasses in a small saucepan. Stirring until molasses dissolves, heat until butter melts and mixture reaches 125° to 130°. With mixer on low speed, beat liquid into flour-yeast mixture until blended. Raise speed to high and beat for 3½ minutes. Add egg and beat 30 seconds longer. With a large spoon, vigorously stir in whole-wheat flour and all but 2 tablespoons of the oats. Then stir in 1⅓ cups white flour to make a stiff and sticky but very light batter.

Cover bowl with plastic wrap. Set aside in a very warm spot (80° to 90°) for 20 minutes. Meanwhile, generously grease two 7⅞ × 3⅞ × 2½-inch aluminum foil (or similar 1-quart) loaf pans. Set aside.

Stir down batter and spoon into pans. Spread and smooth out batter to pan edges with a greased knife. Sprinkle reserved 2 tablespoons oats over loaf tops. Press oats into batter surface with back of tablespoon. Cover loaves with plastic wrap and set aside in a very warm spot (80° to 90°) for 20 minutes. Preheat oven to 375°.

Bake bread, uncovered, for 44 to 49 minutes, or until loaves are well browned and sound hollow when tapped on top. Transfer pans to racks and let stand for 5 minutes. Remove loaves from pans and cool on racks. Serve slightly warm, at room temperature or toasted. Makes 2 small loaves.

Approximate Preparation Time: 20 minutes
Rising/Baking Time: 1 hour 27 minutes

• *Anadama Bread* •

Start to Finish: About 1 hour 40 minutes

The robust taste and texture of good, old-fashioned Anadama bread, but with far less bother and wait.

> *About 2¾ cups all-purpose white or unbleached flour*
> *1 packet fast-rising dry yeast*
> *1 teaspoon salt*
> *1 cup water*
> *3 tablespoons butter or margarine, cut into 3 or 4 pieces*
> *¼ cup light molasses*
> *1 egg, at room temperature*
> *⅔ cup cornmeal, preferably yellow*
> *Additional cornmeal for dusting pan and top of loaf*

Stir together 1⅓ cups flour, the yeast and salt in large mixer bowl. In a small saucepan, combine water, butter and molasses. Stirring until molasses dissolves, heat mixture until butter melts and mixture reaches 125° to 130°. With mixer on low speed, beat liquid into flour-yeast mixture until blended. Raise speed to high and beat for 3½ minutes. Add egg and beat 30 seconds longer. With a large spoon, stir in cornmeal. Then stir in 1¼ cups more flour; batter will be very rubbery.

Cover bowl with plastic wrap. Set aside in a very warm spot (80° to 90°) for 15 minutes. Meanwhile, grease an 8½ × 4½ × 2½-inch (or similar 1½-quart) loaf pan. Generously dust pan with cornmeal, tipping back and forth to evenly coat bottom and sides.

Stir down batter; spoon into pan. Spread out and smooth batter with a greased knife. Generously sprinkle surface with cornmeal. Set pan, uncovered, in a larger pan. Carefully fill larger pan with enough hot water (120° to 130°) to come ⅔ of the way up sides of bread pan. Let batter rise for 20 minutes. Preheat oven to 425°.

Bake bread for 40 to 45 minutes, or until lightly tinged with brown and springy to the touch. Immediately remove loaf from pan and transfer to rack to cool. Anadama Bread is best served warm from the oven, with butter. Makes 1 medium-sized loaf.

Approximate Preparation Time: 20 minutes
Rising/Baking Time: 1 hour 18 minutes

• *No-Knead Seeded Rye Bread* •

Start to Finish: About 1 hour 45 minutes

A pleasant, soft-textured rye bread with a rough, homey look. Use it for sandwiches, or serve along with a salad or seafood.

> 2½ cups all-purpose white or unbleached flour
> 2 packets fast-rising dry yeast
> ⅓ cup instant nonfat dry milk
> 1 tablespoon caraway seeds
> 1¾ teaspoons salt
> 1⅔ cups water
> ¾ cup plain yogurt, preferably lowfat
> ½ cup light or dark molasses
> ¼ cup vegetable oil
> ⅓ cup wheat germ
> 2 cups medium or dark rye flour
> 1½ cups whole-wheat flour

Stir together 2½ cups white flour, the yeast, milk powder, caraway seeds and salt in a large mixer bowl. Stir together water, yogurt, molasses and oil in a medium-sized saucepan. Stirring until molasses dissolves, heat mixture to 125° to 130°. With mixer on low speed, add liquid ingredients to flour-yeast mixture and beat until blended. Raise speed to high and beat for 4 minutes. With a large spoon, vigorously stir in wheat germ and rye flour. Then stir in whole-wheat flour to yield a fairly stiff batter.

Cover bowl with plastic wrap and set aside in a very warm spot (80° to 90°) for 15 minutes. Meanwhile, generously grease two 8½ × 4½ × 2½-inch (or similar 1½-quart) loaf pans and set aside.

Stir down batter. Divide between pans, spreading and smoothing out surface with a greased knife. Cover pans with plastic wrap. Set aside in a very warm spot (80° to 90°) for 25 minutes. Preheat oven to 375°.

Uncover loaves and bake for 40 to 45 minutes, or until tops are well browned and sound hollow when tapped. Place loaves on racks and cool thoroughly before serving. Makes 2 large loaves.

Approximate Preparation Time: 20 minutes
Rising/Baking Time: 1 hour 23 minutes

Herbed Corn and Wheat Batter Bread

Start to Finish: About 1 hour 25 minutes

An unusual combination of herbs, cornmeal and whole-wheat flour gives these loaves their distinctive, savory taste. Good served with roast chicken or turkey.

> 3½ cups all-purpose white or unbleached flour
> 2 packets fast-rising dry yeast
> 3 tablespoons granulated sugar
> 1 teaspoon salt
> 1 teaspoon celery salt
> 2 teaspoons dried basil leaves
> 1 teaspoon dill seed
> 2 cups water
> ½ cup butter or margarine, cut into 5 or 6 pieces
> 2 eggs, at room temperature
> 2 cups whole-wheat flour
> 1 cup yellow or white cornmeal
> Additional cornmeal for dusting loaf pans
> 2 teaspoons poppy seeds for garnishing loaves

Stir together 2½ cups white flour, the yeast, sugar, salt, celery salt, basil and dill seed in a large mixer bowl. Combine water and butter in a small saucepan, and heat to 125° to 130°. With mixer on low speed, beat liquid into flour-yeast mixture until blended. Raise speed to medium and beat for 3 minutes. Add eggs and ½ cup more white flour, and beat for 1 minute longer. With a large spoon, vigorously stir in whole-wheat flour, cornmeal and remaining ½ cup white flour; batter will be stiff.

Cover bowl with plastic wrap and set aside in a very warm spot (80° to 90°) for 10 minutes. Generously grease two 8½ × 4½ × 2½-inch (or similar 1½-quart) loaf pans. Dust pans with cornmeal, tipping back and forth to evenly coat bottoms and sides. Divide batter between pans. Smooth batter out to edges with a greased knife. Sprinkle a teaspoon of poppy seeds over each loaf; press down seeds slightly with the back of a spoon.

142

Cover pans with plastic wrap and set in a larger pan of hot water (120° to 130°) for 25 minutes. Remove plastic wrap, place pans in a cold oven and set thermostat to 425°.

Bake loaves for 30 to 34 minutes, or until tops are nicely browned and sound hollow when tapped. Transfer pans to racks and let stand 5 to 8 minutes. Remove loaves from pans and cool slightly before serving. Serve warm or at room temperature. Makes 2 medium-sized loaves.

Approximate Preparation Time: 18 minutes
Rising/Baking Time: 1 hour 6 minutes

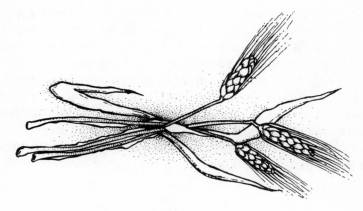

• *Cheese Casserole Bread with Herbs* •

Start to Finish: About 1 hour 25 minutes

A super-savory casserole bread featuring snappy Cheddar cheese and a subtle blend of herbs and seasonings. This recipe is made very quickly with the aid of a blender.

> 3⅓ cups all-purpose white or unbleached flour
> 1 packet fast-rising dry yeast
> 2 tablespoons granulated sugar
> ¾ teaspoon salt
> Scant 1¼ cups water
> 1¼ cups coarsely chopped or cubed sharp Cheddar cheese (about 5 ounces)
> ¼ cup vegetable oil
> 1 egg yolk
> 1 teaspoon Worcestershire sauce
> ¾ teaspoon paprika
> ½ teaspoon dry mustard
> ½ teaspoon instant (dehydrated) minced onions
> ½ teaspoon celery seed
> ¼ teaspoon dried thyme leaves
> ⅛ teaspoon finely crumbled rosemary leaves
> Cornmeal for dusting casserole
> Milk for brushing top of bread

Stir together 1 cup flour, the yeast, sugar and salt in a large cup. Combine water, cheese and oil in a small saucepan. Heat to 125° to 130°; cheese does not have to melt completely. Transfer mixture to blender container. Blend on low speed for 10 seconds. With blender on low speed, add flour-yeast mixture. Raise speed to medium and blend for 30 seconds. Add egg yolk and ⅓ cup more flour, and blend for 10 seconds longer. Pour blended mixture into a large bowl. Stir in all seasonings and herbs. Vigorously stir in remaining 2 cups flour to make a fairly stiff batter. Generously grease a 2-quart flat-bottomed round casserole or soufflé dish. Dust casserole with cornmeal, tipping back and forth to evenly coat bottom and sides. Spoon batter into casserole. Smooth out top with a knife. Cover casserole with plastic wrap and set aside in a very warm spot (80° to 90°) for 25 minutes. Preheat oven to 375°.

Remove plastic wrap and bake bread for 35 minutes. Remove casserole from oven and lightly brush top of loaf with milk, using a pastry brush or paper towel. Return to oven and continue baking for 5 to 10 minutes longer, or until top is slightly springy to the touch and nicely browned. Transfer casserole to rack and let stand for 10 minutes before removing loaf. Bread may be served still warm from the oven and cut into thick wedges, or cooled and cut crosswise into large slices. Makes 1 large loaf.

Approximate Preparation Time: 15 minutes
Rising/Baking Time: 1 hour 8 minutes

◆ *Chilies and Cheese Casserole Bread* ◆

Start to Finish: About 1 hour 30 minutes

A zippy, cheesy, corny bread perfect for serving with a hearty soup or Tex-Mex food. It can also spice up meals featuring hamburgers, meatloaf and other lightly seasoned fare.

> 2¾ cups all-purpose white or unbleached flour
> 1 tablespoon fast-rising dry yeast (about 1½ packets)
> ¼ cup instant nonfat dry milk
> 3 tablespoons granulated sugar
> ¾ teaspoon salt
> ¾ cup water
> ¼ cup butter or margarine, cut into 4 pieces
> 1 8¾-ounce can cream-style corn
> 1 egg, at room temperature
> 3 to 4 tablespoons chopped, well-drained green chilies (use the larger amount for a zippier bread)
> 1¼ cups lightly packed shredded or grated hot pepper cheese (about 5 ounces)
> 2 teaspoons dried chopped chives
> ⅔ cup yellow cornmeal
> Additional cornmeal for coating casserole

Stir together 1¼ cups white flour, the yeast, milk powder, sugar and salt in a large mixer bowl. In a small saucepan, combine water, butter and corn, and heat until butter melts and mixture reaches 125° to 130°. With mixer on low speed, beat liquid mixture into dry ingredients until blended. Raise speed to high and beat for 2½ minutes. Add egg, green chilies, cheese and chives, and beat with mixer on medium speed for 30 seconds longer. With a large spoon, stir in cornmeal and remaining 1½ cups flour until well blended.

Cover bowl with a damp cloth and set aside in a very warm spot (80° to 90°) for 15 minutes. Meanwhile, thoroughly grease a 1¾- to 2-quart casserole. Then sprinkle bottom and sides of dish with cornmeal until thoroughly coated.

Stir down batter and spoon into casserole; smooth out surface with back of spoon. Cover casserole with a slightly damp cloth and

146

set bread aside to rise in a very warm spot (80° to 90°) for 15 minutes. Preheat oven to 375°.

Bake bread for 35 to 40 minutes, or until nicely browned on top and springy to the touch. Let stand for 8 to 10 minutes; then run a knife around the casserole to loosen bread. Chilies and Cheese Casserole Bread is best served warm, either plain or with butter. It may also be frozen and reheated at serving time, if desired. Makes 1 large loaf.

Approximate Preparation Time: 20 minutes
Rising/Baking Time: 1 hour 8 minutes

NOTE: Hot pepper cheese is a commercial cheese product usually featuring a mild-flavored cheese, such as Monterey Jack, made piquant with flecks of jalapeño pepper. It can be purchased in many supermarkets and cheese shops. However, if hot pepper cheese is unavailable, 5 ounces of grated or shredded Monterey Jack and 1 to 2 teaspoons finely chopped jalapeño pepper (or more to taste) may be substituted.

• *Confetti Buffet Bread* •

Start to Finish: About 1 hour 25 minutes

Here is a colorful, savory bread baked in a large ring mold. Encrusted with poppy seeds on the outside and flecked with chopped pimiento and chives on the inside, the slices make a very festive addition to a buffet table. The bread is perfect for serving with a platter of sliced cheeses and meats.

> 3¾ cups all-purpose white or unbleached flour
> 2 packets fast-rising dry yeast
> 1½ tablespoons granulated sugar
> ⅓ cup instant nonfat dry milk
> 1 teaspoon salt
> 1⅓ cups water
> 6 tablespoons butter or margarine, cut into 3 or 4 pieces
> 1 egg, at room temperature
> 2 tablespoons dried chopped chives
> 1 tablespoon spicy prepared mustard
> 2 teaspoons poppy seeds
> 2 teaspoons mustard seed (optional)
> 3 tablespoons drained, finely chopped pimiento
> About 1 tablespoon poppy seeds for coating interior of ring mold

Stir together 1¼ cups flour, the yeast, sugar, milk powder and salt in a large mixer bowl. Combine water and butter in a small saucepan and heat to 125° to 130°. With mixer on low speed, beat liquid mixture into dry ingredients until blended. Raise speed to high and beat for 4 minutes. Add egg, chives, mustard, poppy seeds, mustard seed (if desired) and ¼ cup more flour, and beat for 30 seconds longer. With a large spoon, stir in pimiento and remaining 2¼ cups flour. Batter will be fairly stiff.

Cover bowl with plastic wrap. Set aside in a very warm spot (80° to 90°) for 10 minutes. Meanwhile, very generously grease a large ovenproof ring mold or fluted tube pan (9-cup capacity, minimum). Sprinkle interior lightly but evenly with poppy seeds, tipping back and forth to coat entire surface.

Stir down batter and spoon into mold. Smooth top with back of spoon. Cover mold with plastic wrap and set aside in a very warm spot (80° to 90°) for 20 minutes. Preheat oven to 375°.

Remove plastic wrap and bake bread for 30 to 35 minutes, or until top is nicely browned. Let mold stand for 5 minutes on rack. Then slide loaf from mold; transfer to rack, placing so that the top during baking becomes the bottom for cooling and serving. Serve bread at room temperature; it is very attractive presented sliced, with the slices still arranged in their original ring shape. Very good for making party sandwiches. Makes 1 large ring loaf.

Approximate Preparation Time: 20 minutes
Rising/Baking Time: 1 hour 2 minutes

• *Beer Batter Bread* •

Start to Finish: About 1 hour 20 minutes

Nothing could be easier than this bread, yet it is very light textured and appealing. You don't even have to like beer to enjoy it! Served warm from the oven and cut into thick, fluffy slices, it makes even the simplest meal seem special.

> 2½ cups all-purpose white or unbleached flour
> 2 packets fast-rising dry yeast
> 2 tablespoons granulated sugar
> 1 teaspoon salt
> 1½ cups beer (fresh or flat)
> ⅓ cup water
> ¼ cup butter or margarine, cut into 3 or 4 pieces
> 2 eggs, at room temperature
> 1⅓ cups whole-wheat flour
> 2 teaspoons sesame seeds for garnish (optional)

Stir together 1½ cups white flour, the yeast, sugar and salt in a large mixer bowl. Combine beer, water and butter in a small saucepan. Heat, stirring, until butter melts and mixture reaches 125° to 130°. With mixer on low speed, beat liquid into flour-yeast mixture until blended. Raise speed to medium and beat for 3 minutes. Add eggs and ½ cup more white flour, and beat for 30 seconds longer. With a large spoon, vigorously stir in whole-wheat flour and remaining ½ cup white flour; batter will be stiff.

Cover bowl with plastic wrap and set aside in a very warm spot (80° to 90°) for 15 minutes. Meanwhile, thoroughly grease two 8½ × 4½ × 2½-inch (or similar 1½-quart) loaf pans.

Stir down batter and divide between loaf pans. Smooth batter top out to edges with a greased knife. Sprinkle a teaspoon of sesame seeds over each loaf, if desired. Cover pans with plastic wrap and set aside in a very warm spot (80° to 90°) for 20 minutes.

Uncover pans and place in a cold oven; immediately set thermostat to 400°. Bake bread for 24 to 28 minutes, or until loaves are browned and sound hollow when slipped from pans and tapped on the bottom. (Return loaves to pans and bake several minutes longer if necessary.) Transfer loaves from pans to racks and cool for 5 to 10 minutes before serving. Best served still warm from the oven. Makes 2 medium-sized loaves.

Approximate Preparation Time: 18 minutes   *Rising/Baking Time:* 1 hour

• *Peanut Butter Bread* •

Start to Finish: About 1 hour 30 minutes

Most kids love this easy, nourishing bread. Serve it along with jam or honey.

3 cups all-purpose white or unbleached flour
2 packets fast-rising dry yeast
½ cup granulated sugar
½ cup instant nonfat dry milk
1 teaspoon salt
2 cups water
⅔ cup peanut butter, smooth or chunky
1 cup whole-wheat flour
2 tablespoons chopped peanuts for garnish (optional)

Stir together 2 cups white flour, the yeast, sugar, milk powder and salt in a large mixer bowl. Combine water and peanut butter in a small saucepan. Heat, stirring, to 125° to 130°. With mixer on low speed, beat liquid into flour-yeast mixture until blended. Raise speed to medium and beat for 3½ minutes. With a large spoon, vigorously stir in whole-wheat flour and remaining 1 cup white flour until well mixed; batter will be rubbery and stiff.

Cover bowl with plastic wrap and set aside in a very warm spot (80° to 90°) for 15 minutes. Meanwhile, thoroughly grease two 8½ × 4½ × 2½-inch (or similar 1½-quart) loaf pans.

Stir down batter and divide between loaf pans. Smooth batter out to edges of pans with a greased knife. Sprinkle a tablespoon of chopped peanuts over each loaf, if desired.

Cover pans with plastic wrap. Turn oven on to low for 1 minute; then turn off again. Put pans in oven and let batter rise for 30 minutes.

Remove plastic wrap from pans. Immediately set oven to 375°. Bake loaves for 27 to 30 minutes, or until tops are browned and sound hollow when tapped. Transfer pans to rack and let stand for 5 minutes before removing loaves. Cool loaves for at least 8 to 10 minutes before serving. Peanut Butter Bread may also be used for toast. Makes 2 medium-sized loaves.

Approximate Preparation Time: 15 minutes
Rising/Baking Time: 1 hour 13 minutes

• *Spiced Cottage Cheese Bread* •

Start to Finish: About 1 hour 30 minutes

Most cottage-cheese breads seem to be savory, but this fragrant, spicy casserole loaf has a hint of sweetness. It is very tasty plain, but can be dressed up with an easy confectioners'-sugar glaze, if you wish.

Unlike most breads, this one is just as good the second day. The flavor seems to ripen a bit, and the cottage cheese helps keep the loaf moist. (Of course, there may not be any left by the second day!)

> *2¾ cups all-purpose white or unbleached flour*
> *1 packet fast-rising dry yeast*
> *Generous ⅓ cup dark brown sugar, packed*
> *⅓ cup instant nonfat dry milk*
> *½ teaspoon salt*
> *⅔ cup large- or small-curd cottage cheese, preferably lowfat*
> *¾ cup water*
> *2 tablespoons butter or margarine, cut into 2 pieces*
> *1 egg, at room temperature*
> *1¼ teaspoons freshly grated orange rind*
> *¾ teaspoon ground allspice*
> *½ teaspoon ground mace*
> *½ teaspoon ground ginger*
> *Scant ½ teaspoon anise seed (or ¼ teaspoon ground anise)*
> *⅔ cup seedless raisins*
> GLAZE (optional)
> *½ cup confectioners' sugar (sifted if lumpy)*
> *¼ teaspoon vanilla*
> *1½ to 2 teaspoons water*

Combine 1 cup flour, the yeast, brown sugar, milk powder and salt in a large mixer bowl. Combine cottage cheese and water in a blender container. Whirl on medium speed until well blended and smooth. Transfer blended mixture to small saucepan and add butter. Heat until butter melts and mixture reaches 125° to 130°. With mixer on low speed, beat liquid into dry ingredients until blended. Raise speed to medium and beat for 3 minutes. Add egg, orange rind, allspice, mace, ginger and anise, and beat on medium speed for 30 seconds longer. With a large spoon, stir in raisins and remaining 1¾ cups flour.

Cover bowl with plastic wrap and set aside in a very warm place (80° to 90°) for 10 minutes. Meanwhile, generously grease a 1½- to 1¾- quart soufflé dish or casserole.

Stir down batter and spoon into greased soufflé dish; smooth out top with back of spoon. Cover dish with plastic wrap and set aside in a very warm place (80° to 90°) for 20 minutes.

Place dish, uncovered, in cold oven; immediately set thermostat to 375°. Bake bread for 36 to 40 minutes, or until top is puffy and well browned. (If top begins to brown too rapidly, reduce heat to 350° for the last 10 minutes of baking.)

Transfer dish to rack and let stand for 5 minutes before removing loaf. Run a knife around casserole to loosen loaf; then transfer to rack to cool. Meanwhile, if glaze is desired, prepare as follows: Stir together confectioners' sugar, vanilla and 1 teaspoon water. Gradually stir in enough more water to yield a smooth, liquefied but not runny glaze. Allow loaf to cool for 10 minutes before adding glaze. Spread glaze over top of loaf, letting excess drip decoratively down sides. Bread may be served slightly warm or at room temperature. Makes 1 medium-sized loaf.

Approximate Preparation Time: 25 minutes
Rising/Baking Time: 1 hour 8 minutes

• *Cranberry Batter Bread* •

Start to Finish: About 1 hour 48 minutes

This is a handsome casserole bread enlivened with colorful, tangy bits of cranberry. In combination with the yeast dough, the cranberries taste a little like sour cherries.

> *3 cups all-purpose white or unbleached flour*
> *1 packet fast-rising dry yeast*
> *⅔ cup granulated sugar*
> *¾ teaspoon salt*
> *½ teaspoon ground cinnamon*
> *1 cup hot water (125° to 130°)*
> *2 tablespoons vegetable oil*
> *1 egg, at room temperature*
> *½ teaspoon freshly grated orange rind*
> *1 cup coarsely chopped fresh cranberries (or frozen cranberries thawed to room temperature)*

Stir together 1 cup flour, the yeast, sugar, salt and cinnamon in a large mixer bowl. With mixer on low speed, beat hot water, then oil into dry ingredients until blended. Raise speed to high and beat for 3 minutes. Add egg and orange rind, and beat on high speed for 30 seconds longer. With a large spoon, stir in 2 cups more flour. Batter will be fairly stiff. Cover bowl with plastic wrap. Set aside in a very warm spot (80° to 90°) for 10 minutes. Meanwhile, grease a 1¼- to 1½-quart round casserole or soufflé dish.

Stir down batter. Fold in cranberries until distributed throughout batter. (Don't worry if batter looks slightly pink.) Spoon batter into greased casserole; spread out and smooth surface with a greased knife. Set bowl in a larger bowl. Carefully fill larger bowl with enough hot water (120° to 130°) to come ⅔ of the way up sides of casserole. Lay a sheet of wax paper over casserole. Let batter rise for 25 minutes. Preheat oven to 375°.

Remove wax paper and bake bread for 50 to 55 minutes, or until top is nicely browned and firm to the touch. Remove loaf from casserole and transfer to rack to cool. Bread may be served warm or at room temperature. Makes 1 medium-sized loaf.

Approximate Preparation Time: 20 minutes
Rising/Baking Time: 1 hour 27 minutes

Spiced Casserole Bread with Raisins

Start to Finish: About 1 hour 55 minutes

Easy to make, yet always a favorite, this fluffy bread is lightly spiced and enlivened with raisins.

> 3½ cups all-purpose white or unbleached flour
> 2 packets fast-rising dry yeast
> ½ cup granulated sugar
> ¼ cup instant nonfat dry milk powder
> ¾ teaspoon salt
> ½ teaspoon ground cinnamon
> ¼ teaspoon ground nutmeg
> ¼ teaspoon ground allspice
> ¼ teaspoon ground ginger
> 1¼ cups water
> 2½ tablespoons butter or margarine, cut into 2 or 3 pieces
> 1 egg, at room temperature
> ¾ cup raisins

Stir together 1¼ cups flour, the yeast, sugar, milk powder, salt and spices in a large mixer bowl. Combine water and butter in a small saucepan, and heat until butter melts and mixture reaches 125° to 130°. With mixer on low speed, beat liquid into dry ingredients until well blended. Raise speed to high and beat for 1 minute. Add egg and ½ cup more flour, and beat for 2 minutes longer. With a large spoon, vigorously stir in raisins and remaining 1¾ cups flour until well blended; batter will be fairly stiff.

Cover bowl with plastic wrap. Set aside in a very warm spot (80° to 90°) for 20 minutes. Meanwhile, generously grease a 2-quart soufflé dish or round casserole. Lightly dust casserole with flour, tipping back and forth until bottom and sides are lightly coated; tap out any excess flour.

Stir down batter and spoon into casserole; spread out and smooth surface with a greased knife. Set aside, uncovered, in a very warm spot (80° to 90°) for 25 minutes.

155

Place bread in a cold oven; immediately set thermostat to 350°. Bake loaf for 50 to 55 minutes, or until top is browned and firm to the touch. Transfer casserole from oven to rack and let stand for 5 minutes before removing loaf. Run a knife around loaf to loosen from casserole. Best served still warm from the oven. Makes 1 medium-sized loaf.

Approximate Preparation Time: 18 minutes
Rising/Baking Time: 1 hour 37 minutes

◆ *Almond Casserole Bread* ◆

Start to Finish: About 1 hour 45 minutes

An attractive, delicately flavored bread. Very easy to make, too.

2¾ cups all-purpose white or unbleached flour
1 packet fast-rising dry yeast
⅓ cup instant nonfat dry milk
2 tablespoons granulated sugar
1 teaspoon salt
1 cup water
⅓ cup butter or margarine, cut into 5 or 6 pieces
2 tablespoons honey
1 egg, at room temperature
⅓ cup finely ground blanched almonds (ground in a blender or food
   processor)
¼ teaspoon almond extract
About 2 tablespoons coarsely chopped blanched almonds for garnishing
   top of loaf

Stir together 1¼ cups flour, the yeast, milk powder, sugar and salt in a large mixer bowl. Combine water, butter and honey in a small saucepan. Stirring until honey dissolves and butter melts, heat to 125° to 130°. With mixer on low speed, beat liquid mixture into dry ingredients until blended. Raise speed to high and beat for 3 minutes.

Add egg, ground almonds and almond extract, and beat on medium speed for 30 seconds longer. With a large spoon, stir in 1½ cups more flour; batter will be fairly stiff.

Cover bowl with plastic wrap. Set aside in a very warm spot (80° to 90°) for 20 minutes. Meanwhile, grease a 1½-quart (or similar) round casserole or soufflé dish.

Stir down batter and spoon into greased casserole; spread out and smooth surface with a greased knife. Sprinkle surface with chopped almonds; press almonds into batter slightly with back of a spoon. Cover casserole with plastic wrap and set aside in a very warm spot (80° to 90°) and let batter rise for 15 minutes. Preheat oven to 375°.

Remove plastic wrap and bake bread for 47 to 52 minutes, or until top is golden brown and firm to the touch. Let stand for 2 to 3 minutes; then remove loaf from casserole and transfer to rack to cool. Loaf may be served warm or at room temperature. Makes 1 medium-sized loaf.

Approximate Preparation Time: 18 minutes
Rising/Baking Time: 1 hour 25 minutes

❖ *No-Knead Dinner Rolls* ❖

Start to Finish: About 1 hour 10 minutes

For delicious homemade rolls that require no kneading, mix up these fluffy muffin-shaped creations. You can make plain rolls or the Cinnamon Puffies variation provided below using the same easy batter. (Or double the recipe and prepare a dozen of each!)

> 2⅔ *cups all-purpose white or unbleached flour*
> 1 *packet fast-rising dry yeast*
> ¼ *cup granulated sugar*
> ¼ *cup instant nonfat dry milk*
> ½ *teaspoon salt*
> 1 *cup water*
> 3 *tablespoons butter or margarine, cut into 3 or 4 pieces*
> 1 *egg, at room temperature*

Stir together 1 cup flour, the yeast, sugar, milk powder and salt in a large mixer bowl. In a small saucepan, heat water and butter until butter melts and mixture reaches 125° to 130°. With mixer on low speed, beat liquid into dry ingredients until blended. Raise speed to high and beat for 2½ minutes. Add egg and beat for 30 seconds longer. With large spoon, vigorously stir in remaining 1⅔ cups flour; batter will be stiff.

Cover bowl with plastic wrap and set aside in a very warm spot (80° to 90°) for 20 minutes. Meanwhile, heavily grease twelve standard-sized muffin-tin cups.

Stir down batter and divide among muffin cups. Smooth out batter surface with a greased knife. Set muffin tin aside, uncovered, in a very warm spot (80° to 90°) for 20 minutes. Preheat oven to 400°.

Bake rolls for 14 to 17 minutes, or until nicely browned on top and springy to the touch. Let rolls stand in tins for 3 to 4 minutes. Then run a knife around cups to loosen rolls, and transfer to racks for 5 minutes before serving. Serve still warm from the oven. Makes 12 large muffin-shaped rolls.

Approximate Preparation Time: 15 minutes   *Rising/Baking Time:* 56 minutes

VARIATION: Cinnamon Puffies—Prepare batter and set aside as directed for rolls. Generously grease twelve muffin-tin cups. Stir together ¼ cup sugar and ¾ teaspoon cinnamon. Divide half the cinnamon-sugar mixture equally among the muffin cups and tip back and forth to coat bottoms and sides; reserve remainder for garnishing tops of puffies.

Stir down batter, spoon into cups, and let rise, uncovered, for 15 minutes. Sprinkle reserved cinnamon-sugar mixture over puffies and bake as directed in basic recipe.

• *No-Knead Honey-Wheat Rolls* •

Start to Finish: About 1 hour 10 minutes

The perfect choice when you want to add a little whole-grain goodness to a meal on short notice. Honey gives these easy muffin-shaped rolls a very nice flavor.

1⅔ cups all-purpose white or unbleached flour
1 tablespoon fast-rising dry yeast (about 1½ packets)
2 tablespoons light or dark brown sugar, packed
½ teaspoon salt
1 cup water
3 tablespoons honey
2 tablespoons vegetable oil
1 egg yolk, at room temperature
¾ cup whole-wheat flour

Stir together 1 cup white flour, the yeast, sugar and salt in a large mixer bowl. Combine water, honey and oil in a small saucepan. Stirring until honey dissolves, heat to 125° to 130°. With mixer on low speed, beat liquid mixture into flour-yeast mixture until blended. Raise speed to high and beat for 2½ minutes. Add egg yolk and beat on medium speed for 30 seconds longer. With a large spoon, quickly and vigorously stir in whole-wheat flour and remaining ⅔ cup white flour; batter will be rubbery.

Cover bowl with plastic wrap. Set aside in a very warm spot (80° to 90°) for 10 minutes. Meanwhile, generously grease twelve standard-sized muffin-tin cups.

Spoon batter into greased cups, dividing evenly among them. Smooth out batter surface with a greased knife. Lay a sheet of wax paper over muffin tin. Set tin aside in a very warm place (80° to 90°) for 15 minutes. Remove wax paper and let stand for 10 minutes longer. Preheat oven to 375°.

Bake rolls for 14 to 18 minutes, or until tops are just tinged with brown and slightly springy to the touch. Let rolls stand in cups for 3 to 4 minutes. Then run a knife around cups to loosen rolls, and place on racks. Serve warm from the oven, with butter. Makes 12 rolls.

Approximate Preparation Time: 18 minutes   *Rising/Baking Time:* 52 minutes

Festive Fruit Loaves with Rum Icing

Start to Finish: About 1 hour 28 minutes

Bake these appealing fruit-and-nut-studded loaves when you need a "fancy" bread in a hurry. They're nice on a tea or coffee table, and no one will guess just how easy they were to make!

¼ cup light rum
½ cup diced mixed candied citrus peel
½ cup raisins
½ cup chopped blanched almonds
5 cups all-purpose white or unbleached flour
2 packets fast-rising dry yeast
¼ cup instant nonfat dry milk
½ cup granulated sugar
1 teaspoon salt
1¼ cups water
⅓ cup butter or margarine, cut into 5 or 6 pieces
3 eggs, at room temperature
2 teaspoons freshly grated lemon rind
GLAZE AND GARNISH
¾ cup confectioners' sugar
1 teaspoon lemon juice
2 to 3 teaspoons light rum
2 tablespoons diced mixed candied citrus peel
2 tablespoons chopped blanched almonds

Stir together ¼ cup rum, ½ cup candied citrus peel, raisins and ½ cup almonds in a medium-sized bowl. Set aside. Stir together 1½ cups flour, the yeast, milk powder, granulated sugar and salt in a large mixer bowl. Combine water and butter in a small saucepan, and heat until butter melts and mixture reaches 125° to 130°. With mixer on low speed, beat liquid into flour-yeast mixture until ingredients are blended. Raise speed to medium and beat for 3 minutes. Add eggs and ½ cup more flour, and beat on low speed for 30 seconds. With a large spoon, stir in fruit-rum mixture, grated lemon rind and remaining 3 cups flour until thoroughly incorporated.

161

Cover bowl with plastic wrap. Set aside in a very warm spot (80° to 90°) for 15 minutes. Meanwhile, grease two 8½ × 4½ × 2½-inch (or similar 1½-quart) loaf pans. Dust pans with flour, tipping back and forth until bottoms and sides are evenly coated. Tap out any excess flour and set pans aside.

Stir batter down; it will be very rubbery. Spoon batter into pans; smooth and spread out to edges with greased knife. Cover pans with plastic wrap and set aside in a very warm spot (80° to 90°) for 15 minutes.

Place pans, uncovered, in a cold oven; immediately set thermostat to 375°. Bake bread for 30 to 35 minutes, or until loaves fill pans and tops are browned and sound hollow when tapped. Transfer pans to racks and cool for 5 minutes before removing loaves. Let loaves stand on racks until almost cool, then top with glaze. (If loaves are to be frozen for later use, prepare and add glaze and garnishes shortly before serving.)

Prepare glaze as follows: Stir together confectioners' sugar, lemon juice and 2 teaspoons rum until smooth. Gradually add enough more rum to yield a fairly thick but spreadable glaze. Spread glaze over tops of loaves with a knife, allowing excess to drip decoratively down sides. Immediately sprinkle 2 tablespoons each diced candied peel and chopped almonds evenly over glaze. Before serving, let loaves stand a few minutes until glaze sets. Loaves may be served at room temperature or just barely warm. Makes 2 medium-sized loaves.

Approximate Preparation Time: 25 minutes
Rising/Baking Time: 1 hour 3 minutes

• *Brandied Fruit and Nut Ring* •

Start to Finish: About 1 hour 55 minutes

A handsome ring loaf baked in a tube pan. This impressive-looking bread is enlivened with brandy-soaked dried fruit, nuts and spices. It goes well with autumn meals, especially Thanksgiving, and is also good for brunch or tea.

3½ cups all-purpose white or unbleached flour
2 packets fast-rising dry yeast
⅔ cup instant nonfat dry milk
½ cup granulated sugar
¾ teaspoon salt
½ teaspoon ground cinnamon
½ teaspoon ground allspice
¼ teaspoon ground ginger
2 cups water
¼ cup vegetable oil
2 eggs, at room temperature
1½ cups whole-wheat flour
¼ cup brandy
½ cup finely chopped dates
½ cup finely chopped prunes
½ cup golden raisins
1 cup finely chopped walnuts or pecans

Stir together 2½ cups white flour, the yeast, milk powder, sugar, salt and spices in a large mixer bowl. Combine water and oil in a small saucepan, and heat to 125° to 130°. With mixer on low speed, beat liquid into flour-yeast mixture until blended. Raise speed to high and beat for 2 minutes. Add eggs and beat 1 minute longer. With a large spoon, stir in whole-wheat flour and remaining 1 cup white flour until thoroughly blended; batter will be fairly stiff.

Cover bowl with plastic wrap. Set aside in a very warm spot (80° to 90°) for 25 minutes. Meanwhile, combine brandy, fruit and ⅔ cup nuts in a corrosion-proof bowl, and toss until well mixed; set aside. (Reserve remaining ⅓ cup nuts for lining pan and garnishing top of loaf.) Generously grease a 10-inch-diameter (or similar) tube pan.

163

Sprinkle pan interior with half the remaining ⅓ cup nuts. Set aside.

Vigorously stir down batter. Stir in fruit-and-nut mixture (including any unabsorbed brandy) until distributed throughout batter. Spoon batter into tube pan. Smooth out surface with a greased knife. Sprinkle remaining nuts over batter top. Lightly press nuts into batter with the back of a greased spoon.

Cover pan with plastic wrap and set aside in a very warm spot (80° to 90°) for 15 minutes. Preheat oven to 375°. Bake for 45 to 50 minutes, or until bread fills pan and top is nicely browned and sounds hollow when tapped. Place pan on rack and cool for 10 minutes. Remove bread from pan; loosen sides first, then bottom. Bread may be served slightly warm or at room temperature. Spread with butter, cream cheese or jam. Makes 1 large loaf.

Approximate Preparation Time: 25 minutes
Rising/Baking Time: 1 hour 28 minutes

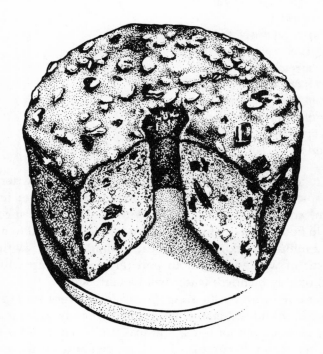

• Sally Lunn •

Start to Finish: About 1 hour 30 minutes

Here's a streamlined version of the classic batter bread, Sally Lunn. The large finished loaf is impressive looking, as well as delicious. It makes a wonderful, yet very easy, special-occasion bread.

5 cups all-purpose white or unbleached flour
2 packets fast-rising dry yeast
⅓ cup instant nonfat dry milk
⅓ cup granulated sugar
1 teaspoon salt
1⅓ cups water
6 tablespoons butter or margarine, cut into 5 or 6 pieces
3 eggs, at room temperature

Stir together 1½ cups flour, the yeast, milk powder, sugar and salt in a large mixer bowl. Combine water and butter in a small saucepan, and heat until butter melts and mixture reaches 125° to 130°. With mixer on low speed, beat liquid into dry ingredients until blended. Raise speed to medium and beat for 3 minutes. Add eggs and ¾ cup more flour, and beat on low speed for 30 seconds. With a large spoon, vigorously stir in remaining 2¾ cups flour until thoroughly incorporated.

Cover bowl with plastic wrap. Set aside in a very warm spot (80° to 90°) for 20 minutes. Meanwhile, grease and lightly flour a 10-inch-diameter (or similar) tube pan.

Stir batter down; it will be very rubbery. Spoon batter into tube pan, smoothing and spreading out to edges. Cover pan with plastic wrap. Set aside in a very warm spot (80° to 90°) for 10 minutes.

Place pan, uncovered, in a cold oven; immediately set thermostat to 375°. Bake bread for 40 to 45 minutes, or until it fills pan, is nicely browned and sounds hollow when tapped on top. Place pan on rack and cool for 10 minutes. Remove bread from pan; loosen sides first, then bottom. Best served warm, cut into wedges and buttered. Makes 1 very large loaf.

Approximate Preparation Time: 15 minutes
Rising/Baking Time: 1 hour 13 minutes

• *Kugelhopf* •

Start to Finish: About 1 hour 50 minutes

Kugelhopf is a classic Alsatian sweet bread baked in a turban, or Turk's-head, mold especially designed for the purpose. However, any tall, fluted tube or turban-style pan can be substituted. The bread is delicious for breakfast or brunch. It can also be dressed up with a syrupy glaze, and perhaps a dollop of whipped cream, and served for dessert.

The following is my updated version of the recipe that was included with the beautiful ceramic kugelhopf form I purchased on a trip to eastern France. Kirsch, a cherry brandy, which is used to soak the raisins, lends a wonderful aroma and subtle taste to the bread.

> *¼ cup kirsch (cherry brandy)*
> *½ cup brown raisins*
> *½ cup golden raisins*
> *4¼ cups all-purpose white or unbleached flour*
> *3 packets fast-rising dry yeast*
> *⅔ cup granulated sugar*
> *⅓ cup instant nonfat dry milk*
> *½ teaspoon salt*
> *1 cup water*
> *⅓ cup butter (or margarine), cut into 5 or 6 pieces*
> *2 eggs, at room temperature*
> *1 teaspoon freshly grated lemon rind*
> *½ cup chopped blanched almonds*
> GLAZE *(optional)*
> *½ cup granulated sugar*
> *2 tablespoons water*
> *2 teaspoons lemon juice*
> *2 tablespoons kirsch*

Stir ¼ cup kirsch and the raisins together in a small bowl and set aside. Stir together 1½ cups flour, the yeast, ⅔ cup sugar, milk powder and salt in a large mixer bowl. Combine 1 cup water and butter in a small saucepan, and heat until butter melts and mixture reaches 125° to 130°. With mixer on low speed, beat liquid into dry ingredients until mixed. Raise speed to medium and beat for 3½ minutes. Add eggs, lemon rind and ¾ cup more flour, and beat on low speed for 30 seconds. With a large spoon, stir in all but 2 tablespoons raisins, any unabsorbed kirsch, and remaining 2 cups flour until thoroughly incorporated.

Cover bowl with a slightly damp towel. Set aside in a very warm spot (80° to 90°) for 10 minutes. Meanwhile, very generously grease a large kugelhopf mold or turban-style pan (at least 9-cup capacity). Sprinkle almonds in mold, tipping back and forth to distribute evenly over interior. Sprinkle reserved 2 tablespoons raisins into mold.

Stir down batter; it will be very stiff and rubbery. Gently spoon batter into mold, taking care not to dislodge almonds from greased surface. Cover mold with a slightly damp towel and set aside in a very warm spot (80° to 90°) for 30 minutes.

Place mold, uncovered, in a cold oven; immediately set thermostat to 375°. Bake for 43 to 48 minutes, or until top is nicely browned and firm to the touch. Place pan on rack and cool for 8 to 10 minutes before removing bread. To cool loaf (and also to serve) turn so that top during baking becomes the bottom. Serve warm, with butter, for breakfast, or with kirsch glaze for dessert.

If glaze is desired, prepare as follows: Stir together all glaze ingredients, except kirsch, in a small saucepan over medium-high heat. Bring to a boil, stirring, and boil for 1 minute. Remove from heat and let stand for 30 seconds. Stir in kirsch. Spoon warm glaze over kugelhopf. Makes 1 large loaf.

Approximate Preparation Time: 23 minutes
Rising/Baking Time: 1 hour 25 minutes

◆ WHOLE-GRAIN BREADS ◆

Most people eat bread just because they like it. How nice that the staff of life is also very healthful fare. In general, bread provides satisfying complex carbohydrates and protein, but without adding large amounts of unhealthful fat and sugar to the diet. (Pastries and other fatty, sugary bread products made with highly refined flour don't count, of course!)

Whole-grain breads, which are the focus of this chapter, also furnish lots of B vitamins, fiber and important trace minerals—not to mention robust good taste. Whole-grain breads don't have to be dark and doormat heavy, however. There are a number of selections included here—the Braided Herb Loaves, Best-Ever Wheat Rolls, and 100 Percent Whole Wheat–Honey Bread, for example—that are lighter in color and airier than many recipes containing no whole-grain products at all. Of course, some folks enjoy denser, stick-to-the-ribs loaves, and a pleasing assortment of these—from Black Bread to Bran Loaves and Pumpernickel—is provided, too.

As you thumb through this chapter, you may notice that nearly all the recipes call for some whole-wheat flour. There are several reasons for this. First, wheat is the only grain that contains large amounts of gluten, that magical material that enables yeast to raise bread. Moreover, whole-wheat flour is the most readily available whole-grain product, and in this book the major emphasis is on recipes that are convenient to use.

Many people are confused about which foodstuffs qualify as

"whole grain" and why they are considered particularly healthful. The term "whole grain" means that all parts of the kernel are retained, not just the starchy portion (endosperm) normally found in refined flours and cereals. Thus, the designation "whole wheat" (as opposed to just "wheat") indicates that the fibrous outer coat, or bran, and the tiny germ are also included. These latter are important because they contain most of the fiber, vitamins and minerals in the kernel. Of the cereal and grain products commonly available today, whole-wheat flour, dark rye flour and brown rice are whole grain. Most other products, such as rolled oats, pearled barley and degerminated cornmeal, are at least partially refined. Even so, all these contribute a variety of appealing textures and flavors—not to mention worthwhile protein and carbohydrate—to breads.

• *Wheat Bread* •

Start to Finish: About 1 hour 28 minutes

A good, all-purpose wheat bread, particularly well suited for toasting.

> 3¼ to 3¾ cups all-purpose white or unbleached flour
> 2 packets fast-rising dry yeast
> ⅔ cup instant nonfat dry milk
> ⅓ cup granulated sugar
> 2 teaspoons salt
> 2 cups water
> ¼ cup butter or margarine, cut into 3 or 4 pieces
> 1 egg, at room temperature
> 2½ cups whole-wheat flour

Stir together 2¼ cups white flour, the yeast, milk powder, sugar and salt in a large mixer bowl. In a small saucepan, combine water and butter, and heat until butter melts and mixture reaches 125° to 130°. With mixer on low speed, beat liquid into flour-yeast mixture until blended. Raise speed to high and beat for 3½ minutes. Add egg and beat 1 minute longer. With a large spoon, vigorously stir in whole-wheat flour. Working in the bowl or on a clean, lightly floured surface, gradually knead in enough more white flour to yield a smooth, malleable dough; kneading should take 3 to 4 minutes. Shape dough into a ball and return to bowl. Cover bowl with a slightly damp towel. Set bowl aside in a very warm spot (80° to 90°) for 20 minutes. Meanwhile, grease two 9 × 5 × 3-inch (or similar 2-quart) loaf pans and set aside.

Punch down dough; divide in half. With well-greased hands, form into two smooth, well-shaped loaves and place in greased pans. Lightly cover pans with a damp towel. Set aside in a very warm place (80° to 90°) for 15 minutes. Preheat oven to 375°.

Cut a ¼-inch-deep slash lengthwise down center of loaves with a sharp knife. Bake loaves for 30 to 35 minutes, or until tops are browned and bottoms sound hollow when tapped. Cool loaves on racks before serving. May be frozen for later use, if desired. Makes 2 large loaves.

Approximate Preparation Time: 20 minutes
Rising/Baking Time: 1 hour 8 minutes

• *Best-Ever Wheat Rolls* •

Start to Finish: About 1 hour 20 minutes

Enjoy these light and tasty rolls along with a meal, or use to make sandwiches. They're delicious!

4 to 4½ cups all-purpose white or unbleached flour
3 packets fast-rising dry yeast
¼ cup granulated sugar
½ cup instant nonfat dry milk
2 teaspoons salt
2 cups hot water (125° to 130°)
2 cups whole-wheat flour
⅓ cup cold butter or margarine
Milk for brushing over tops of rolls

Stir together 2⅓ cups white flour, the yeast, sugar, milk powder and salt in a large mixer bowl. With mixer on low speed, beat water into flour-yeast mixture until blended. Raise speed to medium and beat for 2 minutes. In another bowl combine 2 cups whole-wheat flour and the butter. With two forks or a pastry blender, work butter into whole-wheat flour until mixture resembles very coarse meal. Stir whole wheat–butter mixture into dough with a large spoon until well blended. Working in the bowl, stir and then lightly knead in enough more white flour to yield a fairly soft yet springy dough. Cover bowl with a slightly damp towel and set aside in a very warm spot (80° to 90°) for 30 minutes. Generously grease a 17½ × 15-inch (or similar very large) baking sheet, or two small baking sheets, and set aside.

Punch down dough. Divide dough in half; then divide each half into eight equal portions. With well-greased hands, carefully shape portions into smooth, round balls; for best appearance of finished rolls, be sure excess dough is smoothed and tucked under the bottom. Space rolls at least 2 inches apart on baking sheet. Lightly cover with damp towel and set aside in a very warm spot (80° to 90°) for 15 minutes. Preheat oven to 400°.

Lightly brush tops of rolls with milk, using pastry brush or paper towel. Bake for 14 to 17 minutes, or until nicely browned and rolls sound hollow when tapped on top. Remove from sheet and let stand on racks for 5 minutes before serving, or cool on racks for later use. Rolls may be frozen, if desired. Makes 16 large rolls.

Approximate Preparation Time: 20 minutes   *Rising/Baking Time:* 1 hour

⋄ *Farmhouse Potato-Wheat Bread* ⋄

Start to Finish: About 1 hour 33 minutes

Potatoes add moistness to this springy, full-bodied bread. It's especially good for sandwiches.

> *1½ cups potato cubes (about 2 peeled medium-sized potatoes)*
> *1¾ to 2¼ cups all-purpose white or unbleached flour*
> *2 packets fast-rising dry yeast*
> *Generous ⅓ cup dark brown sugar, packed*
> *1¾ teaspoons salt*
> *3½ tablespoons butter or margarine, cut into 2 or 3 pieces*
> *Reserved potato-cooking liquid*
> *3¼ cups whole-wheat flour*
> *Milk for brushing over tops of loaves (optional)*

Place potato cubes in a small saucepan and just cover with water. Bring to a boil over medium heat and simmer, covered, 7 to 9 minutes, or until potatoes are just tender. Meanwhile, stir together 1½ cups flour, the yeast, sugar and salt in a bowl, and set aside.

Drain potato cubes well, reserving their liquid in a large measuring cup. Place potatoes in large mixer bowl. With mixer on low speed, beat for about 1½ minutes, or until potatoes are well blended and smooth. Add butter and continue beating for 1 minute longer. Add enough water to potato liquid to make 1⅔ cups and, if necessary, return liquid mixture to small saucepan and heat to 125° to 130°.

Add flour-yeast mixture, then liquid mixture to potatoes in mixer bowl. Beat with mixer on low speed until ingredients are blended. Raise speed to high and beat for 4 minutes. With a large spoon, vigorously stir in whole-wheat flour. Working in the bowl or on a clean, lightly floured surface, quickly and vigorously knead in enough more white flour to yield a smooth and malleable, fairly firm dough. Form into a ball and return to mixer bowl. Cover bowl with plastic wrap and set aside in a very warm place (80° to 90°) for 15 minutes. Meanwhile, grease two 8½ × 4½ × 2½-inch (or similar 1½-quart) loaf pans and set aside. Preheat oven to 400°.

Punch dough down and divide in half. With well-greased hands, shape dough into loaves and place in pans. Cover pans with plastic wrap and set aside in a very warm spot (80° to 90°) for 25 minutes.

Brush tops and sides of loaves with milk, if desired. Make a ¼-inch-deep slash lengthwise down center of each loaf. Bake loaves in preheated 400° oven for 28 to 33 minutes, or until tops are nicely browned and sound hollow when tapped. Remove loaves from pans and transfer to racks. Serve bread still warm from the oven, or cool for later use. Makes 2 medium-sized loaves.

Approximate Preparation Time: 28 minutes
Rising/Baking Time: 1 hour 10 minutes

100 Percent Whole Wheat–Honey Bread

Start to Finish: About 1 hour 35 minutes

If you object to whole-wheat loaves because of the "doormat" texture, here is the recipe for you! This bread is light and airy, not to mention delicious and nourishing. It may become one of your all-time favorites.

> 7 to 7½ cups whole-wheat flour
> 3 packets fast-rising dry yeast
> ¼ cup instant nonfat dry milk
> 1½ teaspoons salt
> 2¼ cups water
> Generous ⅓ cup honey
> ⅓ cup butter or margarine, cut into 4 or 5 pieces
> 1 egg, at room temperature
> Milk for brushing tops of loaves

Stir together 2¼ cups flour, the yeast, milk powder and salt in a large mixer bowl. In a small saucepan, combine water, honey and butter. Stirring until honey dissolves and butter melts, heat to 125° to 130°. With mixer on low speed, beat liquid mixture into dry ingredients until blended. Raise mixer speed to high and beat for 3½ minutes. Add egg and beat 1 minute longer. Vigorously stir in 3¼ cups more flour, or enough to yield a kneadable dough. Working on a clean, well-floured surface, gradually knead in enough more flour to yield a light and elastic but still slightly sticky dough; kneading should take 6 to 8 minutes.

Form dough into a ball and transfer to a large, well-greased bowl. Cover bowl with a slightly damp towel and set aside in a very warm spot (80° to 90°) for 25 minutes. Meanwhile, generously grease two 9 × 5 × 3-inch (or similar 2-quart) loaf pans.

Punch down dough; divide in half. With lightly greased hands, form into two smooth, well-shaped loaves and place in greased pans. Cover pans with plastic wrap and set aside in a very warm place (80° to 90°) for 20 minutes. Preheat oven to 400°.

Brush tops of loaves with milk, using a pastry brush or paper towel. Cut a ¼-inch-deep slash lengthwise down center of each loaf with a sharp knife. Bake loaves for 24 to 28 minutes, or until tops are browned and sound hollow when tapped. Immediately remove loaves from pans and transfer to racks to cool. Bread slices best when cool, but may be served slightly warm. It makes good toast. The loaves may be frozen for later use, if desired. Makes 2 large loaves.

Approximate Preparation Time: 25 minutes
Rising/Baking Time: 1 hour 11 minutes

• *Brown-Rice and Wheat Bread* •

Start to Finish: About 1 hour 30 minutes

Brown-rice flour adds not only the nutritional benefits of whole grain but a distinctive and appealing flavor to this bread. Brown-rice flour can be obtained in health food stores, but this recipe is designed so you can make your own by grinding ordinary brown rice in a blender. Homemade flour is usually somewhat coarser than the commercially ground, and will lend your bread a crunchiness reminiscent of cracked wheat. This is a hearty, yet not heavy bread.

1 cup uncooked brown rice
2⅔ to 3¼ cups all-purpose white or unbleached flour
2 packets fast-rising dry yeast
¼ cup light brown sugar, packed
1½ teaspoons salt
1½ cups water
3 tablespoons butter or margarine, cut into 2 or 3 pieces
1¼ cups whole-wheat flour

Put brown rice in a blender container and blend on high speed for several minutes, or until kernels are ground into flour; stop blender several times and redistribute the kernels so flour is as fine as possible.

Stir together 1⅔ cups white flour, the yeast, sugar and salt in a large mixer bowl. Combine water and butter in a small saucepan, and heat until butter melts and mixture reaches 125° to 130°. With mixer on low speed, beat water-butter mixture into flour-yeast mixture until blended. Raise speed to high and beat for 4 minutes. Stir in brown-rice flour, whole-wheat flour and ⅔ cup more white flour until blended. Working in the bowl or on a clean, lightly floured surface, quickly and vigorously knead in enough more white flour to yield a springy and malleable yet not dry dough. Transfer dough to large, well-greased bowl. Cover bowl with plastic wrap and set aside in a very warm spot (80° to 90°) for 15 minutes. Meanwhile, grease two 7⅞ × 3⅞ × 2½-inch aluminum foil (or similar 1-quart) loaf pans.

Punch down dough and divide in half. With well-greased hands, form halves into smooth, well-shaped loaves and place in pans.

Cover pans with plastic wrap and set aside in a very warm place (80° to 90°) for 20 minutes. Preheat oven to 400°.

Bake loaves, uncovered, for 29 to 33 minutes, or until tops are nicely browned and sound hollow when tapped. Place loaves on racks and cool. Serve warm or at room temperature. This is a good toasting bread. When fresh, it can also be used for sandwiches. Loaves can be frozen for later use, if desired. Makes 2 medium-sized loaves.

Approximate Preparation Time: 22 minutes
Rising/Baking Time: 1 hour 7 minutes

• *Whole Wheat–Bulgur Loaves* •

Start to Finish: About 1 hour 35 minutes

Here is a nutritious, 100 percent whole-wheat bread with the added crunchiness of bulgur (parched cracked wheat). The loaves have a rich, nutty flavor, moderately dense texture and nice crispy crust.

5¼ to 5¾ cups whole-wheat flour
2 packets fast-rising dry yeast
¼ cup granulated sugar
1½ teaspoons salt
2½ cups water
3 tablespoons butter or margarine, cut into 2 or 3 pieces
1 cup bulgur wheat (uncooked)

Stir together 2¼ cups flour, the yeast, sugar and salt in a large mixer bowl. In a small saucepan, combine water and butter, and heat to 125° to 130°. With mixer on low speed, beat liquid into dry ingredients until well blended. Raise speed to high and beat for 3½ minutes. With a large spoon, stir in bulgur wheat and about 2¼ cups

177

more whole-wheat flour until well mixed. On a clean, well-floured surface, gradually knead in enough more flour to yield a malleable but still slightly soft and sticky dough; kneading should take 4 to 5 minutes. Form dough into a ball and transfer to large, well-greased bowl. Cover bowl with plastic wrap and set aside in a very warm spot (80° to 90°) for 20 minutes. Generously grease two 8½ × 4½ × 2½-inch (or similar 1½-quart) loaf pans.

Punch down dough; divide in half. With well-greased hands, form into two smooth, well-shaped loaves and place in greased pans. Lightly cover pans with plastic wrap and set aside in a very warm place (80° to 90°) for 20 minutes. Preheat oven to 400°.

Bake loaves for 31 to 36 minutes, or until lightly browned and tops sound hollow when tapped. Remove loaves from pans and transfer to racks to cool. Serve at room temperature or toasted. The bread may be frozen for later use, if desired. Makes 2 medium-sized loaves.

Approximate Preparation Time: 20 minutes
Rising/Baking Time: 1 hour 14 minutes

NOTE: Bulgur wheat is available in health food stores and many super-markets (often in the ethnic or imported foods section). It looks very much like plain cracked wheat, but since it is already partly cooked, is not as hard or tough on the teeth and requires no presoaking.

◆ *Sesame-Wheat Hearth Loaves* ◆

Start to Finish: About 1 hour 30 minutes

Robust, crispy and encrusted with sesame seeds, these hand-some hearth loaves tempt even people who think they don't like whole-wheat bread. The addition of yogurt gives the loaves a pleas-ing "sourdough" taste and bulgur wheat adds an appealing "crunch" to the texture.

3 to 3½ cups all-purpose white or unbleached flour
2 packets fast-rising dry yeast
1¾ teaspoons salt
1 teaspoon granulated sugar
1⅓ cups warm water
1 cup plain lowfat yogurt
3 tablespoons vegetable oil
¾ cup bulgur wheat
2 cups whole-wheat flour
3 tablespoons sesame seeds, approximately
1 egg white beaten with 1 tablespoon water for brushing over loaves

Stir together 1¾ cups white flour, the yeast, salt and sugar in a large mixer bowl. Combine water, yogurt, oil and bulgur wheat in a medium-sized saucepan, and heat to 125° to 130°. Pour liquid over flour-yeast mixture and beat with mixer on high speed for 4 minutes. With a large spoon, vigorously stir in the whole-wheat flour and ½ cup more white flour, or enough to yield a kneadable dough. Work-ing in the bowl or on a clean, lightly floured surface, gradually knead in enough more white flour to yield a smooth, very manageable, springy dough; kneading should take 4 to 5 minutes. Transfer dough to a large, well-greased bowl. Cover bowl with a slightly damp towel. Set aside in a very warm spot (80° to 90°) for 15 minutes. Meanwhile, lightly grease a 17½ × 15-inch (or similar very large) baking sheet and sprinkle with 1 tablespoon sesame seeds.

Punch down dough; divide in half. With well-greased hands, form into two evenly thick, cigar-shaped loaves, each about 10 inches long. Roll loaves back and forth on a clean surface to smooth exteri-ors. Place as far apart as possible on baking sheet. Cover loaves with a

179

damp towel and set aside in a very warm place (80° to 90°) for 20 minutes. Preheat oven to 450°.

Brush loaves with egg white-water mixture, using a pastry brush or paper towel. Sprinkle each loaf with about 1 tablespoon sesame seeds. With a sharp knife, make three ¼-inch-deep, parallel diagonal slashes in tops of loaves. Bake bread for 15 minutes. Lightly spray or brush loaves with water. Continue baking for 12 to 16 minutes, or until loaves are well browned and sound hollow when tapped on the bottom. (If loaves seem to be browning too rapidly, reduce heat to 425° for last 10 minutes of baking.) Immediately transfer loaves to racks and let stand 10 minutes before serving. Loaves may be served warm or at room temperature, preferably with butter. Freeze for later use, if desired. Makes 2 large hearth loaves.

Approximate Preparation Time: 25 minutes
Rising/Baking Time: 1 hour 4 minutes

NOTE: Bulgur wheat is cracked wheat that has been partially cooked and then dried. (Thus it is a little tenderer and easier on the teeth than regular cracked wheat.) Bulgur can be purchased in health food stores and in the "foreign" or "exotic" foods section of some supermarkets.

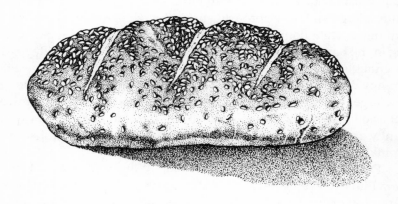

• *Wheat-Triticale Bread* •

Start to Finish: About 1 hour 30 minutes

Triticale is a high-protein grain produced from crossbreeding wheat and rye. It's unfortunate triticale flour isn't more readily available, since it not only boosts nutrition but lends a wonderful flavor and aroma to bread. (It's so good, in fact, that it's worth hunting for.)

In case no source for triticale can be located, in the following recipe rye flour may be substituted and will yield nice loaves. The bread is excellent for sandwiches and toast, and keeps well.

2¾ to 3 cups all-purpose white or unbleached flour
2 packets fast-rising dry yeast
2 teaspoons salt
2 cups water
3 tablespoons honey
3 tablespoons butter or margarine, cut into 2 or 3 pieces
2 cups triticale flour (or medium or dark rye flour)
1¼ cups whole-wheat flour

Stir together 2¼ cups white flour, the yeast and salt in a large mixer bowl. In a small saucepan, combine water, honey and butter. Stirring until honey dissolves and butter melts, heat to 125° to 130°. With mixer on low speed, beat liquid into flour-yeast mixture until blended. Raise speed to high and beat for 4 minutes. With a large spoon, stir in triticale and whole-wheat flour. Working in the bowl, gradually knead in enough more white flour to yield a smooth, malleable dough; kneading should take 3 to 4 minutes. Cover bowl with a slightly damp towel. Set bowl in a very warm spot (80° to 90°) for 20 minutes. And grease two 9 × 5 × 3-inch (or 2-quart) loaf pans.

Punch down dough; divide in half. With well-greased hands, form the halves into smooth, well-shaped loaves and place in greased pans. Lightly cover pans with a damp towel and set aside in a very warm place (80° to 90°) for 25 minutes. Preheat oven to 400°.

Bake loaves for 25 to 29 minutes, or until tops are browned and bottoms sound hollow when tapped. Cool loaves on racks. Slice for sandwiches or toast. The loaves may be frozen for later use, if desired. Makes 2 large loaves.

Approximate Preparation Time: 18 minutes
Rising/Baking Time: 1 hour 12 minutes

181

• *Braided Herb Loaves* •

Start to Finish: About 1 hour 30 minutes

This bread is quite delicious and impressive looking, yet easy to prepare. It is especially good with robust, spicy meals.

3⅓ to 4 cups all-purpose white or unbleached flour
2 packets fast-rising dry yeast
¼ cup instant nonfat dry milk
2 tablespoons granulated sugar
1⅔ cups water
2 teaspoons dried chopped chives
1½ teaspoons celery salt
¾ teaspoon dill seed
¼ teaspoon celery seed
¼ teaspoon dried dill weed
⅛ teaspoon garlic salt or onion salt
3½ tablespoons butter or margarine, cut into 3 or 4 pieces
1 egg, at room temperature
2 cups whole-wheat flour
Milk for brushing over loaves
About ⅛ teaspoon more celery seed for garnishing loaves

Stir together 1¾ cups white flour, the yeast, milk powder and sugar in a large mixer bowl. Combine water, all herbs, seeds and seasoning salts, and butter in a small saucepan. Heat until butter melts and mixture reaches 125° to 130°. With mixer on low speed, beat liquid into flour-yeast mixture until blended. Raise speed to high and beat for 3½ minutes. Add egg and ¼ cup more white flour, and beat 1 minute longer. Stir in whole-wheat flour and 1 cup more white flour, or enough to yield a kneadable dough. Working in the bowl or on a clean, lightly floured surface, gradually knead in enough more white flour to yield a smooth, malleable dough; kneading should take 3 to 4 minutes. Shape dough into a ball and return to mixer bowl. Cover bowl with a slightly damp towel and set aside in a very warm spot (80° to 90°) for 10 minutes. Meanwhile, grease a 17½ × 15-inch (or similar very large) baking sheet.

Punch down dough; divide in half. With well-greased hands,

182

divide each half into three pieces. Shape pieces into 6- to 7-inch logs. Working on a clean surface, gently stretch out and roll logs back and forth with fingertips to form 11-inch-long ropes. Transfer ropes to baking sheet and intertwine into a smooth, well-shaped braid; tuck ends under to form a neat, slightly tapered loaf. (For illustrations on how to braid, see page 210.) Repeat process to form second braided loaf. Lightly cover braids with a damp towel and set aside in a very warm place (80° to 90°) for 25 minutes. Preheat oven to 425°. Generously brush tops and sides of braids with milk, using a pastry brush or a paper towel. Garnish loaf tops with a light sprinkling of celery seed.

Bake loaves for 27 to 32 minutes, or until tops are nicely browned and bottoms sound hollow when tapped. Transfer bread to racks to cool. Braided Herb Loaves may be served still warm from the oven or at room temperature. Freeze for later use, if desired. Makes 2 large braided loaves.

Approximate Preparation Time: 25 minutes
Rising/Baking Time: 1 hour 5 minutes

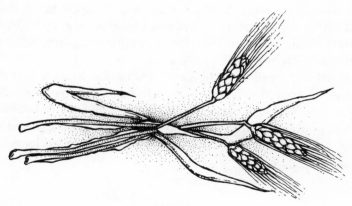

• *Easy Rye Bread* •

Start to Finish: 1 hour 30 minutes

Not too dark, not too light, this all-purpose rye has a chewy crust.

3¾ to 4½ cups all-purpose white or unbleached flour
2 packets fast-rising dry yeast
2 teaspoons salt
2 tablespoons caraway seeds
1 cup water
Generous ⅓ cup light molasses
3 tablespoons butter or margarine, cut into 3 or 4 pieces
2⅔ cups medium or dark rye flour
Milk for brushing tops and sides of loaves

Stir together 2 cups white flour, the yeast, salt and caraway seeds in a large mixer bowl. Combine water, molasses and butter in a small saucepan. Stirring until molasses dissolves and butter melts, heat to 125° to 130°. With mixer on low speed, beat liquid into flour-yeast mixture until blended. Raise speed to high and beat for 4 minutes. Stir in rye flour and 1 cup more white flour, or enough to yield a kneadable dough. Working in the bowl, vigorously knead in enough more white flour to yield a smooth, fairly stiff, slightly sticky dough.

Cover bowl with a slightly damp towel; set aside in a very warm spot (80° to 90°) for 10 minutes. Grease a 17½ × 15-inch (or similar very large) baking sheet and set aside.

Punch down dough; divide in half. With well-greased hands, form halves into smooth lengthened ovals (shaped much like over-sized Idaho baking potatoes) and place on greased pan. Lightly cover loaves with plastic wrap. Set aside in a very warm place (80° to 90°) for 30 minutes. Preheat oven to 400°.

Brush tops and sides of loaves with milk. Make a ⅛-inch-deep slash lengthwise down center of each loaf. Bake loaves for 25 to 30 minutes, or until tops are browned and bottoms sound hollow when tapped. Cool loaves on racks before slicing and serving. Bread may be frozen for later use, if desired. Makes 2 medium-sized loaves.

Approximate Preparation Time: 20 minutes
Rising/Baking Time: 1 hour 7 minutes

• *Molasses Oatmeal Bread* •

Start to Finish: About 1 hour 40 minutes

Homey and nourishing, this well-flavored bread makes delicious toast. Like many oatmeal breads, this has a slightly chewy texture.

1½ *cups quick-cooking rolled oats*
¾ *cup hot tap water*
2¾ *to* 3¼ *cups all-purpose white or unbleached flour*
2 *packets fast-rising dry yeast*
⅔ *cup instant nonfat dry milk*
1½ *teaspoons salt*
1 *cup water*
⅓ *cup molasses, preferably dark*
1½ *tablespoons vegetable oil*
1½ *cups whole-wheat flour*

Combine rolled oats and ¾ cup hot water in a small bowl, stirring to make oatmeal. Set aside. Stir together 1¼ cups white flour, the yeast, milk powder and salt in a large mixer bowl. Combine water, molasses and oil in a small saucepan. Stirring until molasses dissolves, heat mixture to 125° to 130°. With mixer on low speed, beat water-molasses mixture into flour-yeast mixture until blended. Raise speed to high and beat for 3½ minutes. Stir in all but 3 tablespoons of oatmeal, the whole-wheat flour, and 1 cup more white flour, or enough to yield a kneadable dough. (Reserve 3 tablespoons oatmeal for topping loaves.) Working in the bowl, quickly and vigorously knead in enough white flour to yield a springy, malleable, fairly stiff dough.

Cover bowl with plastic wrap and set aside in a very warm spot (80° to 90°) for 15 minutes. Meanwhile, thoroughly grease two 8½ × 4½ × 2½-inch (or similar 1½-quart) loaf pans.

Punch down dough and divide in half. With lightly greased hands, form into two smooth, well-shaped loaves and place in pans. Spread half the reserved oatmeal evenly over top of each loaf, using fingers or a knife. (This may look odd at first, but will ultimately yield attractive results.) Make three parallel, ¼-inch-deep diagonal slashes in top of each loaf with a sharp knife. Place pans in a larger pan, and

185

carefully add enough hot water (120° to 130°) to larger pan to come ⅔ of the way up sides of bread pans. Lay a sheet of wax paper over bread pans. Let dough rise for 25 minutes. Preheat oven to 375°.

Remove plastic wrap and bake bread for 38 to 42 minutes, or until loaves are light brown and sound hollow when tapped on the bottom. Place loaves on racks to cool. Serve warm or at room temperature. Molasses Oatmeal Bread is good served plain or toasted, with butter. Makes 2 medium-sized loaves.

Approximate Preparation Time: 20 minutes
Rising/Baking Time: 1 hour 20 minutes

• *Oats and Honey Loaves* •

Start to Finish: About 1 hour 35 minutes

This makes two handsome loaves with a slightly rough texture and nutty-sweet taste.

> 4 to 4¾ cups all-purpose white or unbleached flour
> 2 packets fast-rising dry yeast
> ⅔ cup instant nonfat dry milk
> 1¾ teaspoons salt
> 2 cups water
> ¼ cup honey
> ¼ cup butter or margarine, cut into 3 or 4 pieces
> 1½ cups whole-wheat flour
> 2 cups old-fashioned rolled oats
> Additional rolled oats for coating bread pans

Stir together 2½ cups white flour, the yeast, milk powder and salt in a large mixer bowl. In a medium-sized saucepan, combine water, honey and butter. Stirring until honey dissolves, heat to 125° to 130°.

186

With mixer on low speed, beat liquid into flour-yeast mixture until blended. Raise speed to high and beat for 3½ minutes. Vigorously stir in 1¼ cups more white flour, the whole-wheat flour and rolled oats. Working in the bowl, gradually knead in enough more white flour to yield a malleable but still slightly soft dough. Cover bowl with plastic wrap. Set aside in a very warm spot (80° to 90°) for 15 minutes. Meanwhile, generously grease two 8½ × 4½ × 2½-inch (or similar 1½-quart) loaf pans. Sprinkle pans with rolled oats; tip pans back and forth until bottoms and sides are lightly coated. Set pans aside.

Punch down dough and divide in half. Form into two smooth, well-shaped loaves and transfer to prepared pans. Lightly cover pans with plastic wrap and set aside in a warm spot (80° to 90°) for 25 minutes. Preheat oven to 375°.

Remove plastic wrap and bake loaves for 34 to 38 minutes, or until tops are well browned and bottoms sound hollow when tapped. (Remove loaves from pans to check.) Transfer loaves to racks to cool. Oats and Honey Loaves slice best when cool, but are delicious served warm from the oven. The bread also makes a pleasant, slightly soft toast. Makes 2 medium-sized loaves.

Approximate Preparation Time: 22 minutes
Rising/Baking Time: 1 hour 16 minutes

• *Miller's Loaves* •

Start to Finish: About 1 hour 40 minutes

Since fresh stone-ground whole-grain flours can lend so much flavor and goodness to bread, it's too bad that the wonderful variety local millers used to produce can't be readily found today. The following loaves, for example, have a subtle, nutty-sweet taste that comes from a blending of whole wheat, oats, rye, brown rice and barley. Brown-rice and barley flours can be obtained in some health food stores, but to save you a trip, this recipe provides directions for making them at home in a blender. In this case, the flours will not be quite as fine, and the resulting loaves will have a crunchiness reminiscent of cracked-wheat bread.

Miller's Loaves go well with soups, stews and similar hearty, homey fare.

> ⅔ cup brown rice (uncooked)
> ¼ cup pearled barley (uncooked)
> 3½ to 4½ cups all-purpose white or unbleached flour
> 2 packets fast-rising dry yeast
> ¼ cup light brown sugar, packed
> 1½ teaspoons salt
> 2½ cups water
> ¼ cup butter or margarine, cut into 3 or 4 pieces
> ¾ cup old-fashioned or quick-cooking rolled oats
> 1 cup whole-wheat flour
> ⅔ cup medium or dark rye flour
> Milk for brushing over loaves (optional)

Combine brown rice and barley in a blender container and blend on high speed for several minutes, or until kernels are ground into flour; stop blender several times and redistribute the kernels so flour is as fine as possible.

Stir together 2¾ cups white flour, the yeast, sugar and salt in a large mixer bowl. Combine water and butter in a small saucepan, and heat until butter melts and mixture reaches 125° to 130°. With mixer on low speed, beat liquid into flour-yeast mixture until blended. Raise speed to high and beat for 4 minutes. Stir in brown-rice and barley flours and rolled oats. Then, stir in whole-wheat flour and rye flour until blended. Working in the bowl, quickly and vigorously stir, then knead in enough more white flour to yield a springy, malleable dough.

Cover bowl with plastic wrap and set aside in a very warm spot (80° to 90°) for 25 minutes. Meanwhile, generously grease two 8½ × 4½ × 2½-inch (or similar 1½-quart) loaf pans.

Punch down dough and divide in half. With well-greased hands, form halves into smooth, well-shaped loaves and place in pans. Cover pans with plastic wrap and set aside in a very warm place (80° to 90°) for 20 minutes. Preheat oven to 400°.

Lightly brush loaf tops with milk, if desired, and bake for 31 to 36 minutes, or until tops are browned and loaves sound hollow when tapped on the bottom. Place loaves on racks to cool. Serve warm or at room temperature. This is a good toasting or sandwich bread. Makes 2 medium-sized loaves.

Approximate Preparation Time: 22 minutes
Rising/Baking Time: 1 hour 18 minutes

◆ *Wholesome Four-Grain Bread* ◆

Start to Finish: About 1 hour 45 minutes

A nourishing, healthful bread that nevertheless is high rising and delicately flavored. The large, handsome loaves are particularly good for toast.

> 3¼ to 3¾ cups all-purpose white or unbleached flour
> 2 packets fast-rising dry yeast
> ¾ cup instant nonfat dry milk
> ⅓ cup granulated sugar
> 2 teaspoons salt
> 2¼ cups water
> ¼ cup vegetable oil
> 1 large egg, at room temperature
> 2¼ cups whole-wheat flour
> 1 cup quick-cooking or old-fashioned rolled oats
> ½ cup medium or dark rye flour
> ⅓ cup white or yellow cornmeal
> Additional cornmeal for coating pans
> Milk for brushing over tops of loaves

Stir together 2¾ cups white flour, the yeast, milk powder, sugar and salt in a large mixer bowl. In a small saucepan, heat water and oil to 125° to 130°. With mixer on low speed, beat liquid into flour-yeast mixture until blended. Raise speed to high and beat for 5 minutes. Add egg and beat 30 seconds longer. With a large spoon, vigorously stir in whole-wheat flour, rolled oats, rye flour and cornmeal. Working in the bowl or on a clean surface, quickly and vigorously knead in enough more white flour to yield a smooth, fairly firm yet still slightly sticky dough. Place dough in a large, well-greased bowl. Cover bowl with plastic wrap and set aside in a very warm spot (80° to 90°) for 20 minutes. Meanwhile, lightly grease two 9 × 5 × 3-inch (or similar 2-quart) loaf pans. Sprinkle pans with cornmeal; then tip back and forth to evenly coat sides and bottom.

Punch down dough and divide in half. With well-greased hands, form halves into smooth, well-shaped loaves and place in pans. Cover pans with plastic wrap and set aside in a very warm spot (80° to 90°) for 25 minutes. Preheat oven to 375°.

Brush loaf tops with milk, using pastry brush or paper towel. Cut 3 parallel, ¼-inch-deep diagonal slashes in top of each loaf with a sharp knife. Bake bread for 33 to 37 minutes, or until loaves are well browned and sound hollow when tapped on the bottom. Transfer loaves to racks to cool. Serve warm or at room temperature. Use for toast or serve along with a meal. Makes 2 large loaves.

Approximate Preparation Time: 23 minutes
Rising/Baking Time: 1 hour 20 minutes

• *Honey Bran Bread* •

Start to Finish: About 2 hours

The following is my slightly modified version of the fine Super-Nutritious Honey Bran Bread recipe developed by the Kansas Wheat Commission. The healthful, very handsome loaves have a relatively light, springy texture and rich flavor. Honey lends a pleasant sweetness.

> *1 cup hot tap water*
> *1 cup 100 percent bran cereal*
> *4⅓ to 5 cups all-purpose white or unbleached flour*
> *3 packets fast-rising dry yeast*
> *2½ teaspoons salt*
> *1 cup water*
> *⅔ cup honey*
> *½ cup butter or margarine, cut into 5 or 6 pieces*
> *2 eggs, at room temperature*
> *½ cup wheat germ*
> *2 cups whole-wheat flour*

Stir together hot water and bran in a small bowl. Set aside. Stir together 2 cups white flour, the yeast and salt in a large mixer bowl.

In a small saucepan, combine 1 cup water, the honey and butter. Stirring until honey dissolves, heat to 125° to 130°. With mixer on low speed, beat liquid into flour-yeast mixture until blended. Raise mixer speed to high and beat for 1 minute. Add eggs and beat for 5 minutes longer. Vigorously stir in bran-water mixture, wheat germ, whole-wheat flour and 2 cups more white flour. Stir; then, working in the bowl, knead in enough more white flour to yield a smooth, elastic yet still slightly sticky dough. (Amount of flour will vary considerably depending on the brand of bran cereal used.) Cover bowl with plastic wrap and set aside in a very warm spot (80° to 90°) for 20 minutes. Meanwhile, generously grease two 9 × 5 × 3-inch (or similar 2-quart) loaf pans. Set pans aside.

Punch down dough; divide in half. With lightly greased hands, form into two smooth loaves and place in greased pans. Cover pans with plastic wrap and set aside in a very warm place (80° to 90°) for 25 minutes. Preheat oven to 375°.

Cut a ¼-inch-deep lengthwise slash down center of loaves with a sharp knife. Bake loaves for 48 to 54 minutes, or until tops are nicely browned and bottoms sound hollow when tapped. Transfer to racks to cool. Honey Bran Bread slices best when cool, but may be served slightly warm. Serve along with a meal, or use for toast. The loaves may be frozen for later use if desired. Makes 2 large loaves.

Approximate Preparation Time: 23 minutes
Rising/Baking Time: 1 hour 36 minutes

• *Bran Loaves* •

Start to Finish: About 1 hour 45 minutes

This is a dense, tawny brown bread with a slightly crisp crust. Bran lends the loaves a rich, sweet taste and pleasant aroma. The bread dries out fairly quickly, so unless it will be used up in a day or two, you may want to cut the loaves in half and freeze portions for later use.

3 to 3½ cups all-purpose white or unbleached flour
2 packets fast-rising dry yeast
⅓ cup instant nonfat dry milk
2 teaspoons salt
2 cups water
½ cup light molasses
½ cup vegetable oil
2 cups whole-wheat flour
2 cups unprocessed (wheat) bran

Stir together 2½ cups white flour, the yeast, milk powder and salt in a large mixer bowl. In a small saucepan, combine water, molasses and oil. Stirring until molasses dissolves, heat to 125° to 130°. With mixer on low speed, beat liquid into flour-yeast mixture until blended. Raise speed to high and beat for 3½ minutes. With a large spoon, stir in whole-wheat flour and bran. Working in the bowl, quickly and vigorously knead in enough more white flour to yield a smooth, malleable dough. Cover bowl with plastic wrap and set aside in a very warm spot (80° to 90°) for 10 minutes. Meanwhile, grease two 8½ × 4½ × 2½-inch (1½-quart) or 9 × 5 × 3-inch (2-quart) loaf pans and set aside.

Knead dough briefly and divide in half. Shape into two loaves and place in greased pans. Place pans in a larger pan. Carefully add enough hot water (120° to 130°) to larger pan to come ⅔ of the way up sides of bread pans. Lay sheets of wax paper over bread pans; let loaves rise for 30 minutes.

Cut three ¼-inch-deep, parallel diagonal slashes in loaf tops with a sharp knife. Place loaves in cold oven; immediately set thermostat to 400°. Bake for 39 to 44 minutes, or until tops are browned and sound hollow when tapped. Transfer to rack and cool. Bran bread is very good toasted or served at room temperature, with butter or jam. Makes 2 large loaves.

Approximate Preparation Time: 20 minutes
Rising/Baking Time: 1 hour 22 minutes

• *Black Bread* •

Start to Finish: About 1 hour 58 minutes

As you might guess, this is a dark, dense bread, a little like pumpernickel in consistency. However, it does not taste at all like pumpernickel—or any other more familiar bread for that matter. Indeed, a special blending of grains and molasses gives Black Bread a wonderful aroma and flavor all its own.

Serve the rough-textured, slightly chewy hearth loaves at room temperature, with butter. They go very well with seafood, salads, robust soups and stews.

> 1¾ cups all-purpose white or unbleached flour
> 2 packets fast-rising dry yeast
> 1¾ teaspoons salt
> 1½ cups water
> ½ cup dark molasses
> 1 tablespoon vegetable oil
> ¾ cup 100 percent bran cereal
> ¼ cup wheat germ
> 1 cup quick-cooking or old-fashioned rolled oats
> ¾ cup medium or dark rye
> 1¾ to 2½ cups whole-wheat flour
> Additional rolled oats for sprinkling baking sheet

Stir together 1¾ cups white flour, the yeast and salt in a large mixer bowl. In a small saucepan, combine water, molasses and oil. Stirring until molasses dissolves, heat to 125° to 130°. With mixer on low speed, beat liquid into flour-yeast mixture until blended. Raise speed to high and beat for 4 minutes. With a large spoon, vigorously stir in bran cereal, wheat germ, rolled oats and rye flour until well blended. Then stir in 1½ cups whole-wheat flour until well mixed. Working in the bowl or on a clean, lightly floured surface, quickly and vigorously knead in enough more whole-wheat flour to yield a smooth and stiff but not dry dough. Form dough into a smooth ball. Put in a medium-sized, well-greased bowl. Set bowl in a larger bowl. Carefully add enough hot water (120° to 130°) to the larger bowl to come ⅔ of the way up sides of bread bowl. Lay a sheet of wax paper

194

over bread bowl and set aside in a very warm spot (80° to 90°) for 15 minutes. Meanwhile, grease a 15 × 10-inch (or similar) baking sheet. Sprinkle baking sheet generously with rolled oats and set aside.

Knead dough briefly and divide in half. Form dough into two very smooth, round loaves and place directly on rolled oats. Cut a small X (about 1½ inches across) in center top of each loaf. Lightly cover loaves with plastic wrap. Turn on oven to low heat for 1 minute; then turn off again. Place loaves in oven and let rise for 35 minutes.

Remove plastic wrap from loaves and return to oven. Immediately set thermostat to 375°. Bake loaves for 20 minutes. Reduce heat to 350° and continue baking for 25 to 30 minutes longer, or until loaves are tinged with brown and sound hollow when tapped on the bottom. Transfer to racks and cool thoroughly before serving. The loaves dry out fairly rapidly, so freeze if not planning to use right away. Makes 2 medium-sized loaves.

Approximate Preparation Time: 20 minutes
Rising/Baking Time: 1 hour 38 minutes

• *Pumpernickel* •

Start to Finish: About 1 hour 55 minutes

A robust, coarse-textured, dense bread with good flavor and slightly chewy crust. Pumpernickel is often presented as a hearth loaf, but this version is baked in bread pans. This makes it not only easier to prepare, but to cut and serve as well.

> *4 cups all-purpose white flour*
> *2 packets fast-rising dry yeast*
> *⅓ cup instant nonfat dry milk*
> *1 tablespoon caraway seeds*
> *2½ teaspoons salt*
> *1½ cups water*
> *½ cup black coffee*
> *¼ cup molasses, preferably dark*
> *½ cup plain yogurt, preferably lowfat*
> *2 tablespoons vegetable oil*
> *½ cup 100 percent bran cereal*
> *⅓ cup wheat germ*
> *2 cups medium or dark rye flour*
> *2 to 2½ cups whole-wheat flour*
> *1 egg beaten with 1 tablespoon water for brushing over loaves*

Stir together 2½ cups white flour, the yeast, milk powder, caraway seeds and salt in a large mixer bowl. In a medium-sized saucepan, combine water, coffee, molasses, yogurt and oil. Stirring until molasses dissolves, heat to 125° to 130°. With mixer on medium speed, beat liquid into flour-yeast mixture until well blended. Raise speed to high and beat for 3 minutes. With a large spoon, vigorously stir in remaining 1½ cups white flour and the bran cereal. Then stir in wheat germ and rye flour. Working in the bowl or on a clean, well-floured surface, gradually knead in enough more whole-wheat flour to yield a very stiff but still slightly sticky dough; kneading should take about 5 minutes. Form dough into a ball and transfer to a large well-greased bowl.

Cover bowl with plastic wrap and set aside in a very warm spot (80° to 90°) for 20 minutes. Meanwhile, generously grease two 8½ ×

4½ × 2½-inch (or similar 1½-quart) loaf pans and set aside.

Punch down dough and divide in half. With well-greased hands, carefully form halves into smooth, well-shaped loaves and place in greased pans. Lightly cover loaves with plastic wrap and set aside in a very warm place (80° to 90°) for 30 minutes. Preheat oven to 375°.

Brush tops of loaves evenly with egg-water mixture. Bake loaves for 40 to 45 minutes, or until tops are well-browned and sound hollow when tapped. Remove loaves from pans and transfer to racks to cool thoroughly. Pumpernickel is good thinly sliced and used for sandwiches. Freeze for later use, if desired. Makes 2 medium-sized loaves.

Approximate Preparation Time: 23 minutes
Rising/Baking Time: 1 hour 33 minutes

• *Fruited Honey-Wheat Braids* •

Start to Finish: About 1 hour 45 minutes

Although these eye-catching sweet braids are quite wholesome, they are tasty and attractive enough to tempt even people who aren't interested in "healthy" fare. (In fact, they probably won't be able to tell this bread is good for them.) Fruited Honey-Wheat Braids will keep well for several days.

3¼ to 3¾ cups all-purpose white or unbleached flour
2 packets fast-rising dry yeast
½ cup instant nonfat dry milk
1¾ teaspoons salt
1¼ teaspoons ground cinnamon
1⅓ cups water
Generous ½ cup honey
1½ tablespoons butter or margarine
2 eggs, at room temperature
½ cup brown raisins
½ cup golden raisins
½ cup dried currants (or substitute ½ cup more raisins, if desired)
3 cups whole-wheat flour
1 egg yolk beaten with 1 tablespoon water for brushing over braids
1½ tablespoons granulated sugar for sprinkling over braids

Stir together 1½ cups white flour, the yeast, milk powder, salt and cinnamon in large mixer bowl. In a small saucepan, combine water, honey and butter. Heat to 125° to 130°. With mixer on low speed, beat liquid into flour-yeast mixture until blended. Raise speed to high and beat for 3½ minutes. Add eggs and 1 cup more white flour. Beat on medium speed for 1 minute. Stir in raisins, currants and whole-wheat flour until incorporated. Working in the bowl or on a clean, lightly floured surface, quickly and vigorously knead in enough more white flour to yield a smooth, malleable, fairly stiff dough. Shape dough into a ball. Place in mixer bowl and cover bowl with a damp towel; set bowl in a very warm spot (80° to 90°) for 10 minutes. Meanwhile, grease a 17½ × 15-inch (or similar very large) baking sheet, or two smaller baking sheets, and set aside.

198

Punch down dough; divide in half. With well-greased hands, divide each half into three pieces. Form pieces into 6- to 7-inch logs. On a clean work surface, gently stretch and roll logs back and forth with fingertips to form 16-inch-long ropes. Transfer ropes to baking sheet and intertwine to form into a smooth, well-shaped braid. Compress braid slightly and tuck ends under to form a neat, slightly plump loaf. (For illustration of how to braid, see page 210.) Repeat process to form second braid. Lightly cover braids with a damp towel. Turn on oven for 1 minute; then turn off again. Place pan in oven and let braids rise for 30 minutes.

Brush egg yolk-water mixture evenly on tops and sides of braids, using a pastry brush or paper towel. Sprinkle half the sugar over each loaf. Return pan to cold oven and immediately set thermostat to 375°. Bake for 34 to 38 minutes, or until tops are nicely browned and loaves sound hollow when tapped on the bottom. Transfer loaves to racks to cool. Serve still warm from the oven or reheated in a warm oven. Freeze for later use, if desired. Makes 2 medium-sized braided loaves.

Approximate Preparation Time: 30 minutes
Rising/Baking Time: 1 hour 15 minutes

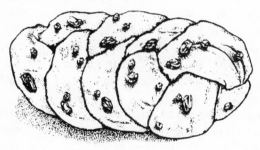

• *Beer and Honey Bread* •

Start to Finish: About 1 hour 30 minutes

The unusual combination of beer and honey gives this loaf an intriguing, slightly malty flavor. It is a fairly dense, compact bread.

2¾ to 3½ cups all-purpose white or unbleached flour
2 packets fast-rising dry yeast
1¼ teaspoons salt
½ cup beer (fresh or flat)
⅔ cups water
Generous ⅓ cup honey
3 tablespoons vegetable oil
1 cup whole-wheat flour
Milk for brushing over loaf top

Stir together 1¼ cups white flour, the yeast and salt in a large mixer bowl. In a small saucepan, combine beer, water, honey and oil. Stirring until honey dissolves, heat to 125° to 130°. With mixer on low speed, beat liquid into flour-yeast mixture until blended. Raise speed to high and beat for 3½ minutes. Vigorously stir in whole-wheat flour and 1¼ cups more white flour, or enough to yield a kneadable dough. Working in the bowl or on a clean, lightly floured surface, quickly and vigorously knead in enough more white flour to yield a smooth and malleable but not dry dough. Form dough into a ball and return to mixer bowl. Cover bowl with a slightly damp towel and set aside in a very warm spot (80° to 90°) for 15 minutes. Meanwhile, grease a 9 × 5 × 3-inch (or similar 2-quart) loaf pan.

Punch down dough. With well-greased hands, form into a smooth, well-shaped loaf and place in greased pan. Lightly cover pan with a damp towel. Set aside in a very warm spot (80° to 90°) for 25 minutes. Preheat oven to 375°.

Brush loaf top with milk, using pastry brush or paper towel. Cut a ¼-inch-deep slash lengthwise down center of loaf with a sharp knife. Bake for 28 to 32 minutes, or until top is nicely browned and loaf sounds hollow when tapped on the bottom. Transfer loaf to rack and cool at least 5 minutes before serving. Beer and Honey Bread is very good warm from the oven, thickly sliced and buttered. It may also be served at room temperature or toasted. Makes 1 large loaf.

Approximate Preparation Time: 18 minutes
Rising/Baking Time: 1 hour 10 minutes

◆ PARTY AND SPECIALTY BREADS ◆

*A*ll manner of party and specialty breads are grouped together in this chapter. Many of the recipes are ideal for informal entertaining, adding interest and taste appeal to buffet tables and party trays. For example, there are a number of unusual, zesty sandwich breads here, like Ranch House Cornmeal and Cheese Loaves, Dilled Casserole Bread and Gary's Peppered Potato Bread. Other selections include little party bread loaves (perfect for cheese platters) and an impressive-looking Tricolor Braid. Or choose rich and savory Walnut Hearth Loaves or Toasty Oat and Cornmeal Bread to add a festive touch to a company one-pot meal.

This chapter also includes some specialty breads, like Bagels, Seeded Onion Twists, Hawaiian Bread, and an unusual "Short-Time" White Bread, based on a British preparation method.

• *Walnut Hearth Loaves* •

Start to Finish: About 1 hour 40 minutes

These savory loaves have a rustic, rough-textured look, some-what crisp crust and a delightful walnutty taste. They add a festive touch to any meal. Walnut Hearth Loaves also make a nice gift for those who prefer savory breads to sweet ones.

> 3½ to 4¼ cups all-purpose white or unbleached flour
> 2 packets fast-rising dry yeast
> ¼ cup instant nonfat dry milk
> 1 tablespoon granulated sugar
> 1¾ teaspoons salt
> 1 cup plus 2 tablespoons water
> 6 tablespoons butter or margarine, cut into 5 or 6 pieces
> 1 egg, at room temperature
> 1¼ cups finely chopped walnuts (about 5 ounces)
> 1 cup whole-wheat flour

Stir together 1¼ cups white flour, the yeast, milk powder, sugar and salt in a large mixer bowl. Combine water and butter in a small saucepan. Heat until butter melts and mixture reaches 125° to 130°. With mixer on low speed, beat liquid into flour-yeast mixture until blended. Raise speed to high and beat for 3 minutes. Add egg and ½ cup more white flour and beat for 30 seconds longer. Stir in walnuts, whole-wheat flour and 1 cup more white flour. Working in the bowl, quickly and vigorously knead in enough more white flour to yield a fairly stiff yet malleable dough. (The dough will feel lumpy and some-what heavy due to the walnuts.) Cover bowl with plastic wrap and set aside in a very warm spot (80° to 90°) for 15 minutes. Meanwhile, grease a 17½ × 15-inch (or similar very large) baking sheet, or two smaller baking sheets.

Punch down dough. Knead dough briefly and divide in half. Shape each half into a high, smooth round and place on baking sheet. Lightly cover loaves with plastic wrap. Set baking sheet aside in a very warm spot (80° to 90°) for 25 minutes. Preheat oven to 425°. Place a shallow pan of hot water on oven floor.

With a very sharp knife, slash a ring about ¼ inch deep and ¼ inch in from edge of each loaf (as shown in background of illustration); this is easiest if the loaf is rotated and the blade is held still. Spray or brush loaves with water. Place loaves in oven. Spray or brush with water twice more during baking. Bake for 35 to 40 minutes, or until tops are nicely browned and bottoms sound hollow when tapped. Remove loaves from oven and let cool on racks. Serve slightly warm or at room temperature, with butter. Makes 2 medium-sized round loaves.

Approximate Preparation Time: 22 minutes
Rising/Baking Time: 1 hour 17 minutes

◆ *Dilled Casserole Bread* ◆

Start to Finish: About 1 hour 25 minutes

A zesty blend of seasonings gives this bread its distinctive and delicious flavor. The homey, dark-crusted loaf is good buttered and served along with robust meals or paired with cold cuts and cheese.

1¾ to 2¼ cups all-purpose white or unbleached flour
1 packet fast-rising dry yeast
1 tablespoon granulated sugar
¾ teaspoon salt
1½ teaspoons dill seed
¾ teaspoon paprika, preferably spicy imported
¼ teaspoon celery seed
½ cup plain yogurt, preferably lowfat
⅓ cup water
2 tablespoons butter or margarine, cut into 2 pieces
2 tablespoons dried chopped chives
1 egg, at room temperature
¾ cup medium or dark rye flour

Stir together ¾ cup white flour, the yeast, sugar, salt, dill seed, paprika and celery seed in large mixer bowl. In a small saucepan, combine yogurt, water, butter and chives, and heat to 125° to 130°. With mixer on low speed, beat liquid into flour-yeast mixture until blended. Raise speed to high and beat for 3 minutes. Add egg and beat on medium speed for 30 seconds longer. Stir in rye flour and ½ cup more white flour, or enough to yield a kneadable dough. Working in the bowl or on a lightly floured surface, gradually knead in enough more white flour to yield a smooth and elastic yet still slightly sticky dough. Shape dough into a ball and transfer to a large greased bowl. Cover bowl with plastic wrap and set aside in a very warm spot (80° to 90°) for 15 minutes. Meanwhile, grease a 1-quart round casserole, soufflé dish or utility pan.

Punch down dough. With well-greased hands, form into a smooth, well-shaped loaf and place in greased casserole or pan. Lightly cover with plastic wrap. Set casserole in a larger bowl. Carefully add enough hot water (120° to 130°) to bowl to come ⅔ of the way up sides of casserole. Let dough rise for 20 minutes. Preheat oven to 400°.

With a very sharp knife, cut a ⅛-inch-deep and about 2-inch-wide grid pattern # in center of loaf top. Bake loaf for 27 to 32 minutes, or until top is well browned and sounds hollow when tapped. Remove loaf from casserole and transfer to rack to cool. Serve at room temperature. Makes 1 medium-sized loaf.

Approximate Preparation Time: 18 minutes
Rising/Baking Time: 1 hour 5 minutes

• *Gary's Peppered Potato Bread* •

Start to Finish: About 1 hour 35 minutes

This unusual, zippy bread goes great with a flavorful pimiento-cheese spread. It can also be served with ham spread, chicken salad or sharp cheese.

> 1 medium-sized potato, peeled and cubed
> 1½ cups water
> 5½ to 6½ cups all-purpose white or unbleached flour
> 2 packets fast-rising dry yeast
> ¾ cup instant nonfat dry milk
> 1 tablespoon granulated sugar
> 2 teaspoons salt
> 1 tablespoon fresh, coarsely ground black pepper
> 1 teaspoon fresh, coarsely ground white pepper
> 2 tablespoons butter or margarine, cut into 2 or 3 pieces
> Reserved potato-cooking liquid
> Milk for brushing over tops of loaves (optional)

Place potato cubes in a small saucepan with water. Bring to a boil over medium heat and simmer, covered, 7 to 10 minutes, or until

205

potatoes are just tender. Meanwhile, stir together 2 cups flour, the yeast, milk powder, sugar, salt, black pepper and white pepper in a bowl, and set aside.

Drain potato cubes well, reserving their cooking liquid in a large measuring cup. Place potatoes in large mixer bowl. With mixer on low speed, beat for about 1½ minutes, or until potatoes are well blended and smooth. Add butter and continue beating for 1½ minutes longer. Add enough water to reserved potato liquid to make 1¾ cups, and, if necessary, return liquid mixture to small saucepan and heat to 125° to 130°.

Add flour-yeast mixture, then liquid mixture to potatoes. Beat with mixer on low speed until blended. Raise speed to high and beat for 4 minutes. Vigorously stir in 2½ cups more flour, or enough to yield a kneadable dough. Working in the bowl or on a clean, lightly floured surface, quickly and vigorously knead in enough more flour to yield a smooth and malleable but not firm dough. Place dough in large, well-greased bowl. Cover bowl with damp towel and set aside in a very warm place (80° to 90°) for 20 minutes. Meanwhile, grease two 9 × 5 × 3-inch (or similar 2-quart) loaf pans and set aside.

Punch dough down and divide in half. With well-greased hands, shape into two loaves and place in pans. Cover pans with plastic wrap and set aside in a very warm spot (80° to 90°) for 15 minutes. Preheat oven to 375°.

Bake loaves for 34 to 38 minutes, or until tops are nicely browned and sound hollow when tapped. Remove loaves from pans and transfer to racks. Serve bread still warm from the oven, or cool for later use. Makes 2 large loaves.

Approximate Preparation Time: 23 minutes
Rising/Baking Time: 1 hour 10 minutes

• *Seeded Onion Twists* •

Start to Finish: About 1 hour 20 minutes

Despite the seemingly lengthy directions, these attractive, chewy twists are easy to make.

> 1½ *tablespoons butter or margarine*
> 1 *small onion, finely chopped*
> 3½ *to 4 cups all-purpose white or unbleached flour*
> 1 *packet fast-rising dry yeast*
> 1 *tablespoon granulated sugar*
> *Generous* ¾ *teaspoon salt*
> ¾ *cup water*
> ⅓ *cup plain yogurt*
> 1 *egg white*
> ½ *cup medium or dark rye flour*
> 1 *egg yolk beaten with 1 tablespoon water*
> *About 3 tablespoons poppy seeds or sesame seeds (or half of each) for garnishing twists*
> *About* ¼ *teaspoon coarse salt crystals for garnishing twists (substitute table salt, if necessary)*

Combine butter and onion in a small saucepan over medium heat. Cook, stirring occasionally, for 5 to 6 minutes, or until onion is transparent and golden. Meanwhile, stir together ¾ cup white flour, the yeast, sugar and salt in a large mixer bowl.

Add water and yogurt to onion and heat, stirring, to 125° to 130°. Add liquid to flour-yeast mixture and beat on low speed to blend ingredients. Raise speed to high and beat for 3 minutes. Add egg white and beat for 30 seconds longer. Vigorously stir in rye flour and about 1¾ cups more white flour, or enough to yield a kneadable dough. Working in the bowl, quickly and vigorously knead in enough more white flour to yield a smooth, malleable and firm dough. Cover bowl with plastic wrap and set aside in a very warm place (80° to 90°) for 20 minutes. Meanwhile, thoroughly grease two 17 × 11½-inch (or similar large) baking sheets and set aside.

Punch down dough. On a lightly floured work surface, roll or press out dough to an evenly thick 12 × 5-inch rectangle. With a

207

sharp knife, trim away uneven dough edges and discard. Mark and then cut rectangle crosswise to produce seventeen or eighteen 5-inch-long strips. Stretch out strips slightly and form into a U shape. Entwine and twist the lengths of the U together as though forming crullers. (See page 134 for illustration of how to form crullers.) Space onion twists 2 inches apart on baking sheets. Two or three at a time, brush tops of twists with egg yolk-water mixture, using a pastry brush or paper towel, and sprinkle with some of the seeds and salt. Set twists aside, uncovered, in a very warm spot (80° to 90°) for 15 minutes. Preheat oven to 450°.

Bake twists for 12 to 15 minutes, or until tops are golden brown and sound hollow when tapped. Serve warm from the oven, or place on racks until cool. Makes 17 or 18 twists.

Approximate Preparation Time: 28 minutes   *Rising/Baking Time:* 49 minutes

• *Tricolor Braid* •

Start to Finish: About 1 hour 40 minutes

Each strand of this very attractive novelty braid features a different, complementing color. However, the bread is actually easier to prepare than its appearance suggests, since one basic dough is used for all three strands.

> 4 to 4½ cups all-purpose white or unbleached flour
> 2 packets fast-rising dry yeast
> 1 teaspoon salt
> 1 cup water
> Scant ⅓ cup honey
> 2 tablespoons vegetable oil
> 2 eggs, at room temperature
> ¾ to 1 cup medium or dark rye flour
> ½ tablespoon unsweetened cocoa powder
> ¾ to 1 cup whole-wheat flour
> 1 egg yolk beaten with 1 tablespoon lukewarm water
> 2 teaspoons sesame seeds (optional)

Stir together 1¼ cups white flour, the yeast and salt in a large mixer bowl. In a small saucepan, combine water, honey and oil. Stirring until honey dissolves, heat to 125° to 130°. With mixer on low speed, beat liquid into flour-yeast mixture until blended. Raise speed to high and beat for 2 minutes. Add eggs and ¾ cup more white flour and beat for 1½ minutes longer. Stir in 1¼ cups more white flour until well mixed. Transfer one-third of the dough to a medium-sized bowl. Transfer another third to another bowl. To one-third of the dough, knead in about ¾ to 1 cup more white flour to yield a smooth, elastic and fairly firm dough. To a second third of the dough, stir in ½ cup rye flour mixed with cocoa powder. Knead in enough more rye flour to yield an elastic, fairly firm dough. To the final third, knead in about ¾ to 1 cup whole-wheat flour to yield a smooth, elastic and fairly firm dough. Cover bowls with plastic wrap and set aside in a very warm spot (80° to 90°) for 20 minutes. Meanwhile, grease a 17½ × 11½-inch (or similar large) baking sheet.

With lightly greased hands, punch down dough portions, one at a time. Shape portions into 8- to 9-inch logs. Then gently stretch and roll logs back and forth on a clean work surface to form 18-inch-long ropes. Lay ropes side by side on baking sheet and intertwine to form braid (see illustration). Tuck ends under and compress loaf slightly. Cover braid with plastic wrap and set pan aside in a very warm spot (80° to 90°) for 20 minutes. Preheat oven to 375°.

Evenly brush loaf with egg yolk–water mixture. Sprinkle lightly with sesame seeds, if desired. Bake bread for 29 to 34 minutes, or until braid is golden brown and sounds hollow when lightly tapped. Remove pan from oven and, with spatula, transfer braid to rack. Let stand at least 8 to 10 minutes before serving, or serve at room temperature. Makes 1 large braid.

Approximate Preparation Time: 30 minutes
Rising/Baking Time: 1 hour 11 minutes

How to Braid

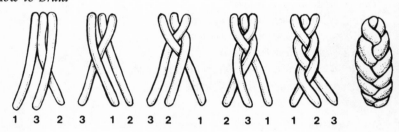

1　3　2　3　1　2　3　2　1　2　3　1　1　2　3

• *Party Bread Loaves* •

Start to Finish: About 1 hour 30 minutes

This recipe features a basic yeast dough that is turned into three different, very attractive little party loaves—plain, herbed and caraway. Although easy to make, the loaves are tasty and quite festive looking.

> 2⅔ to 3 cups all-purpose white or unbleached flour
> 1 tablespoon fast-rising dry yeast (about 1½ packets)
> ⅓ cup light brown sugar, packed
> 1 teaspoon salt
> 1⅓ cups water
> 3 tablespoons butter or margarine, cut into 3 or 4 pieces
> 1½ cups medium or dark rye flour
> 2 teaspoons caraway seeds
> 2 teaspoons dried chopped chives
> 2 teaspoons dried parsley flakes
> ⅛ teaspoon garlic salt (optional)
> 1 egg beaten with 1 tablespoon water for brushing over loaves

Stir together 2 cups white flour, the yeast, brown sugar and salt in a large mixer bowl. Combine water and butter in a small saucepan and heat to 125° to 130°. With mixer on low speed, beat liquid into flour-yeast mixture until blended. Raise speed to high and beat for 3 minutes. Stir in rye flour until well blended. Working in the bowl or on a clean, lightly floured surface, quickly and vigorously knead in enough more white flour to yield a very smooth, elastic and stiff dough. Shape dough into a ball. Transfer to a large, well-greased bowl. Grease the dough top well. Cover with a damp cloth and set aside in a very warm spot (80° to 90°) for 20 minutes. Meanwhile, generously grease a 15½ × 11-inch (or similar large) baking sheet and set aside.

Punch down dough and divide into three equal portions. With lightly greased hands and on a clean work surface, roll first dough portion back and forth into a smooth log about 9 inches long. For the most attractive appearance, be sure the log is completely smooth and well shaped. For second dough portion, gradually work 1½ teaspoons of caraway seeds into dough, sprinkling some seeds over surface, then kneading, then adding more seeds, and repeating process until seeds are evenly incorporated. (Reserve remaining ½ teaspoon seeds for garnish.) Shape dough into a 9-inch log. Knead chives, parsley and garlic salt (if desired) into the final dough portion and shape into a 9-inch-long log. Transfer logs to baking sheet, spacing as far apart from one another as possible. Lightly cover with greased sheets of wax paper. Set aside in a very warm spot (80° to 90°) for 15 minutes. Preheat oven to 350°.

Evenly brush loaves with egg-water mixture, using pastry brush or paper towel. Sprinkle reserved caraway seeds over caraway loaf. With a sharp knife, gently make a ¼-inch-deep slash lengthwise down center of each loaf. Bake loaves for 28 to 33 minutes, or until they are dark golden brown and sound hollow when lightly tapped. Remove pans from oven and, with spatula, transfer loaves to racks. Let stand until completely cold. At serving time, use a sharp bread knife to cut loaves into ¼-inch-thick slices. Bread may be made ahead, frozen, then thawed shortly before serving time, if desired. Makes 3 party sandwich bread loaves.

Approximate Preparation Time: 25 minutes
Rising/Baking Time: 1 hour 5 minutes

◆ *Bagels* ◆

Start to Finish: About 1 hour 30 minutes

Homemade bagels won't be quite as evenly shaped as commercial ones, but they'll have a matchless fresh-baked taste. The fastest and easiest way to form your bagels is to use a doughnut cutter. However, for a more authentic look, try the alternate method given below.

3¼ to 3¾ cups all-purpose white or unbleached flour
1 tablespoon fast-rising dry yeast
2½ tablespoons granulated sugar
2 teaspoons salt
1 cup hot water (125° to 130°)
1 tablespoon vegetable oil
1 egg, at room temperature
1 egg beaten with 1 tablespoon water for brushing over bagels
Sesame seeds and poppy seeds for sprinkling over bagels (optional)

Stir together 1 cup flour, the yeast, 1½ tablespoons sugar and the salt in large mixer bowl. With mixer on low speed, beat hot water and oil into dry ingredients until blended. Raise speed to high and beat for 2½ minutes. Add egg and ¼ cup more flour, and beat for 1 minute longer. Vigorously stir in 1¾ to 2 cups more flour, or enough to yield a kneadable dough. Working in the bowl, quickly and vigorously knead in enough more flour to yield a firm and malleable but not dry dough. Cover bowl with plastic wrap. Set aside in a very warm spot (80° to 90°) for 20 minutes. Meanwhile, lightly grease a 17½ × 15-inch (or similar very large) baking sheet, or two small baking sheets.

Punch down dough. To ready dough for cutting out with doughnut cutter, roll out ½ inch thick on clean, lightly floured surface. Cut out bagels with cutter; reroll scraps and "holes," and cut out additional bagels. (Alternatively, for a more professional appearance, divide dough in half. Divide each half into eight equal parts. One at a time, shape each into a smooth ball, tucking excess dough underneath. Flatten ball into a 2½-inch-diameter disc. With floured hands, poke a hole through center of disc with finger, as shown in illustration on page 214. Enlarge hole to about 1 inch in diameter by twirling

213

dough on finger. See illustration.) Transfer bagels to baking sheets, spacing at least ½ inch apart. Cover with plastic wrap. Set aside in very warm spot (80° to 90°) for 15 minutes. Preheat oven to 375°. Prepare to boil bagels by stirring remaining 1 tablespoon sugar into 2 quarts water in a large pot. Bring to a boil over medium-high heat.

Transfer bagels to pot with slotted spoon and boil in batches of three or four for about 1 minute; turn over and boil for 1 minute longer. Use slotted spoon to return bagels to baking sheet. Brush bagels with egg-water mixture, using a pastry brush or paper towels. Sprinkle with poppy or sesame seeds, if desired.

Bake bagels for 27 to 32 minutes, or until they are golden brown and sound hollow when tapped. Transfer to racks and cool well before serving. Makes about 16 bagels.

Approximate Preparation Time: 25 minutes
Rising/Baking Time: 1 hour 5 minutes

Making Bagels

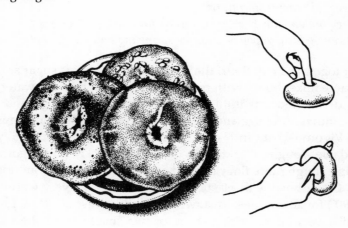

VARIATION: Onion-Pumpernickel Bagels—Prepare as for plain bagels except replace the 1¾ cups white flour to be stirred into dough with ¼ cup whole-wheat flour, ½ cup medium or dark rye flour and 1 cup white flour. While bagels are rising, sauté ⅓ cup finely chopped onion in 1 tablespoon butter for 4 to 5 minutes, or until transparent and golden. Set aside. Proceed as for plain bagels. When bagels have baked for 20 minutes, remove from oven and top each with a sprinkling of onions. Return bagels to oven and bake for 8 to 12 minutes longer, or until golden brown.

VARIATION: Cinnamon-Raisin Bagels—Prepare as for plain bagels except add ¼ teaspoon cinnamon along with sugar and salt. Stir in ⅓ cup finely chopped raisins along with egg. Proceed as for plain bagels. Very good served with date-and-walnut cream-cheese spread.

• *Hawaiian Bread* •

Start to Finish: About 1 hour 50 minutes

Here's the homemade version of a popular commercial loaf called Hawaiian Bread. It is a fairly sweet, light and very aromatic bread.

> 1 large potato, peeled and cubed
> 5 to 5½ cups all-purpose white or unbleached flour
> 2 packets fast-rising dry yeast
> ⅓ cup instant nonfat dry milk
> 1 cup granulated sugar
> ¾ teaspoon salt
> Reserved potato-cooking liquid
> 6 tablespoons butter or margarine, cut into 4 or 5 pieces
> 2 eggs plus 1 egg yolk, at room temperature
> Milk for brushing over tops of loaves

Place potato cubes in a small saucepan and just cover with water. Bring to a boil over medium heat and simmer, covered, for 6 to 9 minutes, or until potatoes are just tender. Meanwhile, stir together 1½ cups flour, the yeast, milk powder, sugar and salt in a bowl and set aside.

Drain potato cubes well, reserving their cooking liquid in a large measuring cup. Place potatoes in a large mixer bowl. Beat with mixer on low speed for 1½ to 2 minutes, or until potatoes are well blended and smooth. Add butter to potatoes and beat on medium speed for 1 minute longer. Add enough water to potato liquid to make 1¼ cups, and, if necessary, return liquid mixture to small saucepan and heat to 125° to 130°. Add flour-yeast mixture, then liquid to potatoes. Beat with mixer on low speed to blend ingredients. Raise speed to medium and beat for 2 minutes. Add eggs and yolk, and beat for 1 minute longer. Vigorously stir in about 3½ cups flour, or enough to yield a kneadable dough. Working in the bowl, quickly and vigorously knead in enough more flour to yield a smooth, slightly soft dough. Cover bowl with plastic wrap and set aside in a very warm place (80° to 90°) for 15 minutes. Meanwhile, generously grease two 8-inch cake pans (or similar) and set aside.

Punch dough down and divide in half. With well-greased hands, shape dough into two soft balls. Place each ball in a greased pan and flatten out almost to pan edges. Cover pans with plastic wrap and set aside in a very warm spot (80° to 90°) for 25 minutes.

Brush tops of loaves with milk. Place loaves in a cold oven; immediately set thermostat to 375°. Bake for 45 to 50 minutes, or until tops are puffy and deep golden brown. (If tops begin to brown too rapidly, reduce heat to 350° for the last 15 minutes of baking.) Transfer pans to racks and let stand for 5 to 8 minutes before removing loaves. Serve bread immediately, or cool on racks for later use. Makes 2 round loaves.

Approximate Preparation Time: 23 minutes
Rising/Baking Time: 1 hour 27 minutes

• *"Short-Time" White Bread* •

Start to Finish: About 1 hour 15 minutes

Here is a good, fast white bread made by a rather unusual method. It is roughly based on a special "short-time method" of bread making sometimes seen in British bread books and in use by some British commercial bakers. Although the technique I've devised is easier and faster than the British version, it does involve adding the same "magic ingredient" to the dough—a small amount of vitamin C. This simple, harmless addition helps the dough mature at an accelerated rate, which means that rising periods can be very short and still yield bread with good texture. (There are no nutritional advantages to including vitamin C in yeast breads, because it is destroyed during baking.)

Vitamin C can be purchased very inexpensively in 100-milligram tablets and then broken into quarters for use in bread making.

> *3½ to 4 cups all-purpose white or unbleached flour*
> *1 tablespoon fast-rising dry yeast (about 1½ packets)*
> *⅓ cup instant nonfat dry milk*
> *¼ cup granulated sugar*
> *1¼ teaspoons salt*
> *25 milligrams vitamin C (¼ 100-milligram tablet)*
> *Generous 1 cup water*
> *2½ tablespoons butter or margarine*
> *Milk for brushing over top of loaf (optional)*

Stir together 1½ cups flour, the yeast, milk powder, sugar and salt in a large mixer bowl. In a small saucepan, crush vitamin C with a spoon. Add water and stir until vitamin C dissolves. Add butter and heat until it melts and mixture reaches 125° to 130°. With mixer on low speed, beat liquid into dry ingredients until blended. Raise speed to high and beat for 3½ minutes longer. Working in the bowl, vigorously stir and then knead in enough more flour to yield a smooth, malleable dough. Cover bowl with a slightly damp towel and set aside in a very warm spot (80° to 90°) for 5 minutes. Meanwhile, grease a 9 × 5 × 3-inch (or similar 2-quart) loaf pan.

Punch down dough. With well-greased hands, form into a

smooth, well-shaped loaf and place in greased pan. Lightly cover pan with a damp towel and set aside in a very warm place (80° to 90°) for 20 minutes.

Brush loaf top with milk, if desired. Make a ¼-inch-deep cut lengthwise down center of loaf with a sharp knife. Place loaf in a cold oven; immediately set thermostat to 400°. Bake loaf for 30 to 35 minutes, or until top is browned and bottom sounds hollow when tapped. Cool loaf on rack. Slice and serve with a meal, or use for sandwiches or toast. Makes 1 large loaf.

Approximate Preparation Time: 15 minutes   *Rising/Baking Time:* 57 minutes

• *Toasty Oat and Cornmeal Bread* •

Start to Finish: About 1 hour 30 minutes

This is a pleasantly light and fragrant bread with the mild, intriguing flavor of toasted oats and cornmeal.

>   1 cup quick-cooking or old-fashioned rolled oats
>   ½ cup cornmeal, preferably white
>   5½ to 6 cups all-purpose white or unbleached flour
>   2 packets fast-rising dry yeast
>   ⅔ cup instant nonfat dry milk
>   ⅓ cup granulated sugar
>   1¾ teaspoons salt
>   2 cups water
>   ¼ cup vegetable oil
>   1 egg, at room temperature
>   Additional cornmeal for sprinkling pans and loaves

Toast rolled oats and cornmeal by combining in a large skillet over high heat. Heat grains, stirring to prevent burning, for 2 to 3 minutes. Turn down heat slightly and continue toasting about 1 to 2

218

minutes longer, or until mixture is very fragrant and just starts to turn brown; lower heat further or lift pan from heat, if necessary, to prevent from smoking. Remove pan from heat and continue stirring mixture for 30 seconds. Set aside.

Stir together 2 cups flour, the yeast, milk powder, sugar and salt in a large mixer bowl. Combine water and oil in a small saucepan and heat to 125° to 130°. With mixer on low speed, beat liquid into flour-yeast mixture until blended. Raise speed to high and beat for 3½ minutes longer. Add egg and ½ cup more flour, and beat for 30 seconds longer. Vigorously stir in toasted oats and cornmeal and 2 cups more flour. Set dough aside to rest for 3 to 4 minutes. Working in the bowl or on a clean surface, quickly and vigorously knead in enough more flour to yield a smooth and elastic yet still slightly moist dough. Cover bowl with plastic wrap and set aside in a very warm spot (80° to 90°) for 15 minutes. Meanwhile, lightly grease two 9 × 5 × 3-inch (or similar 2-quart) loaf pans. Sprinkle pans with cornmeal; then tip back and forth to evenly coat sides and bottom.

Punch down dough and divide in half. With greased hands, form halves into smooth, well-shaped loaves and place in pans. Dust tops of loaves lightly with cornmeal. Cover pans with plastic wrap. Set aside in a very warm spot (80° to 90°) for 15 minutes. Preheat oven to 375°.

Cut four or five parallel, ¼-inch-deep diagonal slashes in top of each loaf with a sharp knife. Bake loaves for 31 to 36 minutes, or until they are lightly browned and bottoms sound hollow when tapped. Transfer loaves to racks to cool. Serve warm or at room temperature. Good for sandwiches and toast, or served along with a meal. Makes 2 large loaves.

Approximate Preparation Time: 23 minutes
Rising/Baking Time: 1 hour 6 minutes

• *Herbed Cheese Bread* •

Start to Finish: About 1 hour 45 minutes

The herbs and cheese in this loaf lend an unusual and savory flavor, as well as nice color to the slices. The bread makes delicious sandwiches.

> 2⅓ to 3 cups all-purpose white or unbleached flour
> 1 packet fast-rising dry yeast
> ¾ teaspoon salt
> 1⅓ cups hot water (125° to 130°)
> 1 tablespoon olive or vegetable oil
> 1 egg, at room temperature
> 2 tablespoons dried chopped chives
> ¾ teaspoon dry mustard
> ½ teaspoon finely crumbled dried rosemary
> ¼ teaspoon dried marjoram leaves
> ¼ teaspoon dried oregano leaves
> 1 cup lightly packed shredded or finely grated sharp Cheddar cheese
>   (4 ounces)
> 1 cup whole-wheat flour
> Milk for brushing over top of loaf

Stir together 1 cup white flour, the yeast and salt in a large mixer bowl. With mixer on low speed, beat water and oil into flour-yeast mixture until blended. Raise speed to high and beat for 3 minutes. Add egg, chives, mustard, rosemary, marjoram, oregano and Cheddar, and beat for 30 seconds longer. Vigorously stir in whole-wheat flour and 1 cup more white flour, or enough to yield a kneadable dough. Working in the bowl, quickly and vigorously knead in enough more white flour to yield a moderately stiff dough. Shape dough into a ball and transfer to a large greased bowl. Grease dough top. Cover bowl with plastic wrap and set aside in a very warm place (80° to 90°) for 25 minutes. Meanwhile, grease a 9 × 5 × 3-inch (or similar 2-quart) loaf pan and set aside.

Punch dough down. On a clean, lightly floured work surface, roll dough back and forth into a smooth, evenly thick log about 8¾ inches long. Transfer to loaf pan. Lightly cover pan with wax paper and set aside in warm spot (80° to 90°) for 20 minutes. Preheat oven to 375°.

Evenly brush loaf top with milk. With a sharp knife, gently make a ⅛-inch-deep slash lengthwise down center of loaf. Bake for 38 to 43 minutes, or until loaf is lightly browned and sounds hollow when tapped on the bottom. Remove loaf to rack to cool. Serve warm or at room temperature. Makes 1 large loaf.

Approximate Preparation Time: 20 minutes
Rising/Baking Time: 1 hour 25 minutes

◆ *Ranch House Cornmeal and Cheese* ◆ *Loaves*

Start to Finish: About 1 hour 35 minutes

Try this hearty and attractive corn-and-cheese-flavored bread with Tex-Mex food or other robust fare.

1¼ cups yellow cornmeal
1½ cups boiling water, approximately
4¼ to 5 cups all-purpose white or unbleached flour
2 packets fast-rising dry yeast
⅓ cup instant nonfat dry milk
3 tablespoons granulated sugar
2¾ teaspoons salt
1 cup water
¼ cup butter or margarine, cut into 3 or 4 pieces
1¼ cups grated or shredded longhorn cheese (about 5 ounces)
Additional flour for dusting baking sheets and loaves

Put cornmeal in a medium-sized bowl. Gradually stir in enough boiling water to yield a smooth but not mushy paste. Set aside. Stir together 1¼ cups flour, the yeast, milk powder, sugar and salt in

221

large mixer bowl. Combine 1 cup water and butter in a small saucepan, and heat until butter melts and mixture reaches 125° to 130°. With mixer on low speed, beat liquid into dry ingredients until blended. Raise speed to high and beat for 3½ minutes. With a large spoon, stir in cheese, cornmeal-water mixture and 2½ cups more flour until well blended. Working in the bowl, quickly and vigorously knead in enough more flour to yield a firm, malleable but not dry dough. Cover bowl with plastic wrap and set aside in a very warm spot (80° to 90°) for 10 minutes. Meanwhile, lightly grease two 8½ × 4½ × 2½-inch (or similar 1½-quart) loaf pans. Generously dust pans with flour; tap out any excess flour and set pans aside.

Punch down dough and divide in half. Shape halves into smooth loaves and place in pans. Sprinkle loaves with flour. Cover pans with plastic wrap and set aside in a very warm spot (80° to 90°) for 25 minutes. Preheat oven to 425°.

With a sharp knife, slash four ¼-inch-deep X's in a lengthwise line down center of each loaf. (Space X's so their tips just touch and form a diamond pattern in dough surface.) Bake loaves for 35 to 40 minutes, or until tops are lightly browned and sound hollow when tapped. Remove loaves from pans and transfer to racks. Serve slightly warm or at room temperature. Makes 2 medium-sized loaves.

Approximate Preparation Time: 21 minutes
Rising/Baking Time: 1 hour 12 minutes

◆ FOOD-PROCESSOR BREADS ◆

*F*or the cook looking for virtually fuss-free yeast breads, food-processor recipes fill the bill. In literally seconds, this handy machine can mix together ingredients and "knead" dough sufficiently to yield very light, fine-textured bread. And the variety of breads that can be prepared with a processor is nearly endless. This chapter, for example, contains everything from crispy Onion-Garlic Bread Sticks, Soft Pretzels and Granola-Pecan Coffee Cake to Crusty Swiss Cheese Braid and fancy Apricot-filled Twist Loaves. In fact, the only real limitation in processor bread making is that the bowl size prevents preparation of large quantities at once.

If you haven't used a food processor for bread making before, you may notice that the recipe directions are a bit different from what you're used to. For one thing, instructions always indicate how many *seconds* (not minutes!) to processs ingredients. Mere seconds might not seem to matter much but they make a noticeable difference in texture in processor breads. Be particularly careful not to overprocess doughs that are to be fried, as this causes toughness.

Another unfamiliar feature of processor-bread recipes is the instruction to "process until the dough cleans the bowl." During preparations, it will quickly become obvious what this means: as a sufficient amount of flour is added and the dough becomes stiff, it will mass into a ball on the blade and then sweep around the bowl, cleaning the sides as it goes.

The recipes that follow have been tested using several different

223

brands of food processors, and most standard models can be expected to yield similar results. However, since different batches of flour have different moisture contents, it's not usually possible to specify exactly how much flour will be needed for the dough to "clean the bowl." If you find that the amount indicated in a recipe leaves the dough too soft, simply add a bit more until the desired stage is reached.

If all this sounds a bit tricky, be assured that it really isn't. Most people find processor breads a lot of fun to prepare, and some enthusiasts won't make bread any other way.

• *Vienna Bread* •

Start to Finish: About 1 hour 25 minutes

A quick and easy way to make Vienna Bread. This recipe yields two small loaves.

3⅔ to 4½ cups all-purpose white or unbleached flour
1 packet fast-rising dry yeast
1 teaspoon granulated sugar
1¾ teaspoons salt
1 cup hot water (125° to 130°)
2 tablespoons vegetable oil
Cornmeal for dusting baking sheet

Combine 1¼ cups flour, the yeast, sugar and salt in processor fitted with steel blade. Pulse on/off for 5 seconds to mix. With processor motor running, quickly add water, then oil, through feed tube and process for 15 seconds. Sprinkle 2 cups more flour over processed mixture. Process for 5 to 8 seconds longer, or until dough masses around blade and cleans the bowl. Processing in on/off bursts, gradually add about ¼ cup more flour through feed tube until dough is fairly stiff. Cap feed tube. Set closed processor bowl aside in a very warm spot (80° to 90°) for 20 minutes. Meanwhile, generously sprinkle a 17½ × 11-inch (or similar large) baking sheet, or two small baking sheets, with cornmeal.

Turn dough out onto a clean, lightly floured surface. Quickly and vigorously knead in enough more flour to yield a very stiff dough. Divide dough in half; shape each half into a smooth 6- to 7-inch log. On a clean work surface, roll each log back and forth until about 10 inches long and slightly tapered at the ends. Transfer loaves to baking sheet. Lightly cover with wax paper and set aside in a very warm spot (80° to 90°) for 25 minutes. Preheat oven to 425°. Place a shallow pan of hot water on oven floor.

With a sharp knife, make a ⅛-inch-deep slash lengthwise down center of each loaf. Lightly brush or spray loaves with water. Place in oven; brush or spray loaves several more times during baking. Bake for 21 to 25 minutes, or until loaves are a light tan color and sound

225

hollow when tapped on the bottom. Transfer loaves to rack and let stand 5 minutes before serving. Vienna Bread may be served warm or at room temperature, or frozen for later use. Makes 2 small loaves.

Approximate Preparation Time: 18 minutes
Rising/Baking Time: 1 hour 8 minutes

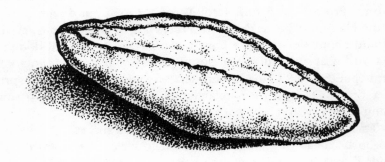

◆ *Tan Wheat Processor Loaves* ◆

Start to Finish: About 1 hour 20 minutes

This recipe produces a light wheat bread with just a hint of sweetness. The loaves are evenly shaped and tan in color.

3⅓ to 3¾ cups all-purpose white or unbleached flour
2 packets fast-rising dry yeast
¼ cup instant nonfat dry milk
1¼ teaspoons salt
Scant 1 cup water
⅓ cup vegetable oil
¼ cup honey
1 egg, at room temperature
1 cup whole-wheat flour
1 egg beaten with 1 tablespoon water for brushing over loaves

Combine 1½ cups white flour, the yeast, milk powder and salt in processor fitted with steel blade. Pulse on/off for 5 seconds to mix. Combine water, oil and honey in a small saucepan. Stirring until honey dissolves, heat to 125° to 130°. With processor motor running, quickly add liquid mixture through feed tube and process for 15 seconds. Add egg and process for 5 seconds longer. Remove lid and sprinkle whole-wheat flour and 1½ cups more white flour over processed mixture. Process for 5 to 8 seconds longer, or until dough begins to mass around blade. Processing in on/off bursts, gradually add more white flour until dough is smooth and cleans the bowl. Remove dough from processor and shape into a ball. Place in large, well-greased bowl. Cover with plastic wrap and set aside in a very warm spot (80° to 90°) for 20 minutes. Lightly grease two 8 × 4½ × 2½-inch (or similar 1½-quart) loaf pans.

Punch down dough. Knead in the bowl briefly, adding a bit more flour if needed to yield a fairly firm but not dry dough. Divide in half. With well-greased hands, carefully shape each half into a plump, smooth loaf, and place in greased pans. Cover pans with plastic wrap and set aside in a very warm place (80° to 90°) for 25 minutes. Preheat oven to 375°.

Brush tops of loaves with egg-water mixture, using a pastry brush or paper towel. Cut three or four ¼-inch-deep parallel diagonal slashes in loaf tops, using sharp knife. Bake loaves for 26 to 30 minutes, or until tops are golden brown and sound hollow when lightly tapped. Remove loaves from pans and transfer to racks to cool. The loaves may be served warm, if desired, although they slice better when thoroughly cooled. The cooled, sliced bread is good for toasting. Makes 2 medium-sized loaves.

Approximate Preparation Time: 17 minutes
Rising/Baking Time: 1 hour 13 minutes

◆ *Potato Casserole Bread* ◆

Start to Finish: About 1 hour 55 minutes

Potato breads are always tasty, but most are a bit of trouble to prepare because the potato has to be boiled and mashed first. In the following recipe the potato still has to be cooked, but the mashing is completed in a few seconds in the food processor. Not only is this simple bread delicious and light textured, but the aroma that wafts from the oven during baking is incredible! The loaf also has a nice crispy crust.

> *1 medium-sized potato, peeled and cubed*
> *3⅓ to 3½ cups all-purpose white or unbleached flour*
> *1 tablespoon fast-rising dry yeast (about 1½ packets)*
> *⅓ cup granulated sugar*
> *1¼ teaspoons salt*
> *¼ cup butter or margarine, cut into 3 or 4 pieces*
> *Reserved potato-cooking liquid*

Place potato cubes in a small saucepan and just cover with water. Bring to a boil over medium heat and simmer, covered, for 6 to 9 minutes, or until potatoes are just tender. Meanwhile, stir together 1 cup flour, the yeast, sugar and salt in a small, deep bowl. Drain potatoes well, reserving their cooking liquid in a measuring cup. Transfer potatoes to processor fitted with steel blade. Pulse on/off for 5 seconds; then process for 10 seconds. Scrape down sides of bowl and add butter. Process for 5 seconds longer, or until mixture is completely smooth. Add enough more water to reserved potato liquid to make a generous 1 cup, and, if necessary, return liquid mixture to saucepan, and heat to 125° to 130°. Sprinkle flour-yeast mixture over potatoes in processor bowl.

With processor motor running, quickly add liquid mixture through feed tube and process for 10 seconds, or until ingredients are blended. Sprinkle 2 cups more flour over processed mixture. Process for 10 seconds longer. Processing in on/off bursts, gradually add about ⅓ to ½ cup more flour until batter is very thick and begins to mass around blade. Transfer batter to large, well-greased bowl. Cover with plastic wrap and set aside in a warm place (80° to 90°) for 15 minutes. Meanwhile, heavily grease, then flour a 1¾- to 2-quart soufflé dish or similar round casserole. Tap out any excess flour.

Vigorously stir down batter and spoon into casserole. Smooth top and spread out to edges with a well-greased knife. (Smoothing will be difficult since batter is very rubbery.) Set casserole aside, uncovered, in a very warm spot (80° to 90°) for 20 minutes. Preheat oven to 375°.

Bake loaf for 60 to 65 minutes, or until top is very well browned and sounds hollow when tapped. Remove from oven and let stand on rack for at least 5 minutes. Run a knife around casserole to loosen loaf and transfer to rack to cool for 5 minutes longer. Serve bread warm and cut into wedges. It does not freeze well. Makes 1 large round loaf.

Approximate Preparation Time: 18 minutes
Rising/Baking Time: 1 hour 37 minutes

229

• *Puffy Potato Rolls* •

Start to Finish: About 1 hour 10 minutes

These are high-rising, muffin-shaped rolls with a lovely aroma and rich taste that always seems to please.

> *1 medium-sized potato, peeled and cubed*
> *3⅔ to 4 cups all-purpose white or unbleached flour*
> *1 tablespoon fast-rising dry yeast (about 1½ packets)*
> *½ cup instant nonfat dry milk*
> *¼ cup granulated sugar*
> *1½ teaspoons salt*
> *Reserved potato-cooking liquid*
> *2 tablespoons butter or margarine, cut into 2 or 3 pieces*
> *1 egg, at room temperature*

Place potato cubes in a small saucepan and just cover with water. Bring to a boil over medium heat and simmer, covered, for 6 to 9 minutes, or until potatoes are just tender. Meanwhile, combine 1 cup flour, the yeast, milk powder, sugar and salt in processor fitted with steel blade. Pulse on/off for 5 seconds to mix.

Drain potato cubes well, reserving their liquid in a measuring cup. Set potatoes aside to cool. Add enough more water to potato-cooking liquid to make ¾ cup. Return liquid mixture to small saucepan and add butter; heat to 125° to 130°.

With processor motor running, quickly add liquid mixture through feed tube and process for 5 seconds. Remove lid and sprinkle 1 cup more flour, egg and potatoes over processed mixture. Process for 30 seconds longer until potato is pureed and mixture is smooth. Add 1¾ cups more flour to bowl, and process for 5 to 8 seconds longer, or until dough masses around blade and cleans the bowl. Processing in on/off bursts, gradually add up to ½ cup more flour through feed tube until dough is smooth and fairly stiff. Cap feed tube. Set closed processor aside in a very warm place (80° to 90°) for 10 minutes. Meanwhile, generously grease sixteen standard-sized muffin-tin cups.

Turn dough out onto a clean, lightly floured surface and knead briefly. Divide dough in half. Then divide first portion into eight equal pieces. With well-greased hands, shape pieces into round balls and place in muffin cups. Repeat process with other half of dough. Lay a sheet of wax paper over muffin tins. Set aside in a very warm spot (80° to 90°) for 15 minutes.

Place rolls in a cold oven; immediately set thermostat to 425°. Bake rolls for 17 to 21 minutes, or until tops are very puffy and nicely browned. Puffy Potato Rolls are best served still hot from the oven. They do not freeze well. Makes 16 large rolls.

Approximate Preparation Time: 25 minutes   *Rising/Baking Time:* 44 minutes

◆ *Onion Bread* ◆

Start to Finish: About 1 hour 15 minutes

Although this bread is extremely easy to prepare, it has good flavor, fine texture and looks very attractive, too. It makes a nice sandwich bread.

3 to 3½ cups all-purpose white or unbleached flour
1 packet fast-rising dry yeast
¼ cup instant nonfat dry milk
2 teaspoons granulated sugar
¾ teaspoon salt
3 tablespoons instant (dehydrated) minced onions
¾ cup water
3 tablespoons vegetable oil
1 egg, at room temperature
1 egg beaten with 1 tablespoon water for brushing over loaf

Combine 1 cup flour, the yeast, milk powder, sugar, salt and 2½ tablespoons onions in food processor fitted with steel blade. (Reserve

231

remaining onions for garnishing loaf.) Pulse on/off for 5 seconds to mix. Combine water and oil in a small saucepan and heat to 125° to 130°. With processor motor running, quickly add liquid mixture through feed tube and process for 10 seconds. Add ½ cup more flour and 1 egg, and process for 6 to 8 seconds. Add 1½ cups more flour and process 6 to 8 seconds longer, or until dough masses around blade and cleans the bowl; dough will be stiff. Let dough stand in closed processor for 5 minutes. Meanwhile, lightly grease a small baking sheet or 12-inch-diameter pizza pan.

Turn dough out onto a lightly floured surface. Knead briefly, working in as much more flour as is needed to yield a smooth, elastic, fairly stiff dough. Shape dough into a smooth, round loaf and transfer to baking sheet. Brush loaf top and sides with beaten egg-water mixture. (Reserve remaining mixture for brushing again during baking.) Set loaf aside, uncovered, in a very warm spot (80° to 90°) for 25 minutes. Preheat oven to 400°.

Make a ⅛-inch-deep cut across diameter of loaf top with a sharp knife. Bake loaf for 20 minutes. Remove from oven and brush either side of slash with egg-water mixture. Lightly sprinkle top with reserved instant minced onion. Return to oven and continue baking 8 to 12 minutes longer, or until loaf is tinged with brown and sounds hollow when tapped on the bottom. Transfer loaf to rack to cool. Serve warm or at room temperature, with butter, or use for sandwiches. Makes 1 medium-sized loaf.

Approximate Preparation Time: 15 minutes   *Rising/Baking Time:* 60 minutes

◆ *Dill and Onion Rye Bread* ◆

Start to Finish: About 1 hour 50 minutes

This dark, attractive loaf has an unusual flavor, dense chewy texture and a nice crispy crust. It is good for sandwiches.

> 2 to 2¼ cups all-purpose white or unbleached flour
> 2 packets fast-rising dry yeast
> 2½ teaspoons dill seed
> 1¼ teaspoons salt
> ⅔ cup water
> 3 tablespoons dark molasses
> 2 tablespoons pickle brine, preferably from dill pickles
> 1 tablespoon butter or margarine
> 2½ teaspoons instant (dehydrated) minced onion
> 1 egg, at room temperature
> 1⅔ cups medium or dark rye flour
> 1 egg white beaten with 1 tablespoon water for brushing over loaf

Combine 1 cup white flour, the yeast, 2 teaspoons dill seed and salt in processor fitted with steel blade. (Reserve ½ teaspoon dill seed for garnish.) Pulse on/off for 5 seconds to mix. Put water, molasses, pickle brine, butter and minced onion in a small saucepan. Stirring until molasses dissolves, heat to 125° to 130°. With processor motor running, quickly add liquid mixture through feed tube and process for 10 seconds. Add egg and process for 10 seconds longer. Remove lid and add rye flour and ¾ cup more white flour. Process for 5 to 8 seconds, or until dough masses around blade and cleans bowl. (Gradually add a bit more white flour, if necessary.) Cap feed tube. Set closed processor aside in a very warm spot (80° to 90°) for 15 minutes. Meanwhile, grease a 12-inch-diameter pizza pan or small baking sheet.

Turn dough out onto a lightly floured work surface. Knead briefly, adding a bit more white flour, as necessary, to yield a firm and manageable but not dry dough. Shape dough into a high, smooth oval loaf about 7½ inches long. Cover with plastic wrap and set aside in a very warm place (80° to 90°) for 30 minutes. Preheat oven to 375°.

233

Brush loaf top and sides with egg white–water mixture, using pastry brush or paper towel. Then sprinkle top with reserved ½ teaspoon dill seed. With a sharp knife, cut a checkerboard pattern (as shown in illustration) about ⅛ inch deep in loaf top.

Bake loaf for 45 to 50 minutes, or until top is well browned and bottom sounds hollow when tapped. Remove loaf from oven and let stand on rack until completely cold. Cut crosswise into ⅛- to ¼-inch-thick slices before serving. Makes 1 large oval loaf.

Approximate Preparation Time: 20 minutes
Rising/Baking Time: 1 hour 32 minutes

• *Vegetable-Pesto Bread* •

Start to Finish: About 1 hour 35 minutes

Enlivened with savory herbs and vegetable juice, this unusual bread is very good spread with cream cheese. It also makes an interesting sandwich bread. The juice gives the handsome hearth loaf a distinctive, tawny gold color.

> 3½ to 4 cups all-purpose white or unbleached flour
> 1 packet fast-rising dry yeast
> 1 tablespoon granulated sugar
> 3 tablespoons coarsely chopped fresh parsley leaves
> 2 teaspoons dried basil leaves
> ½ teaspoon salt
> ¼ teaspoon celery salt
> Pinch of hot red pepper flakes
> Pinch of garlic powder (optional)
> 1 cup V-8 juice or similar vegetable juice
> 2 tablespoons vegetable oil
> 1 egg white beaten with 1 tablespoon water for brushing over loaf
> About 1 tablespoon Parmesan cheese for sprinkling over loaf

Combine 1 cup flour, the yeast, sugar, parsley, basil, salt, celery salt, pepper flakes (and garlic powder, if desired) in food processor fitted with steel blade. Pulse on/off for 5 seconds to mix. Combine vegetable juice and oil in a small saucepan and heat to 125° to 130°. With processor motor running, quickly add liquid mixture through feed tube and process for 10 seconds. Remove lid and sprinkle 2¼ cups more flour over processed mixture. Process for 7 to 8 seconds longer, or until dough masses around blade and cleans the bowl. Turn mixture out onto lightly floured surface and knead in enough more flour to yield a smooth, elastic and fairly stiff dough. Transfer dough to a large, well-greased bowl. Grease dough top. Cover bowl and set aside in a very warm spot (80° to 90°) for 20 minutes. Meanwhile, grease a 12-inch-diameter pizza pan or small baking sheet.

Punch down dough and knead briefly. Form into a smooth, plump, evenly shaped round loaf and place on greased pan. Cover with plastic wrap and set aside in a very warm spot (80° to 90°) for 20 minutes. Preheat oven to 375°.

Brush loaf with egg white-water mixture. Sprinkle loaf top lightly with Parmesan cheese. Cut a ⅛-inch-deep and 4-inch-long X in loaf top, using a sharp knife. Bake bread for 30 to 35 minutes, or until loaf is nicely browned and bottom sounds hollow when tapped. Transfer loaf to rack until cool. Serve at room temperature. Makes 1 large loaf.

Approximate Preparation Time: 22 minutes
Rising/Baking Time: 1 hour 12 minutes

• *Crusty Swiss Cheese Braid* •

Start to Finish: About 1 hour 40 minutes

The crusty, cheesy exterior of this loaf gives it a special appeal. It's a very attractive bread, too.

> *8 ounces Swiss (Emmentaler) or Gruyère cheese*
> *2⅔ to 3 cups all-purpose white or unbleached flour*
> *1 packet fast-rising dry yeast*
> *¼ cup instant nonfat dry milk*
> *2 teaspoons granulated sugar*
> *¾ teaspoon salt*
> *½ cup water*
> *⅓ cup vegetable oil*
> *2 eggs, at room temperature*

Coarsely grate or shred cheese in food processor fitted with grater/shredder blade. Transfer cheese to a bowl; cover and set aside. Wipe out processor bowl and fit with steel blade.

Combine 1 cup flour, the yeast, milk powder, sugar and salt in processor bowl. Pulse on/off for 5 seconds to mix. Combine water and oil in a small saucepan and heat to 125° to 130°. With processor motor running, quickly add liquid mixture through feed tube and process for 5 seconds. Add eggs and process for 5 seconds longer. Add 1½ cups more flour to bowl and process for 4 to 7 seconds longer, or until dough masses around blade. Processing in on/off bursts, add flour a tablespoon at a time through feed tube until dough stiffens enough to clean the bowl. Cap feed tube and set closed processor aside in a very warm spot (80° to 90°) for 20 minutes. Meanwhile, lightly grease a 17 × 11-inch (or similar) baking sheet.

Turn dough out onto a lightly floured surface and punch down. Gradually knead all except 1 tablespoon cheese into dough, distributing evenly; kneading will take about 5 minutes. Divide dough into three equal parts. Gently stretch out and roll portions back and forth on work surface with fingertips to form 16-inch ropes. Lay ropes side by side on baking sheet and intertwine to form braid (see page 210 for illustration). Tuck ends under to seal. Compress braid slightly to about 15 inches long. Sprinkle braid with remaining 1 tablespoon cheese. Cover braid lightly with plastic wrap. Set baking sheet aside in a very warm spot (80° to 90°) for 25 minutes. Preheat oven to 375°.

Remove plastic wrap and bake bread for 25 to 30 minutes, or until braid is nicely browned and sounds hollow when tapped on the bottom. Transfer to rack to cool. Serve warm or at room temperature, with butter. Makes 1 large braided loaf.

Approximate Preparation Time: 25 minutes
Rising/Baking Time: 1 hour 13 minutes

• *Granola-Pecan Coffee Cake* •

Start to Finish: About 1 hour 10 minutes

A delicious, no-knead, one-rise coffee cake to whip up in time for breakfast or brunch.

GRANOLA-PECAN TOPPING
½ cup plain, raisin or date granola
⅓ cup all-purpose white or unbleached flour
⅓ cup light or dark brown sugar, packed
1½ teaspoons ground cinnamon
¼ cup very cold butter or margarine, cut into 7 or 8 pieces
⅓ cup chopped pecans

BATTER
2 cups all-purpose white or unbleached flour
½ cup plain, raisin or date granola
1 packet fast-rising dry yeast
3 tablespoons light or dark brown sugar, packed
¾ teaspoon salt
¼ teaspoon ground nutmeg
¾ cup water
¼ cup vegetable oil
1 egg, at room temperature

To prepare topping, combine granola, flour, sugar and cinnamon in processor fitted with steel blade. Pulse on/off for 8 to 10 seconds, or until ingredients are well mixed and granola is in fine pieces. Sprinkle butter and nuts over dry ingredients. Pulse on/off for 4 to 6 seconds until butter is just cut into dry ingredients and mixture resembles very coarse meal; be careful not to overprocess. Transfer topping to bowl and set aside. Wipe out processor bowl.

To prepare batter, combine 1 cup flour, the granola, yeast, sugar, salt and nutmeg in processor fitted with steel blade. Pulse on/off for 5 seconds to mix. Combine water and oil in a small saucepan, and heat to 125° to 130°. With processor motor running, quickly add liquid mixture through feed tube and process for 5 seconds. Add egg and process for 5 seconds longer. Remove lid and sprinkle remaining 1 cup flour over processed mixture. Process for 4 to 6 seconds longer, or until batter thickens and begins to mass around blade. Grease a 10-inch pie plate or 8-inch square by *3-inch* deep baking pan. Spoon batter into pan, spreading evenly out to edges. Sprinkle topping mixture evenly over batter. Cover pan with plastic wrap, and set aside in a very warm spot (80° to 90°) for 20 minutes. Preheat oven to 375°.

Remove plastic wrap and bake coffee cake for 28 to 33 minutes, or until nicely browned and slightly springy to the touch. Serve warm from the oven. Makes large coffee cake.

Approximate Preparation Time: 18 minutes   *Rising/Baking Time:* 50 minutes

• *Apple Swirl Coffee Ring* •

Start to Finish: About 1 hour 55 minutes

This apple-and-raisin-filled coffee ring is both delicious and impressive looking.

3¾ to 4¼ cups all-purpose white or unbleached flour
2 packets fast-rising dry yeast
2 tablespoons granulated sugar
¼ cup instant nonfat dry milk
½ teaspoon salt
1 cup apple juice
¼ cup butter or margarine, cut into 3 or 4 pieces
1 egg, at room temperature
FILLING
3 to 4 medium-sized tart, peeled apples (enough to yield 2¼ cups,
    finely chopped)
½ cup light or dark brown sugar, packed
1 tablespoon all-purpose white or unbleached flour
1 tablespoon ground cinnamon
½ teaspoon ground allspice
2 teaspoons lemon juice
1 cup raisins
½ cup finely chopped walnuts
GLAZE
1 cup confectioners' sugar (sifted if lumpy)
1 tablespoon butter or margarine, softened
½ teaspoon vanilla extract
2 to 3 teaspoons water

Combine 1 cup flour, the yeast, granulated sugar, milk powder and salt in processor fitted with steel blade. Pulse on/off for 5 seconds to mix. Heat apple juice and butter in a small saucepan until butter melts and mixture reaches 125° to 130°.

With processor motor running, quickly add liquid mixture through feed tube and process for 10 seconds. Add egg through feed tube and process for 5 seconds longer. Remove lid and sprinkle 2½ cups more flour over processed mixture. Process for 5 to 8 seconds longer, or until dough masses around blade and begins to clean bowl.

Continuing to process in on/off bursts, gradually add more flour through feed tube until dough is smooth and cleans the bowl. Form dough into a ball and transfer to a large, well-greased bowl. Cover bowl with plastic wrap. Set aside in a very warm spot (80° to 90°) for 20 minutes.

Meanwhile, prepare filling as follows: Rinse out and dry processor. Peel, core and quarter apples. With processor fitted with steel blade, finely chop enough apples to yield 2¼ cups. In a medium-sized bowl, stir together brown sugar, flour and spices until well mixed. Add apples, lemon juice, raisins and nuts, and stir until well combined. Very generously grease a 12-cup or larger ovenproof ring mold or Bundt pan (or *one-piece* tube pan).

Turn dough out onto a clean, lightly floured surface and punch down. Knead briefly; add a bit more flour, if needed, to yield a smooth, malleable, but not dry dough. Roll out dough to form an evenly thick 17 × 12-inch rectangle. Spread filling mixture over the rectangle. Working from a longer side, tightly roll up dough jelly-roll style. Gently but firmly stretch out to produce an evenly thick log about 22 inches long. Place the log in pan, seam side up, pressing and smoothing ends together to form unbroken ring. Cover with a damp cloth. Set aside in a very warm spot (80° to 90°) for 20 minutes.

Place coffee ring in cold oven; set thermostat to 375°. Bake for 38 to 44 minutes, or until ring is browned on top and slightly springy to the touch. (If top begins to brown too rapidly, reduce heat to 350° for last 10 minutes of baking.) Transfer pan to rack; let ring stand in pan for 10 minutes. Carefully run a knife around edges and center hole to loosen ring. Then invert ring and slide out onto rack; the bottom during baking becomes top of finished ring. Let coffee ring cool for 5 minutes longer. Meanwhile, prepare glaze by stirring together confectioners' sugar, butter, vanilla and enough water to yield a thick but spreadable glaze. Spread over warm (but not hot) ring, allowing excess to drip decoratively down sides. Let ring stand until glaze sets, then serve. Makes 1 very large coffee ring.

Approximate Preparation Time: 35 minutes
Rising/Baking Time: 1 hour 20 minutes

• *Honey Buns* •

Start to Finish: About 1 hour 10 minutes

These are not really buns at all, but delicious spiral-shaped honey doughnuts. They are reminiscent of the honey buns sold by an old-fashioned, German-style bakery near my home.

Don't be put off by the length of this recipe; it's actually rather easy to prepare.

1 small potato, peeled and cubed
2¾ to 3 cups all-purpose white or unbleached flour
1 tablespoon fast-rising dry yeast (about 1½ packets)
¼ cup instant nonfat dry milk
½ teaspoon salt
Reserved potato-cooking liquid
3 tablespoons butter or margarine, cut into 3 pieces
3 tablespoons honey
1 egg, at room temperature
Oil for deep-frying doughnuts
GLAZE
1½ cups confectioners' sugar (sifted if lumpy)
3 tablespoons water
1 tablespoon honey
1 teaspoon vanilla extract

Place potato cubes in small saucepan and just cover with water. Bring to a boil over medium heat and simmer, covered, for 7 to 9 minutes, or until potatoes are just tender. Meanwhile, stir together ¾ cup flour, the yeast, milk powder and salt in a small bowl. Set aside. Drain potatoes well, reserving their liquid in a measuring cup. Put potatoes in processor fitted with steel blade. Process for 10 seconds. Scrape down sides of bowl with rubber spatula and process for 15 to 20 seconds longer, or until potatoes are pureed. Add enough more water to reserved potato liquid to measure ½ cup, and, if necessary, reheat mixture to 125° to 130°. With processor motor running, add potato-liquid mixture, then butter and honey through feed tube, and process for 5 to 6 seconds, or until mixture is completely smooth.

Remove lid and sprinkle flour-yeast mixture over potato mixture. Process for 3 seconds.

Scrape down sides of bowl and add egg. Process for 3 seconds. Sprinkle 1¾ cups more flour over processed mixture. Process for 4 to 7 seconds longer, or until dough masses around blade and cleans bowl. (Add a bit more flour, if necessary.) Cap feed tube. Set closed processor aside in a very warm spot (80° to 90°) for 10 minutes. Meanwhile, set out a large tray or baking sheet and line with wax paper.

Turn dough out onto a lightly floured board and knead briefly with well-greased hands. Press or roll dough out to an evenly thick, 12 × 14-inch rectangle. Working from a longer side, roll up jelly-roll style to form an evenly thick 14-inch-long log. Cut log crosswise into thirteen or fourteen evenly thick pinwheel slices. Space pinwheels about 2½ inches apart on wax-paper-lined tray. Cover loosely with wax paper. Set aside in a very warm spot (80° to 90°) for 20 minutes.

Meanwhile, ready a kettle or pot for deep-frying by filling 3 to 3½ inches deep with oil. Set aside. Prepare honey glaze by stirring together all ingredients in a small bowl until smooth. Cover and set aside. Set out a large rack over a tray or sheet of wax paper (to catch drips when honey buns are dipped in glaze).

When honey buns have risen for about 15 minutes, place oil over medium-high heat and gradually bring to 360° to 365°. Fry honey buns in batches of three or four; cook for about 2 minutes, or until golden brown on first side. Then turn over and fry until browned, about 1½ minutes longer. Immediately transfer to rack. Adjust heat as necessary to maintain constant temperature. When all honey buns are cooked, dip each in glaze until completely coated; then hold up and allow excess glaze to drip back into bowl. Return buns to rack to drain. Let stand for 5 to 10 minutes until glaze is set. Honey Buns are best served while still warm. However, they may be kept several hours and gently reheated in a warm oven, if desired. They do not freeze well. Makes 13 or 14 spiral-shaped doughnuts.

Approximate Preparation Time: 25 minutes
Rising/Frying Time: 45 minutes

• *Gary's Creole Coffee Knots* •

Start to Finish: About 1 hour 30 minutes

Creole coffee—strong Louisiana coffee sweetened with molasses—was the inspiration for this unusual recipe. Coffee knots are a bit like European sweet pretzels in texture and appearance. They are good for breakfast or brunch, or any time coffee is served.

> 2¾ to 3¼ cups all-purpose white or unbleached flour
> 1 packet fast-rising dry yeast
> ⅓ cup instant nonfat dry milk
> 1 teaspoon salt
> 1 cup strong coffee
> ¼ cup molasses, preferably dark
> 2 tablespoons butter or margarine, cut in half
> 1 egg, at room temperature
> 1 tablespoon freshly grated orange rind
> 1 cup whole-wheat flour
> 1 egg yolk beaten with 1 tablespoon water for brushing over knots
> ORANGE GLAZE
> 1 cup confectioners' sugar
> 1 teaspoon freshly grated orange rind
> 1½ to 2 tablespoons orange juice, approximately

Combine 1 cup white flour, the yeast, milk powder and salt in processor fitted with steel blade. Pulse on/off for 5 seconds to mix. Combine coffee, molasses and butter in a small saucepan. Stirring until molasses dissolves, heat to 125° to 130°. With processor motor running, quickly add liquid mixture through feed tube and process for 6 to 7 seconds. Add egg, orange rind and ½ cup more white flour to bowl, and process for 5 seconds longer. Remove lid and sprinkle whole-wheat flour and 1¼ cups more white flour over processed mixture. Process for 5 to 8 seconds longer, or until dough masses around blade and cleans the bowl. Turn dough out on a clean, lightly floured surface and knead in enough more white flour to yield a smooth and elastic but still moist dough. Transfer dough to well-greased bowl. Cover bowl with plastic wrap and set aside in a very warm spot (80° to 90°) for 20 minutes. Meanwhile, generously grease two 15 × 10-inch (or similar) baking sheets and set aside.

Punch down dough. On a clean, lightly floured surface, roll out dough to an evenly thick rectangle about 20 × 8 inches. With a sharp knife, mark and then cut rectangle crosswise into about twenty 8 × 1-inch strips. Tie a loose knot (overhand) in middle of each strip. (Don't bother trying to tighten knots; you can't, and they will expand during rising anyway.) Space coffee knots as far apart as possible on baking sheets. Cover loosely with plastic wrap. Set aside in a very warm spot (80° to 90°) for 25 minutes. Preheat oven to 375°.

Carefully brush knots with egg yolk–water mixture. Bake in preheated oven for 18 to 22 minutes, or until deep brown and springy to the touch. Meanwhile, prepare glaze as follows: Stir together confectioners' sugar and orange rind until blended. Gradually stir in enough orange juice to yield a smooth, almost runny glaze. Set out racks over sheets of wax paper.

Transfer coffee knots from pans to racks and let cool for 5 minutes. Dip top surface of knots in glaze and return to racks to drain. Let cool for 5 minutes longer before serving. Creole Coffee Knots may be frozen for later use, if desired. Makes 20 coffee knots.

Approximate Preparation Time: 25 minutes
Rising/Baking Time: 1 hour 5 minutes

• *Apricot-filled Twist Loaves* •

Start to Finish: About 2 hours

A pretty breakfast or tea bread featuring the delectable flavors of apricots, oranges and raisins. This is a special-occasion bread.

FILLING
1 cup dried apricots
⅔ cup golden raisins
⅔ cup brown raisins
½ cup light brown sugar, packed
¼ cup cornstarch
½ cup orange juice
DOUGH
3 to 3½ cups all-purpose white or unbleached flour
1 packet fast-rising dry yeast
¼ cup granulated sugar
¼ teaspoon salt
1 teaspoon freshly grated orange rind
¾ cup water
¼ cup butter or margarine, cut into 3 or 4 pieces
1 egg
¼ teaspoon almond extract
GLAZE
¾ cup confectioners' sugar
¼ teaspoon vanilla extract
2 to 2¾ teaspoons orange juice

Filling: Very coarsely chop apricots and place in processor fitted with steel blade. Process in on/off bursts for 20 to 30 seconds, or until apricots are chopped medium fine. Add raisins to processor bowl and process in bursts for 15 to 20 seconds longer, or until raisins are coarsely chopped. Combine brown sugar and cornstarch in a small saucepan, stirring until well blended. Gradually add orange juice to pan, stirring until mixture is smooth. Stir chopped apricots and raisins into juice mixture. Bring mixture to a boil over medium heat, stirring constantly. Simmer for 3 to 4 minutes, stirring occasionally,

246

until filling is slightly thickened and clear. Set aside to cool to room temperature. Clean processor.

Dough: Combine 1½ cups flour, the yeast, granulated sugar, salt, and orange rind in processor fitted with steel blade. Pulse on/off for 5 seconds to mix. Combine water and butter in small saucepan. Heat until butter melts and mixture reaches 125° to 130°.

With processor motor running, quickly add water-butter mixture through feed tube and process for 10 seconds. Add egg and almond extract through feed tube, and process for 10 seconds longer. Remove lid and add 1¼ cups more flour to bowl. Process for 4 to 6 seconds, or until dough masses around the blade. Gradually add up to ¾ cup more flour through feed tube, processing in on/off bursts until dough is fairly stiff and cleans the bowl. Cap feed tube. Set closed processor aside in a very warm spot (80° to 90°) for 20 minutes. Meanwhile, grease a 17½ × 15-inch (or similar very large) baking sheet, or two smaller baking sheets. Set aside.

Turn dough out onto a clean, lightly floured surface. Knead briefly, adding a bit more flour if needed to yield a slightly stiffer and less sticky dough. Divide dough into four equal parts. Roll out first portion to form a 12 × 8-inch rectangle. Spread one-quarter of the apricot-raisin filling over dough surface. Working from a longer side, roll up dough to form an evenly thick 12-inch-long log. Repeat shaping and filling process with second dough portion to form another log. Lay logs together on baking sheet and entwine back and forth over one another to form an evenly thick twist. Tuck ends underneath to prevent logs from untwisting. Repeat process with remaining two dough portions and form second twist. Cover twists lightly with a slightly damp cloth and set aside to rise in a very warm spot (80° to 90°) for 25 minutes. Preheat oven to 375°.

Bake twists for 29 to 34 minutes or until loaves are golden brown and sound hollow when lightly tapped on top. Transfer twists to racks and let cool for 10 minutes. While twists cool, prepare orange glaze. (If loaves are to be frozen, do not add glaze until just before serving.) Combine confectioners' sugar, vanilla and enough orange juice to form a liquefied but not thin glaze. Stir until completely smooth. Drizzle glaze over twists. Let twists stand 5 minutes longer and serve. Apricot-filled Twist Loaves may also be frozen for later use and then reheated and iced at serving time. Makes 2 12-inch-long twists.

Approximate Preparation Time: 45 minutes
Rising/Baking Time: 1 hour 17 minutes

• *Sweet Ginger Pinwheels* •

Start to Finish: About 1 hour 25 minutes

These zesty sweet rolls are a nice change of pace from cinnamon buns.

2¾ to 3¼ cups all-purpose white or unbleached flour
1 packet fast-rising dry yeast
¼ cup instant nonfat dry milk
¼ cup granulated sugar
½ teaspoon salt
½ teaspoon ground ginger
Scant 1 cup water
3½ tablespoons vegetable oil
FILLING
½ cup light or dark brown sugar, packed
1 teaspoon freshly grated orange rind
½ teaspoon ground ginger
⅛ teaspoon ground allspice
3 tablespoons butter or margarine, softened
⅓ cup golden raisins (optional)

Combine 1 cup flour, the yeast, milk powder, granulated sugar, salt and ginger in processor filled with steel blade. Pulse on/off for 5 seconds to mix. Combine water and oil in a small saucepan and heat to 125° to 130°. With processor motor running, quickly add liquid mixture through feed tube and process for 10 seconds. Remove lid and add 1⅔ cups more flour. Process for 6 to 10 seconds longer, or until dough masses around blade and cleans the bowl. Processing in on/off bursts, gradually add, by tablespoonfuls, enough more flour to yield a smooth and malleable but still moist dough. Cap feed tube. Set processor bowl aside in a very warm spot (80° to 90°) for 15 minutes. Meanwhile, generously grease two 9- or 10-inch round or square baking pans and set aside. To make filling, stir together brown sugar, orange rind and spices, and set aside.

Turn dough out onto a lightly floured board and knead briefly

249

with lightly greased hands. Press or roll out dough to an evenly thick 13 × 10-inch rectangle. Spread butter, then brown sugar-spice mixture evenly over dough surface. Top with raisins, if desired. Working from a longer side, tightly roll up dough jelly-roll style. Gently stretch out and adjust dough to yield an evenly thick 16- to 17-inch log. Cut log crosswise into about sixteen pinwheels. Arrange, slightly separated, in greased pans. Press down pinwheels to flatten slightly. Cover pans with plastic wrap. Turn oven on for 1 minute; turn off again. Let pinwheels rise in oven for 20 minutes.

Remove plastic wrap and immediately set oven to 375°. Bake pinwheels for 24 to 27 minutes, or until golden brown and springy to the touch. Serve warm from the oven. Makes about 16 sweet rolls.

Approximate Preparation Time: 23 minutes   *Rising/Baking Time:* 1 hour

Preparing Beignets

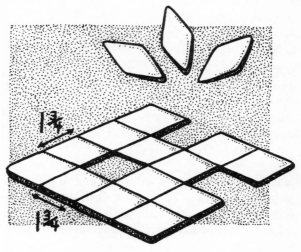

• *Spiced Beignets* •

Start to Finish: About 1 hour 28 minutes

Beignets, an European specialty introduced into America by French settlers, are half doughnut, half fritter. This recipe is for diamond-shaped beignets like the ones sold in and about New Orleans. They are good freshly fried and served for breakfast. They also make an irresistible snack.

> 2¾ to 3¼ cups all-purpose white or unbleached flour
> 1 tablespoon fast-rising dry yeast (about 1½ packets)
> 3 tablespoons granulated sugar
> ¾ teaspoon salt
> 1 teaspoon ground allspice
> ¼ teaspoon ground nutmeg
> ¾ cup hot water (125° to 130°)
> 2 tablespoons vegetable oil
> 1 egg, at room temperature
> Oil for deep-frying beignets
> Confectioners' sugar for dusting beignets

Combine ¾ cup flour, the yeast, sugar, salt and spices in a processor fitted with steel blade. Pulse on/off for 5 seconds to mix. With processor motor running, add water and oil through feed tube and process for 3 seconds. Remove lid and add egg and 2 cups more flour to processed mixture. Process for 4 to 6 seconds, or until dough masses around blade and cleans the bowl (add a bit more flour if needed). Cap feed tube. Set closed processor aside in a very warm spot (80° to 90°) for 20 minutes. Meanwhile, grease a 17½ × 15-inch (or similar very large) baking sheet, or two smaller baking sheets.

Turn dough out onto a lightly floured board and punch down. Knead briefly, adding a bit more flour if necessary to yield a smooth and elastic yet still slightly moist dough. Roll out dough ¼ inch thick. Cut diamonds, about 3½ × 2 inches, by preparing a 1¾-inch grid (as shown in illustration on page 250); cut grid cleanly with a sharp knife. Lay beignets, slightly separated, on baking sheet, cover with damp towels, and set aside in a very warm spot (80° to 90°) for 25 minutes. Meanwhile, ready a large saucepan or pot for deep-frying by filling 3 to 3½ inches deep with oil. Set out a rack and top with a layer of paper towels.

When beignets have risen for about 20 minutes, place oil over medium-high heat and bring to about 365°. In batches of five or six, transfer beignets to pot and fry on first side until golden brown (about 1½ minutes). Then using tongs, turn over and fry second side (about 1 minute). Raise or lower heat as necessary to maintain temperature at about 365°. Transfer beignets to prepared rack to cool. When all are cooked, place (in batches) in a paper bag with confectioners' sugar and shake until thoroughly dusted. Beignets are best served still warm. If absolutely necessary, however, they may be kept several hours and gently reheated in a low oven. Makes about 30 to 35 beignets.

Approximate Preparation Time: 25 minutes
Rising/Frying Time: 1 hour 3 minutes

◆ *Onion-Garlic Bread Sticks* ◆

Start to Finish: About 1 hour 10 minutes

Savory with onion and garlic flavor and pleasantly crisp, these go well with Italian food.

2½ to 3 cups all-purpose white or unbleached flour
1 packet fast-rising dry yeast
1½ teaspoons granulated sugar
1½ teaspoons instant (dehydrated) minced onions
¼ teaspoon salt
¼ teaspoon garlic salt
¾ cup hot water (125° to 130°)
2 tablespoons vegetable oil
1 egg beaten with 1 tablespoon water for brushing over bread sticks
Scant ½ teaspoon coarse salt (or substitute regular table salt, if necessary)

252

Combine 1 cup flour, the yeast, sugar, onions, salt and garlic salt in food processor fitted with steel blade. Pulse on/off for 5 seconds to mix. Combine hot water and oil in a cup. With processor motor running, quickly add liquid mixture through feed tube and process for 5 seconds. Add 1¼ cups more flour to bowl. Process for 4 to 6 seconds, or until dough masses around blade and begins to clean the bowl. Processing in on/off bursts, gradually add more flour through feed tube until dough cleans the bowl and stiffens slightly. Cap feed tube and set processor aside in a very warm spot (80° to 90°) for 20 minutes. Meanwhile, lightly grease a 17½ × 15-inch (or similar very large) baking sheet. Preheat oven to 400°.

Turn dough out onto a clean, well-floured surface. Punch down. Gradually knead in enough more flour to yield a smooth, elastic, fairly stiff dough. With well-floured hands, divide dough into twelve portions. Roll portions back and forth on a lightly floured work surface to form evenly thick sticks about 11 inches long. Space sticks about ½ inch apart on baking sheet. One or two at a time, brush tops and sides lightly with egg-water mixture; immediately sprinkle lightly with salt crystals.

Bake bread sticks for 18 to 22 minutes, or until tops are nicely browned and sound hollow when tapped. Transfer to racks to cool. Bread sticks may be served still warm from the oven, with butter, or at room temperature. They may also be frozen and then thawed before serving, if desired. Makes 12 large bread sticks.

Approximate Preparation Time: 30 minutes   *Rising/Baking Time:* 40 minutes

• *Soft Pretzels* •

Start to Finish: About 1 hour 10 minutes

> *3 to 3½ cups all-purpose white or unbleached flour*
> *1 packet fast-rising dry yeast*
> *1 teaspoon granulated sugar*
> *¾ teaspoon salt*
> *1 cup hot water (125° to 130°)*
> *1 tablespoon vegetable oil*
> *1 egg beaten with 1 tablespoon water*
> *3 cups water*
> *3 tablespoons baking soda*
> *Coarse salt for sprinkling on pretzels*

Combine 1 cup flour, the yeast, sugar and salt in processor fitted with steel blade. Pulse on/off for 5 seconds to mix. With processor motor running, quickly add hot water through feed tube and process for 10 seconds. Remove lid and add 2 cups more flour, oil and 1 tablespoon beaten egg-water mixture to processor bowl. (Reserve remaining egg-water mixture for brushing over pretzels.) Process for 5 to 7 seconds longer, or until dough masses around blade. Processing in on/off bursts, gradually add more flour through feed tube until dough cleans the bowl. Cap feed tube. Set closed processor bowl aside in a very warm spot (80° to 90°) for 15 minutes. Meanwhile, thoroughly grease two 15 × 10-inch (or similar) baking sheets and set aside.

Turn dough out onto a clean, well-floured surface. Gradually knead in enough more flour to yield a smooth and fairly stiff yet still slightly sticky dough. Divide dough in half. Divide each half into six equal portions. With lightly floured hands, roll each portion into an 18-inch-long rope. Begin forming pretzel by laying rope in a U shape, then crossing and twisting the ends about halfway down their length (as shown in illustration). Complete pretzel by lifting up the loop and laying it over the ends. Lay finished pretzels several inches apart, six to each baking sheet. Cover with plastic wrap and set aside in a very warm spot (80° to 90°) for 15 minutes. Preheat oven to 400°. Bring 3 cups of water to a rolling boil in a medium-sized saucepan. Stir in 3 tablespoons baking soda.

In batches of three or four, put pretzels into boiling water and cook for 3 to 4 seconds. Remove with slotted spoon and return to baking sheet. Brush boiled pretzels with reserved egg-water mixture and sprinkle lightly with coarse salt.

Bake pretzels for 9 to 10 minutes, or until golden brown and tops sound hollow when lightly tapped. Let pretzels stand for several minutes before removing to racks or serving. Pretzels may be frozen for later use and reheated, if desired. Makes 12 large pretzels.

Approximate Preparation Time: 30 minutes   *Rising/Baking Time:* 39 minutes

Forming a Pretzel

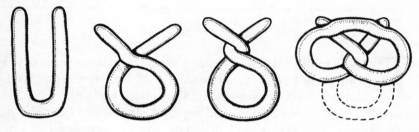

MAKE-AHEAD, BAKE-AHEAD
BREADS

*T*his chapter is aimed at making the bread-baking process not only quick and easy, but exceptionally convenient as well. Thanks to a variety of modern techniques, it's now possible to divide preparations into several separate stages. For example, in some recipes, the mixing and kneading can be completed at one point, and the shaping and baking of the dough at another. In other recipes, everything except the baking can be done ahead; then hours—or even several days—later, the bread is simply slipped into the oven and baked. This wonderful convenience makes these recipes ideal for serving to company. And it means that home bread baking can be fitted into nearly every schedule and life-style.

Among the make-ahead, bake-ahead recipes included in this chapter are refrigerator-rise breads, which are put "on hold" in the refrigerator for up to several days; some unique slow-rise breads, which are simply set aside on a counter for up to 12 hours; and "brown-and-serve" loaves, which are partially baked, frozen and then reheated as needed.

In addition to being convenient, all the techniques employed here yield excellent bread—just as tasty as that made from all the other recipes in the book.

256

• *Refrigerator-Rise Buttermilk Bread* •

Start to Finish: About 1 hour 20 minutes (plus refrigeration)

Put this easy-to-prepare dough "on hold" in the refrigerator for from 3 to 24 hours. It can then be used to make two large loaves of bread or, if you prefer, about 2½ dozen pan rolls. Or use half the dough for a loaf and the other half for rolls.

> *6 to 6½ cups all-purpose white or unbleached flour*
> *1 packet fast-rising dry yeast*
> *1 tablespoon granulated sugar*
> *2 teaspoons salt*
> *2 cups commercial buttermilk*
> *⅔ cup water*
> *¼ cup vegetable oil*
> *¼ teaspoon baking soda*

Stir together 2 cups flour, the yeast, sugar and salt in a large mixer bowl. Combine buttermilk, water, oil and soda in a small saucepan. Heat mixture to 125° to 130°. With mixer on low speed, beat liquid into dry ingredients until blended. Raise speed to high and beat for 3½ minutes. Vigorously stir in 3½ cups more flour, or enough to yield a kneadable dough. Working in the bowl or on a clean surface, quickly and vigorously knead in enough more flour to yield a smooth and elastic but not dry dough. Cover bowl with plastic wrap and set aside in a very warm spot (80° to 90°) for 20 minutes. Meanwhile, lightly grease two 9 × 5 × 3-inch (or similar 2-quart) loaf pans.

Punch down dough and divide in half. With well-greased hands, form halves into smooth, well-shaped loaves and place in pans. Brush loaf tops generously with oil. Cover loaves loosely with plastic wrap. Refrigerate for 3 to 24 hours.

Fifteen minutes before baking time, remove pans from refrigerator; gently remove plastic wrap. Preheat oven to 425°.

Carefully cut a ¼-inch-deep lengthwise slash down center of each loaf, using a sharp knife. Bake bread for 37 to 42 minutes, or until loaves are lightly browned and sound hollow when tapped on the bottom. Transfer to racks and cool thoroughly. Very good sliced and used for sandwiches. Makes 2 large loaves.

Approximate Preparation Time: 20 minutes
Rising/Baking Time: 59 minutes (plus 3–24 hours refrigeration)

VARIATION: Refrigerator-Rise Buttermilk Rolls—Prepare dough and set aside for 20 minutes as directed. Meanwhile, grease four 8-inch round or square baking pans and set aside. Divide dough in half. With very well-greased hands, divide each half into sixteen walnut-sized balls and space, well separated, eight to a pan. Brush roll tops generously with oil. Loosely cover pans with plastic wrap. Refrigerate rolls as directed for loaves. Bake in preheated 425° oven for 28 to 33 minutes, or until lightly browned and springy to the touch. Serve warm or at room temperature, with butter. Makes 32 rolls.

• *Refrigerator-Rise Wheat Bread* •

Start to Finish: About 1 hour 30 minutes (plus refrigeration)

Here is a good basic wheat bread designed for maximum convenience. The dough is mixed up and given a short rising. Then, it is simply put in bread pans and stashed in the refrigerator. Finally, any time in the next 3 to 24 hours, it is popped into the oven and baked. Fresh, tasty loaves of light wheat bread with no last-minute fuss! This bread keeps well.

> *3¾ to 4¼ cups all-purpose white or unbleached flour*
> *1 packet fast-rising dry yeast*
> *¼ cup granulated sugar*
> *2 teaspoons salt*
> *2 cups water*
> *¼ cup vegetable oil*
> *2 cups whole-wheat flour*

Stir together 2 white cups flour, the yeast, sugar and salt in a large mixer bowl. Combine water and oil in a small saucepan, and heat to 125° to 130°. With mixer on low speed, beat liquid into flour-yeast mixture until blended. Raise speed to high and beat for 3½ minutes. Vigorously stir in whole-wheat flour and about 1 cup more white flour, or enough to yield a kneadable dough. Working on a clean, well-floured surface, quickly and vigorously knead in enough more white flour to yield a smooth and elastic but still moist dough.

Cover bowl with plastic wrap and set aside in a very warm spot (80° to 90°) for 20 minutes. Meanwhile, thoroughly grease two 8 × 4½ × 2½-inch (or similar 1½-quart) loaf pans. Punch down dough and divide in half. With greased hands, form halves into smooth, well-shaped loaves and place in pans. Brush loaf tops generously with oil. Cover loaves loosely with plastic wrap. Refrigerate for 3 to 24 hours.

Fifteen minutes before baking time, remove pans from refrigerator. Gently remove plastic wrap. Let loaves stand in a very warm spot (80° to 90°) for 15 minutes.

Carefully cut a ¼-inch-deep lengthwise slash down center of loaves using a sharp knife. Put pans in cold oven; immediately set thermostat to 400°. Bake for 33 to 38 minutes, or until loaves are well browned and sound hollow when tapped on top. Remove loaves from pans, transfer to racks and cool thoroughly. This bread is good for sandwiches and toast. Makes 2 medium-sized loaves.

Approximate Preparation Time: 18 minutes
Rising/Baking Time: 70 minutes (plus 3–24 hours refrigeration)

◆ *Sweet 'n' Wheaty* ◆
Brown-and-Serve Loaves

Start to Finish: About 1 hour 50 minutes (plus freezing and thawing time)

Hearty wheat loaves that are partly baked and then frozen for later use. When you're in the mood for the taste of homemade bread, pull one of these brown-and-serve loaves from the freezer and briefly pop it into the oven.

> 3½ to 4¼ cups all-purpose white or unbleached flour
> 2 packets fast-rising dry yeast
> ⅓ cup instant nonfat dry milk
> ¼ cup light brown sugar, packed
> 2½ teaspoons salt
> 1¾ cups water
> ¼ cup honey
> ¼ cup butter or margarine, cut into 3 or 4 pieces
> 1¾ cups whole-wheat flour

Stir together 2 cups white flour, the yeast, milk powder, sugar and salt in a large mixer bowl. Combine water, honey and butter in a medium-sized saucepan. Stirring until honey dissolves and butter

260

melts, heat to 125° to 130°. With mixer on low speed, beat liquid into flour-yeast mixture until blended. Raise speed to high and beat for 3 minutes. With a large spoon, vigorously stir in whole-wheat flour and about 1 cup more white flour, or enough to yield a kneadable dough. Working in the bowl, quickly and vigorously knead in enough more white flour to yield a smooth and malleable dough. Cover bowl with a damp towel. Set dough aside to rise in a very warm spot (80° to 90°) for 15 minutes. Meanwhile, generously grease three 7⅞ × 3⅞ × 2½-inch aluminum foil (or similar 1-quart) loaf pans.

Punch dough down. With well-greased hands, divide dough into three equal portions. Shape each portion into a smooth loaf. Transfer to pans. Put pans in a larger pan. Carefully add enough hot water (120° to 130°) to larger pan to come ⅔ of the way up sides of bread pans. Lay a sheet of wax paper over bread pans. Let dough rise for 30 minutes.

Cut a ¼-inch-deep lengthwise slash down center of each loaf using a sharp knife. Put loaves in a cold oven; immediately set thermostat to 400°. Bake loaves for 22 to 24 minutes, or until lightly tinged with brown. Transfer pans to rack and cool for 5 minutes. Remove loaves from pans and transfer to rack to cool thoroughly. Pack loaves in plastic bags and freeze for later use.

To serve a loaf, remove from freezer and let stand for 15 minutes. Preheat oven to 375°. Place loaf on a lightly greased small baking sheet and bake for 18 to 22 minutes, or until loaf is lightly browned and sounds hollow when tapped on the bottom. Makes 3 small loaves.

Approximate Preparation Time: 20 minutes
Rising/Baking Time: 1 hour 25 minutes (plus 15 minutes to complete baking and browning)

• *Refrigerator-Rise Potato Bread* •

Start to Finish: About 1 hour 40 minutes (plus refrigeration)

This refrigerator-rise recipe yields fine-textured, flavorful loaves suitable for sandwich making or toasting. Or use it to make delicious hamburger buns, following instructions given in the variation below. (Or divide the dough and use half for a loaf and half for buns.)

> 6 to 7 cups all-purpose white or unbleached flour
> 2 packets fast-rising dry yeast
> ¾ cup granulated sugar
> ⅓ cup instant nonfat dry milk
> 1½ teaspoons salt
> 1½ cups water
> ⅔ cup vegetable oil
> 1 cup freshly made or leftover mashed potatoes (preferably prepared
>   from fresh rather than dehydrated potatoes)
> 2 eggs, at room temperature

Combine 1¾ cups flour, the yeast, sugar, milk powder and salt in a large mixer bowl. Combine water, oil and mashed potatoes in medium-sized saucepan and heat to 125° to 130°. With mixer on low speed, beat liquid into dry ingredients until blended. Raise speed to high and beat for 2 minutes. Add eggs and beat for 2 minutes longer. Vigorously stir in about 3 to 3¼ cups more flour, or enough to yield a kneadable dough. Turn dough out onto a clean, lightly floured surface. Gradually knead in enough more flour to yield a smooth and manageable but still slightly moist dough. Shape dough into a ball and transfer to a very large, well-greased bowl. Grease dough top. Cover bowl with plastic wrap and set aside in a warm spot (70° to 80°) for 20 minutes.

Punch down dough and knead in bowl for 30 seconds. Reshape dough into a ball and grease top well. Cover bowl tightly with plastic wrap. Refrigerate for at least 3 hours and up to 36 hours before using.

When ready to shape and bake, grease two 8½ × 4½ × 2½-inch (or similar 1½-quart) baking pans. Remove dough from refrigerator and punch down. Knead in the bowl for about 1 minute with well-greased hands. Divide dough in half. Form each portion into a smooth, well-shaped loaf and place in pans. Cover pans with plastic wrap. Set aside in a very warm spot (80° to 90°) for 25 minutes. Preheat oven to 375°.

Bake loaves for 30 to 36 minutes, or until tops are well browned and sound hollow when tapped. Remove loaves from pans and transfer to racks to cool. Slice and serve for sandwiches or toast. Makes 2 large loaves.

Approximate Preparation Time: 18 minutes
Rising/Baking Time: 1 hour 20 minutes (plus 3–36 hours refrigeration)

VARIATION: Hamburger Buns—Prepare dough as for Refrigerator-Rise Potato Bread. Refrigerate for 3 to 36 hours as directed. Punch down dough and knead. Divide dough in half. With greased hands, divide each half into nine pieces. Carefully shape pieces into smooth balls, tucking excess dough underneath. Transfer balls to two 17½ × 11-inch (or similar) greased baking sheets, spacing at least 2½ inches apart, nine to each pan. Press dough balls to flatten somewhat. Cover buns lightly with wax paper. Set pans aside in a very warm spot (80° to 90°) for 25 minutes.

Remove wax paper and bake buns in preheated 375° oven for 14 to 18 minutes, or until golden brown and springy to the touch. Transfer to racks to cool. Makes 18 large hamburger buns.

• Slow-Rise White Bread •

Start to Finish: About 1 hour 20 minutes (plus standing period)

This convenient bread is mixed up, then simply set aside in a cool spot (but not the refrigerator) and allowed to slowly rise for 8 to 12 hours. At that point, it is shaped, given a 30-minute rising and baked. The recipe is designed to fit into a typical work schedule. It yields two very good all-purpose loaves. It's also quite economical to prepare.

You'll notice that the recipe calls for only ½ teaspoon of yeast! Don't be tempted to add extra; this is all that is required. The long rising period gives the yeast organisms plenty of time to multiply. Unlike most recipes in this book, the following one also calls for barely warm rather than hot water to be added to dry ingredients. This is because there's no need to get the yeast off to a fast start.

> *6 to 6¾ cups all-purpose white or unbleached flour*
> *½ teaspoon fast-rising dry yeast*
> *½ cup instant nonfat dry milk*
> *⅓ cup granulated sugar*
> *2¼ teaspoons salt*
> *Scant 2 cups barely warm water (85° to 95°)*
> *¼ cup vegetable oil*

Stir together 2 cups flour, the yeast, milk powder, sugar and salt in a large mixer bowl. With mixer on low speed, beat water and oil into dry ingredients until blended. Raise speed to medium and beat for 3½ minutes. Vigorously stir in 3½ cups more flour, or enough to yield a kneadable dough. Working in the bowl, quickly and vigorously knead in enough more flour to yield a smooth, malleable, fairly firm dough. Transfer dough to a very large, well-greased bowl. Turn dough to grease all surfaces. Cover bowl tightly with plastic wrap. Set aside in a cool spot (65° to 70°) for 8 to 12 hours.

When ready to complete bread making, lightly grease two 8½ × 4½ × 2½-inch (or similar 1½-quart loaf pans). Punch down dough and knead briefly. Divide in half. Shape each half into a smooth loaf and place in pan. Cover pans with plastic wrap. Set pans in a larger pan. Carefully add enough hot water (120° to 130°) to larger pan to come ⅔ of the way up sides of bread pans. Let loaves rise, uncovered, for 30 minutes.

Make a ¼-inch-deep lengthwise slash down center of each loaf. Place pans in cold oven; immediately set thermostat to 400°. Bake loaves for 31 to 35 minutes, or until tops are nicely browned and sound hollow when tapped. Remove loaves from pan and transfer to rack to cool. Serve warm, if desired, or allow to cool thoroughly. Makes 2 medium-sized loaves.

Approximate Preparation Time: 17 minutes
Rising/Baking Time: 1 hour 3 minutes (plus 8–12 hours standing time)

• *Slow-Rise French-style Bread* •

Start to Finish: About 1 hour 30 minutes (plus standing period)

Like the Slow-Rise White Bread in this chapter, the following French-style bread recipe is designed to fit into the typical work or sleep schedule. The dough can be quickly mixed up either before going to bed at night or before going to work in the morning. Then it is simply set aside in a cool spot for 8 to 12 hours. (The long, slow rising gives the yeast plenty of time to multiply and lets the dough develop maximum flavor.) Finally, the dough is formed into loaves, allowed to rise and baked.

The preparation method for this recipe is somewhat different from the one most often used in the book, so be sure to follow all directions carefully. You will be rewarded with crusty, flavorful loaves.

> *5¾ to 6¼ cups all-purpose white or unbleached flour*
> *½ teaspoon fast-rising dry yeast*
> *2¼ teaspoons salt*
> *1 teaspoon granulated sugar*
> *2 cups barely warm water (85° to 95°)*
> *2 tablespoons vegetable oil*
> *Cornmeal for sprinkling on baking sheet*
> *1 egg white beaten with 2 tablespoons water for brushing over loaves*

Stir together 2¼ cups flour, the yeast, salt and sugar in a large mixer bowl. With mixer on low speed, beat barely warm water and the oil into dry ingredients until blended. Raise speed to high and beat for 4 minutes. Vigorously stir in about 3 cups more flour, or enough to yield a kneadable dough. Working in the bowl or on a clean surface, quickly and vigorously knead in enough more flour to yield a smooth, malleable and fairly firm dough. Shape into a ball. Transfer dough to a large well-greased bowl, turning to grease all surfaces. Cover bowl tightly with plastic wrap. Set aside in a cool spot (65° to 70°) for 8 to 12 hours.

When ready to complete bread making, lightly grease a 17½ × 15½-inch (or similar very large) baking sheet. Sprinkle lightly with cornmeal. Punch down dough and knead briefly. Divide into thirds.

On a clean, very lightly floured surface, roll or press out each third into a 12 × 9-inch rectangle. Working from a longer side, roll up tightly jelly-roll style. Smooth exterior of loaf by rolling it back and forth on work surface. Taper ends by rolling them back and forth briefly. Lay loaf seam side down on one end of baking sheet. Repeat shaping process with remaining dough portions. Space loaves on sheet as far apart from one another as possible. Brush loaves with water. Set aside, uncovered, in a very warm spot (80° to 90°) for 30 minutes. Preheat oven to 425°.

Make three or four ⅛-inch-deep and 4- or 5-inch-long random diagonal slashes along top of each loaf. Bake for 20 minutes. Remove loaves from oven and carefully brush with egg white-water mixture, using pastry brush or paper towel. Bake for 18 to 23 minutes longer, or until loaves are lightly browned and sound hollow when tapped on the bottom. Remove loaves from baking sheet and transfer to rack to cool. Cool for at least 5 minutes before serving. Loaves do not keep well, but may be frozen for later use. Makes 3 medium-sized French-bread loaves.

Approximate Preparation Time: 20 minutes
Rising/Baking Time: 1 hour 10 minutes (plus 8–12 hours standing time)

• *Butterhorn Rolls* •

Start to Finish: About 1 hour 15 minutes (plus refrigeration)

Buttery, tender and fragrant rolls perfect for serving with a fancy dinner. The dough can be held in the refrigerator for up to 36 hours.

4½ to 5 cups all-purpose white or unbleached flour
1 packet fast-rising dry yeast
⅓ cup granulated sugar
¾ teaspoon salt
1 cup hot water (125° to 130°)
½ cup butter (or margarine), softened
2 eggs, at room temperature
About 1½ tablespoons melted butter for brushing over rolls

Combine 1½ cups flour, the yeast, sugar and salt in a large mixer bowl. With mixer on low speed, beat water into dry ingredients until blended. Raise speed to high and beat for 1½ minutes. Add butter, eggs and ½ cup more flour, and beat for 1 minute longer. Vigorously stir in 2½ to 2⅔ cups more flour, or enough to yield a soft dough. Working in the bowl, knead in more flour, as needed, to yield a manageable yet moist and still slightly sticky dough. Cover bowl and set aside for 20 minutes.

Punch down dough. Shape into a ball and transfer to a large, well-greased bowl. Grease dough top. Cover bowl with plastic wrap. Refrigerate dough for at least 3 hours and up to 36 hours before baking.

To shape dough into rolls, remove from refrigerator and punch down. Turn out onto a clean, lightly floured surface and knead for about 1 minute. Divide dough into three equal portions. One at a time, shape portions into smooth rounds. Press them down on work surface to flatten slightly. Roll out into an 11- to 11½-inch round. Brush surface lightly with melted butter. Using a pastry wheel, pizza cutter or sharp knife cut dough into twelve equal triangles (as shown in illustration). Starting at wider end, roll up triangles to form rolls. Space rolls at least 1¼ inches apart on two lightly greased 15 × 11½-inch baking sheets; lay rolls with point underneath to prevent unrolling. Brush rolls lightly with melted butter. Cover with plastic wrap and set aside in a very warm spot (80° to 90°) for 15 minutes. Preheat oven to 350°.

Uncover rolls and bake for 13 to 17 minutes, or until brown on top and slightly springy to the touch. Serve still warm from the oven, with butter, or cool on racks and freeze for later use. Makes about 36 butterhorn rolls.

Approximate Preparation Time: 28 minutes
Rising/Baking Time: 50 minutes (plus 3–36 hours refrigeration)

Cutting and Forming Butterhorn Rolls

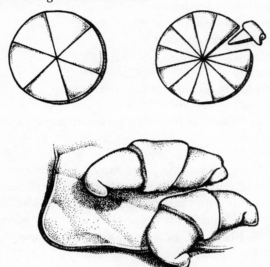

• *Icebox Pan Rolls* •

Start to Finish: About 1 hour 25 minutes (plus refrigeration)

These icebox rolls are wonderfully light and flavorful, as well as convenient. Since they can be made and shaped up to 36 hours in advance of baking, they are great for entertaining.

> *4¼ to 5 cups all-purpose white or unbleached flour*
> *1 packet fast-rising dry yeast*
> *⅓ cup granulated sugar*
> *⅓ cup instant nonfat dry milk*
> *1¼ teaspoons salt*
> *1¼ cups water*
> *¼ cup butter or margarine, cut into 3 or 4 pieces*
> *1 egg, at room temperature*
> *About 1½ tablespoons butter or margarine, softened, for brushing over roll tops*

Combine 1¼ cups flour, the yeast, sugar, milk powder and salt in a large mixer bowl. Combine water and butter in small saucepan, and heat until butter melts and mixture reaches 125° to 130°. With mixer on low speed, beat liquid into dry ingredients until blended. Raise speed to high and beat for 2½ minutes. Add egg and ¼ cup more flour, and beat for 1 minute longer. Vigorously stir in 2½ cups more flour, or enough to yield a kneadable dough. Turn dough out onto a clean, lightly floured surface. Gradually knead in enough more flour to yield a smooth and manageable but still slightly moist dough. Shape dough into a ball and transfer to a large well-greased bowl. Grease dough top. Cover bowl with plastic wrap and set aside in a very warm spot (80° to 90°) for 25 minutes. Meanwhile, grease three 8- or 9-inch cake pans or pie plates.

Punch down dough and knead in bowl for 1 minute. With well-greased hands, divide dough into three equal portions. Divide each portion into eight or nine balls; shape balls into smooth rolls, carefully tucking excess dough underneath. Space rolls, almost touching, in prepared pans. Generously brush tops of rolls with softened butter. Cover pans lightly with plastic wrap. Refrigerate rolls for at least 3 hours and up to 36 hours before baking.

About 15 minutes before baking time, remove rolls from refrigerator to warm up slightly. Preheat oven to 350°.

Bake rolls for 19 to 23 minutes, or until golden brown on top and slightly springy to the touch. Rolls are best served warm from the oven, with butter. They may also be frozen and reheated at serving time, if desired. Makes 24 to 27 large pan rolls.

Approximate Preparation Time: 23 minutes
Rising/Baking Time: 1 hour 2 minutes (plus 3–36 hours refrigeration)

• *Little Brioches* •

Start to Finish: About 1 hour 30 minutes (plus refrigeration)

Enjoy the rich, buttery taste of classic French brioches, but with far less work than traditional recipes require. These little topknot rolls are perfect for entertaining.

> *2 to 2¾ cups all-purpose white or unbleached flour*
> *1 packet fast-rising dry yeast*
> *2 tablespoons granulated sugar*
> *2 tablespoons instant nonfat dry milk*
> *¼ cup hot water (125° to 130°)*
> *2 eggs plus 1 egg yolk, at room temperature*
> *⅓ cup butter (or margarine), at room temperature*
> *1¼ teaspoons salt*
> *1 egg beaten with 1 tablespoon water for brushing over brioches*

Stir together ¾ cup flour, the yeast, sugar and milk powder in a large mixer bowl. With mixer on low speed, beat in hot water, then eggs and yolk until well blended. Raise speed to high and beat for 3½ minutes. Add butter and salt, and beat until completely blended and smooth. Vigorously stir in about 1 cup more flour, or enough to yield a kneadable dough. Working in the bowl or on a clean, lightly floured surface, knead in enough more flour to yield a smooth and manageable but still soft, moist dough. Cover bowl with plastic wrap. Set aside in a warm spot (75° to 80°) for 30 minutes. Meanwhile, generously grease sixteen standard-sized muffin-tin cups.

Punch down dough. With lightly greased hands, divide dough in 2 parts, one consisting of three-quarters of the dough, the other the remaining one-quarter. Divide larger part into sixteen equal portions about the size of small walnuts. Shape into smooth balls, tucking excess dough underneath, and place in muffin cups. Divide smaller dough portion into sixteen equal parts about the size of marbles. One at a time, shape into smooth balls. Then press down thumb in center of a larger ball all the way to bottom of muffin cup to make a deep well; immediately tuck smaller ball into indentation, smooth side facing up, to form topknot. (See illustration.) Repeat. Lightly cover muffin tins with plastic wrap. Set aside in a very warm spot (80° to

90°) for 20 minutes. Place tins in refrigerator and let brioches rest for 4 to 18 hours.

About 15 minutes before baking time, remove brioches from refrigerator and let stand, uncovered, to warm up slightly. Preheat oven to 375°. Lightly brush brioches with egg-water mixture, using pastry brush or paper towel.

Bake brioches for 13 to 16 minutes, or until tops are golden brown. Remove from cups and cool on racks for 4 to 5 minutes before serving. Brioches may also be frozen and reheated before serving, if desired. Makes 16 brioches.

Approximate Preparation Time: 30 minutes
Rising/Baking Time: 1 hour 5 minutes (plus 4–18 hours refrigeration)

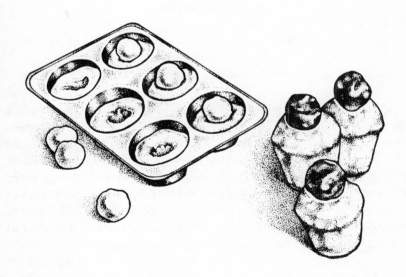

Refrigerator-Rise Swiss-Swirl Loaves

Start to Finish: About 1 hour 30 minutes (plus refrigeration)

Enriched with Swiss cheese, eggs and herbs, these delectable, make-ahead loaves are ideal for serving at a brunch or luncheon. The finished loaves are also very handsome, garnished with a dusting of cheese and herbs outside and an eye-catching swirl of the mixture inside.

5¼ to 5¾ cups all-purpose white or unbleached flour
1 packet fast-rising dry yeast
1 tablespoon granulated sugar
1½ teaspoons salt
⅛ teaspoon ground nutmeg
1¼ cups water
⅓ cup butter or margarine, cut into 4 or 5 pieces
3 eggs, at room temperature
1¾ cups lightly packed shredded or grated top-quality Gruyère or Swiss cheese (about 6½ to 7 ounces)
2½ tablespoons dried chervil or parsley flakes
2½ tablespoons dried chives
Vegetable oil for brushing over loaves
1 egg beaten with 1 tablespoon water for brushing over loaves
Additional dried chervil or parsley flakes for garnish

Stir together 1¼ cups flour, the yeast, sugar, salt and nutmeg in a large mixer bowl. Combine water and butter in a small saucepan. Heat until butter melts and mixture reaches 125° to 130°. With mixer on low speed, beat liquid into dry ingredients until blended. Raise speed to high and beat for 3 minutes. Add eggs and ¾ cup more flour, and beat for 1 minute longer. Vigorously stir in 1 cup cheese and about 2 cups more flour, or enough to yield a kneadable dough. Working in the bowl or on a clean, lightly floured surface, quickly and vigorously knead in enough more flour to yield a smooth and elastic but still slightly moist dough. Cover bowl with plastic wrap and set aside in a very warm spot (80° to 90°) for 20 minutes. Meanwhile, lightly grease two 8½ × 4½ × 2½-inch (or similar 1½-quart) loaf pans.

With greased hands, punch down dough and divide in half. On a lightly floured surface, press or roll out first half to an evenly thick 15 × 8-inch rectangle. Sprinkle dough surface with half the chervil and chives and ¼ cup of remaining cheese. Working from a shorter side, tightly roll up dough jelly-roll style to form an 8-inch log. Place in greased loaf pan. Repeat process with second loaf. Cover and refrigerate remaining ¼ cup cheese. (It will be used to garnish loaves just prior to baking.) Brush loaf tops generously with oil. Cover loaves loosely with plastic wrap or place in large plastic bags. Refrigerate for 3 to 24 hours.

To prepare loaves for baking, remove pans from refrigerator. Gently remove plastic wrap or bags. Let loaves stand, uncovered, in a very warm spot (80° to 90°) for 15 minutes.

Brush loaves with egg-water mixture, using a pastry brush or paper towel. Sprinkle reserved ¼ cup cheese over loaf tops. Add a sprinkling of chervil (or parsley) over cheese. Place loaves in cold oven; immediately set thermostat to 375°. Bake loaves for 30 to 35 minutes, or until loaves are golden brown and sound hollow when tapped on the bottom. Transfer loaves to racks and cool for 5 minutes before serving. Loaves may also be frozen and reheated before serving, if desired. Makes 2 medium-sized loaves.

Approximate Preparation Time: 23 minutes
Rising/Baking Time: 1 hour 5 minutes (plus 3–24 hours refrigeration)

• *Icebox Cinnamon-Nut Sticky Buns* •

Start to Finish: About 1 hour 20 minutes (plus refrigeration)

Tasty cinnamon sticky buns you make ahead and pop into the oven when you're ready for a treat. These may be held in the refrigerator for up to 36 hours.

> *4¾ to 5¼ cups all-purpose white or unbleached flour*
> *1 packet fast-rising dry yeast*
> *⅓ cup granulated sugar*
> *⅓ cup instant nonfat dry milk*
> *1 teaspoon salt*
> *1¼ cups water*
> *¼ cup vegetable oil*
> *1 egg, at room temperature*
> STICKY BUN SAUCE AND FILLING
> *½ cup butter or margarine, softened*
> *½ cup light corn syrup*
> *⅔ cup light brown sugar, packed*
> *2½ teaspoons ground cinnamon*
> *¾ cup chopped pecans or walnuts*

Combine 1¾ cups flour, the yeast, granulated sugar, milk powder and salt in a large mixer bowl. Combine water and oil in a small saucepan and heat to 125° to 130°. With mixer on low speed, beat liquid into dry ingredients until blended. Raise speed to high and beat for 2½ minutes. Add egg and beat for 1 minute longer. Vigorously stir in about 2½ cups more flour, or enough to yield a kneadable dough. Turn dough out on a clean, lightly floured surface. Gradually knead in enough more flour to yield a smooth and manageable but not dry dough. Shape dough into a ball and transfer to a large well-greased bowl. Grease dough top. Cover bowl with plastic wrap and set aside in a very warm spot (80° to 90°) for 25 minutes.

Meanwhile, prepare two 9- or 10-inch by *3-inch* round or square baking pans or *deep dish* pie plates as follows: Grease each pan with 2½ tablespoons softened butter. (Reserve remaining butter for brushing on dough.) Drizzle ¼ cup corn syrup in each pan; tip pans back and forth to coat with syrup. Sprinkle 2½ tablespoons brown sugar over corn syrup in each pan; reserve remainder for sprinkling over dough. Set pans aside.

Punch down dough and turn out onto a clean, lightly floured surface. Knead for 1 minute, adding a bit more flour if required to make dough slightly firmer and more manageable. Roll out dough to an 18 × 12-inch rectangle. Brush reserved butter evenly over dough surface. Sprinkle cinnamon, then reserved brown sugar, then nuts over dough. Working from a longer side, roll up dough jelly-roll style. Stretch out and adjust dough slightly, as needed, to yield an evenly thick log. Cut crosswise into eighteen to twenty slices. Lay slices in prepared pans and cover pans with plastic wrap. Refrigerate for at least 3 and up to 36 hours.

About 15 minutes before baking time, remove buns from refrigerator to warm up slightly. Preheat oven to 375°.

Bake buns for 28 to 33 minutes, or until tinged with brown on top and slightly springy to the touch. Immediately invert each pan of buns over a platter and serve. Buns are best served warm from the oven. Makes about 18 to 20 large sticky buns.

Approximate Preparation Time: 23 minutes
Rising/Baking Time: 55 minutes (plus 3–36 hours refrigeration)

• *Jelly Gem Breakfast Buns* •

Start to Finish: About 1 hour 25 minutes (plus refrigeration)

The name for these colorful sweet buns comes from the fact that teaspoonfuls of jelly sink down in the center and adorn them like jewels. Make ahead and then simply pop in the oven in time for breakfast or brunch. Jelly Gems are easy to prepare, yet irresistibly good. If you can't decide which jelly to use, try two flavors and prepare a pan of buns with each.

> *3½ to 4 cups all-purpose white or unbleached flour*
> *1 packet fast-rising dry yeast*
> *⅓ cup granulated sugar*
> *⅓ cup instant nonfat dry milk*
> *¾ teaspoon salt*
> *1 cup water*
> *¼ cup butter or margarine, cut into 3 or 4 pieces*
> *About ½ cup raspberry or currant jelly; apricot, cherry or plum preserves (or ¼ cup each of two kinds)*
> GLAZE
> *¾ cup confectioners' sugar (sifted if lumpy)*
> *1 tablespoon butter or margarine, softened*
> *¼ teaspoon vanilla extract*
> *1 to 1½ tablespoons warm water, approximately*

Combine 1¼ cups flour, the yeast, granulated sugar, milk powder and salt in a large mixer bowl. Combine water and butter in small saucepan, and heat until butter melts and mixture reaches 125° to 130°. With mixer on low speed, beat liquid into dry ingredients until blended. Raise speed to high and beat for 2½ minutes. Stir in 2 cups more flour, or enough to yield a kneadable dough. Working in the bowl or on a clean, lightly floured surface, gradually knead in enough more flour to yield a smooth and manageable but still slightly moist dough. Shape dough into a ball and return to mixer bowl. Cover bowl with plastic wrap. Set aside in a very warm spot (80° to 90°) for 20 minutes. Meanwhile, grease two 9- or 10-inch round or square baking pans and set aside.

278

Punch down dough and knead in bowl for 1 minute. Divide dough in half. Shape each half into a log and roll back and forth until about 9 inches long. Cut logs crosswise into about nine slices each. Space slices, almost touching, in greased pans; press down buns to flatten slightly. Make a deep well for jelly by pressing down firmly in center of each bun with a finger; immediately spoon a generous tea-spoonful of jelly into well. Cover pans with plastic wrap and set aside in a very warm spot (80° to 90°) for 10 minutes. Transfer to refrigerator and refrigerate buns for at least 3 hours and up to 36 hours before baking.

About 10 minutes before baking time, remove rolls from re-frigerator and set aside, uncovered, to warm up slightly.

Place buns in a cold oven; immediately set thermostat to 350°. Bake buns for 24 to 29 minutes, or until lightly browned on top and slightly springy to the touch. Meanwhile, prepare glaze as follows: Stir together confectioners' sugar, butter, vanilla and 1 tablespoon warm water. A bit at a time, stir in enough more water to yield a liquefied but not runny glaze.

Remove buns from oven and let stand for 5 to 10 minutes. Drizzle glaze over buns and serve. Jelly Gems are best served warm from the oven. They may also be frozen, then reheated in a warm oven and glazed at serving time, if desired. Makes about 18 large buns.

Approximate Preparation Time: 23 minutes
Rising/Baking Time: 57 minutes (plus 3–36 hours refrigeration)

Refrigerator-Rise All-Purpose Sweet Dough

Start to Finish: About 40 minutes (for dough preparation and first rising)

The following all-purpose sweet dough can be used to prepare various different yeast pastry recipes, including Easy Lemon Twist Loaves, which follows, and Scandinavian Coffee Rings and Swaddling Bread in the chapter on Festive Breads. The recipe is especially convenient when you wish to complete initial mixing and kneading at one point and final shaping and baking at another. The dough can be refrigerated for up to 36 hours prior to baking.

4¾ to 5¼ cups all-purpose white or unbleached flour
2 packets fast-rising dry yeast
½ cup granulated sugar
⅓ cup instant nonfat dry milk
1¼ teaspoons salt
1¼ cups water
½ cup butter or margarine, cut into 6 or 7 pieces
1 egg, at room temperature

Combine 1½ cups flour, the yeast, sugar, milk powder and salt in large mixer bowl. Combine water and butter in small saucepan and heat until butter melts and mixture reaches 125° to 130°. With mixer on low speed, beat liquid into dry ingredients until blended. Raise speed to high and beat for 2½ minutes. Add egg and beat for 1 minute longer. Stir in about 2¾ cups more flour, or enough to yield a kneadable dough. Turn dough out onto a clean, lightly floured surface. Gradually knead in enough more flour to yield a smooth and manageable but still slightly moist dough. Shape dough into a ball and transfer to a large, well-greased bowl. Grease dough top. Cover bowl with plastic wrap. Set aside in a warm spot (70° to 80°) for 20 minutes.

Punch down dough and knead in bowl for 30 seconds. Re-form dough into a ball and grease top. Cover bowl tightly with plastic wrap. Refrigerate for at least 3 hours and up to 36 hours before using.

Approximate Preparation Time: 20 minutes   *Rising Time:* 20 minutes

• *Easy Lemon Twist Loaves* •

Start to Finish: About 1 hour 15 minutes

Although Easy Lemon Twist Loaves are quite simple to make, they are attractive and have a deliciously zesty flavor.

> *1 recipe Refrigerator-Rise All-Purpose Sweet Dough (see page 280)*
> *⅓ cup chopped candied lemon peel*
> *Freshly grated rind of 1 well-washed medium-sized lemon*
> *1 egg beaten with 1 tablespoon water for brushing over loaves*
> LEMON GLAZE
> *1 cup confectioners' sugar (sifted if lumpy)*
> *1½ teaspoons freshly grated lemon rind*
> *4 to 5 teaspoons fresh lemon juice, approximately*

Remove dough from refrigerator and let stand, covered, in a very warm spot (80° to 90°) for 10 minutes. Meanwhile, grease two 8½ × 4½ × 2½-inch loaf pans. Punch down dough. Turn out onto a lightly floured surface. Gradually knead in candied lemon peel and grated rind from one lemon. Divide dough in half. With lightly greased hands, form first half into an 8-inch log. Grasp each end of log and twist dough three or four times to form a plump, corkscrew-shaped loaf. Compressing loaf slightly and tucking in ends to prevent dough from untwisting, place in pan. Repeat process with second half of dough. Cover loaves and set aside in a very warm place (80° to 90°) for 20 minutes. Preheat oven to 375°.

Brush loaf tops with egg-water mixture, using a pastry brush or paper towel. Bake loaves for 26 to 30 minutes, or until tops are nicely browned and sound hollow when tapped. Immediately remove loaves from pans and transfer to racks to cool. Meanwhile, prepare glaze as follows: Stir together confectioners' sugar and 1½ teaspoons lemon rind in a small bowl. Gradually stir in enough lemon juice to yield a smooth, fairly thick glaze. Spread glaze over loaves while still warm, but not hot. Allow glaze to set for 2 to 3 minutes before serving loaves. Easy Lemon Twist Loaves are best served warm. They may be frozen (without the glaze) and gently reheated in a warm oven, then glazed, if desired. Makes 2 medium-sized loaves.

Approximate Preparation Time: 15 minutes   *Rising/Baking Time:* 58 minutes

NOTE: Time does not include preparation of basic make-ahead dough. See Refrigerator-Rise All-Purpose Sweet Dough for total time required.

FESTIVE AND FANCY
SWEET BREADS AND PASTRIES

*E*ven the simplest homemade bread is special. But sometimes the occasion calls for particularly festive, fancy fare. With this in mind, the following recipe collection was assembled. It features a delectable and eye-catching assortment of sweet breads suitable for holiday serving and giving, as well as a selection of interesting and unusual yeast pastries and desserts.

For example, choose from among beautiful breads such as traditional fruit-studded stollen, King's Crown Coffee Ring and Alsatian Holiday Prune and Fig Log. Or whip up fancy desserts or pastries like Strawberry Shortcakes, luscious Pineapple "Jelly Rolls," or classic Babas au Rhum. Although some of these treats require more preparation time than other recipes in the book, they all feature the same time-saving techniques and methods—making them far quicker and easier to create than comparable, conventionally prepared yeast-bread recipes. Moreover, every one is worth the extra bit of attention required. Enjoy!

• *Peach-Almond Galette* •

Start to Finish: About 1 hour 20 minutes

Peach-Almond Galette is a pretty and delicious fruit dessert somewhat like a kuchen or a fruit tart. It combines the irresistible taste of fresh peaches, almonds and an almond-flavored liqueur in a rich yeast crust. (This crust is easier to work with than many pastry doughs and doesn't get soggy.) Although the finished creation looks as though it took a lot of time and skill to make, it is in fact rather simple to prepare.

> 2⅔ to 3 cups all-purpose white or unbleached flour
> 1 packet fast-rising dry yeast
> ¼ cup granulated sugar
> ½ teaspoon salt
> ½ cup hot water (125° to 130°)
> ⅓ cup blanched slivered almonds
> 1 egg, at room temperature
> 1 tablespoon Amaretto (almond-flavored liqueur) or orange juice
> ½ teaspoon almond extract
> ⅓ cup cold butter or margarine, cut into 4 to 5 pieces
> FILLING
> ¼ cup light cream
> ¼ cup blanched slivered almonds
> 2 tablespoons Amaretto liqueur or orange juice
> ⅓ cup granulated sugar
> 1½ teaspoons all-purpose white or unbleached flour
> ¼ teaspoon almond extract
> 2 eggs, at room temperature
> 5 to 6 medium-sized ripe peaches (about 1¼ pounds)

Stir together ½ cup flour, the yeast, ¼ cup sugar and salt in a measuring cup. Put hot water and ⅓ cup almonds in blender container. Blend on high speed for 1 to 1½ minutes, or until almonds are completely pureed. With motor running, add flour-yeast mixture to blender and blend on low speed for 45 seconds. Add egg, 1 tablespoon liqueur, ½ teaspoon almond extract and ¼ cup more flour to blender. Blend for 15 seconds longer. Set aside.

284

Put 1¾ cups more flour in a medium-sized bowl. With pastry blender or two forks work butter into flour until mixture resembles coarse meal. Stir blended almond mixture into flour-butter mixture to make a soft dough. A bit at a time, stir and then knead in enough more flour to yield a manageable but still fairly soft dough. Cover bowl with plastic wrap. Set aside in a warm spot (70° to 80°) while filling is prepared. Preheat oven to 375°.

Wash out blender container. To make filling, combine cream, ½ cup almonds and 2 tablespoons liqueur in blender. Blend on high speed for 1 to 1½ minutes, or until almonds are completely pureed. Add all remaining ingredients, except peaches, and blend on medium speed for 15 to 20 seconds, or until well blended. Thoroughly grease an 11¾ × 7½ × 1¾-inch (or similar) flat baking dish.

Punch down dough. Press into an evenly thick layer in bottom and 1 inch up sides of dish. Press away any excess thickness of dough at point where bottom and sides join. Pour blended filling mixture evenly into dough "crust."

Peel and pit peaches. Cut into ¼-inch-thick slices. Lay slices in tight crosswise or lengthwise rows until entire surface of crust is covered. Carefully transfer galette to oven and bake for 15 minutes. Reduce heat to 350° and bake for 20 to 25 minutes longer, or until crust is lightly browned and filling seems "set" in the middle when tapped. Transfer baking dish to rack and allow galette to cool. With wide spatulas, carefully lift entire pastry and transfer to serving platter; or cut and serve from baking dish, if desired. Peach-Almond Galette should be served cold or at room temperature. It may be prepared several days ahead and refrigerated, but should not be frozen. Makes about 8 servings.

Approximate Preparation Time: 35 minutes   *Rising/Baking Time:* 47 minutes

• *Aunt Theresa's Long Johns* •

Start to Finish: About 1 hour 25 minutes

A funny name for a wonderful regional specialty. Prepared by bakeries in some parts of the South, these delectable fried dough pastries feature a raspberry jelly filling, chocolate icing and chopped nuts.

> 3½ to 4 cups all-purpose white or unbleached flour
> 1 packet fast-rising dry yeast
> ⅓ cup granulated sugar
> ½ teaspoon salt
> ¾ cup water
> ⅓ cup vegetable oil
> ½ cup freshly made or leftover mashed potatoes (prepared from fresh or dehydrated potatoes)
> 1 egg, at room temperature
> ICING, FILLING AND GARNISH
> 1½ tablespoons butter or margarine
> 1½ ounces unsweetened baking chocolate
> 1½ cups confectioners' sugar (sifted if lumpy)
> ½ teaspoon vanilla extract
> ½ cup milk, approximately
> About ½ to ⅔ cup raspberry or other fruit jelly
> ½ cup chopped walnuts or pecans
> Oil for deep-frying

Stir together 1 cup flour, the yeast, granulated sugar and salt in a large mixer bowl. Stir together water, oil and mashed potatoes in a small saucepan. Heat to 125° to 130°. With mixer on low speed, beat liquid into dry ingredients until blended. Raise speed to high and beat for 1 minute. Add egg and beat for 30 seconds longer. Stir in 2 cups more flour, or enough to make a kneadable dough. Turn dough out onto a clean, lightly floured surface. Gradually knead in enough more flour to yield a smooth and elastic but still slightly moist dough. Shape dough into a ball and transfer to a large well-greased bowl. Grease dough top. Cover bowl with plastic wrap. Set aside in a very

warm spot (80° to 90°) for 20 minutes. Meanwhile, grease two 15 ×
11½-inch (or similar large) baking sheets and set aside.

Punch down dough and knead in bowl for 1 minute. Divide
dough in half. Divide each half into twelve equal portions. With
lightly greased hands, roll portions back and forth to form smooth
logs about 4 inches long. Transfer logs to baking sheets, spacing as far
apart from one another as possible. Flatten logs slightly until about 2
inches wide. Cover logs with damp towels and set aside in a very
warm spot (80° to 90°) for 15 minutes.

Meanwhile, prepare icing as follows: Melt butter in a medium-
sized heavy saucepan. Add chocolate and melt, stirring, over very
low heat until smooth. Remove from heat. Stir in confectioners'
sugar, vanilla and enough milk to yield a fairly thin but not runny
glaze. Set aside. Ready jelly and nuts and set aside. Set out rack over
paper towels. Ready a kettle or pot for deep-frying by filling about 2½
to 3 inches deep with oil. Bring oil to about 368° over medium-high
heat.

In batches of three or four, fry logs for about 30 seconds on one
side, or until golden. Then turn over and fry for another 30 seconds
on second side. Adjust heat as necessary to maintain oil temperature
at about 368°. Transfer fried pastries to rack to drain.

When pastries are cool enough to handle, make a ¾-inch-deep
slit lengthwise down center of each with a sharp knife. Insert a tea-
spoonful of jelly into slit. Then, with a knife, neatly spread icing over
pastries' tops and sprinkle lightly with chopped nuts. (If icing begins
to stiffen on standing, stir in a few drops of warm water.) Long Johns
are best served very fresh. However, they may be frozen completely
prepared (including icing and jelly) and slowly reheated in a warm
oven, if desired. Makes 24 pastries.

Approximate Preparation Time: 35 minutes   *Rising/Frying Time:* 48 minutes

• *Babas au Rhum* •

Start to Finish: About 1 hour 25 minutes

Here is an incredibly easy yet delicious blender version of a classic French dessert, Babas au Rhum. The dessert features wonderfully light and puffy yeast pastries (the babas), which are soaked in a rum sauce (the "au rhum"). While traditional recipes often require 3½ to 4 hours, this equally good one takes about one-third the time.

> *2 to 2¼ cups all-purpose white or unbleached flour*
> *1 packet fast-acting dry yeast*
> *1 tablespoon granulated sugar*
> *¼ teaspoon salt*
> *⅓ cup water*
> *⅓ cup butter, cut into 4 to 5 pieces*
> *2 eggs plus 1 egg yolk, at room temperature*
> SYRUP AND GARNISHES
> *1½ cups water*
> *¾ cup granulated sugar*
> *½ cup dark rum*
> *About ½ cup strained apricot preserves or jelly*
> *4 candied cherries, cut into quarters*

Stir together ½ cup flour, the yeast, 1 tablespoon sugar and salt in a measuring cup. Heat ⅓ cup water and butter in a small saucepan until butter melts and mixture reaches 125° to 130°. Transfer water-butter mixture to blender container. With motor on low speed, add flour-yeast mixture to blender and blend for 30 seconds. Add eggs and yolk and ¼ cup more flour to blender. Blend for 30 seconds longer. Transfer blended mixture to medium-sized bowl. With a large spoon, vigorously stir in 1 cup more flour. Working in the bowl or on a lightly floured surface, knead in enough more flour to yield a smooth, manageable yet still moist dough. Cover bowl with plastic wrap and set aside in a very warm spot (80° to 90°) for 20 minutes. Meanwhile, generously grease fifteen or sixteen standard-sized muffin-tin cups.

Punch down dough. One at a time, break off fifteen or sixteen small walnut-sized pieces of dough and shape into rounds. Put in greased muffins cups. Turn oven on to low for 1 minute; then turn off again. Place babas in oven and let rise, uncovered, for 25 minutes. Meanwhile, prepare rum sauce as follows: Stir 1½ cups water and ¾ cup sugar together in a small saucepan over medium-high heat until sugar dissolves. Bring to a boil and boil gently for 1½ minutes. Remove from heat and cool to lukewarm. Stir in rum and set aside.

With babas still in the oven, set thermostat to 375°. Bake babas for 14 to 17 minutes, or until puffy and nicely browned. Run a knife around babas to loosen from cups. Transfer to racks to cool slightly.

Gently prick top of each baba two or three times with tines of fork. Put babas, puffy side up, in large serving bowl or in individual serving dishes. Slowly spoon rum syrup over babas; occasionally drain off syrup collecting in bottom of bowl and spoon over babas again. Let stand for 15 to 20 minutes so pastries can absorb additional syrup. Using a pastry brush, generously brush tops of babas with apricot preserves. Top each baba with a bit of candied cherry and serve.

Babas may also be made ahead and frozen for later use. In this case, thaw babas and warm before spooning warm syrup over them and adding apricot preserves. Makes 15 to 16 babas au rhum.

Approximate Preparation Time: 25 minutes   *Rising/Baking Time:* 1 hour

• *Sultan's Morning Buns* •

Start to Finish: About 1 hour 35 minutes

A touch of coriander adds an exotic note to these sumptuous, fruit-laden sweet buns. The large pinwheel rolls are topped off with a luscious honey glaze. The recipe was inspired by several varieties of sweet rolls produced by the Ovens of Brittany restaurant and bakery in Madison, Wisconsin.

> 4¾ to 5¼ cups all-purpose white or unbleached flour
> 2 packets fast-rising dry yeast
> ¼ cup instant nonfat dry milk
> 1 teaspoon salt
> 1⅓ cups water
> Generous ⅓ cup honey
> 3 tablespoons butter or margarine, cut into 2 or 3 pieces
> 1 egg, at room temperature
> FILLING
> ½ cup golden raisins
> ½ cup currants
> ⅓ cup finely chopped dates
> ⅓ cup finely chopped prunes
> ⅓ cup light or dark brown sugar, packed
> 1 tablespoon ground cinnamon
> ½ teaspoon ground coriander
> ½ teaspoon ground mace
> ¼ cup butter or margarine, softened
> GLAZE
> ⅓ cup confectioners' sugar (sifted if lumpy)
> ⅓ cup honey
> 1½ tablespoons butter or margarine, softened
> ⅛ teaspoon freshly grated orange rind

Stir together 1¼ cups flour, the yeast, milk powder and salt in a large mixer bowl. Combine water, ⅓ cup honey and 3 tablespoons butter in a small saucepan. Stirring until honey dissolves, heat to 125° to 130°. With mixer on low speed, beat liquid into dry ingredients until blended. Raise speed to high and beat for 2½ minutes. Add egg and beat for 1 minute longer. Vigorously stir in 2¼ cups more flour, or enough to yield a kneadable dough. Working on a lightly floured surface, quickly and vigorously knead in enough more flour to yield a smooth and malleable yet still moist dough. Cover bowl with plastic wrap and set aside in a very warm spot (80° to 90°) for 25 minutes. Meanwhile, generously grease eighteen standard-sized muffin-tin cups and set aside. Combine all filling ingredients, except butter, in a medium-sized bowl. Stir until well blended and set aside.

Punch down dough. On a clean, lightly floured surface, press or roll dough out to form an evenly thick, 18 × 12-inch rectangle. Spread ¼ cup softened butter evenly over dough with a knife. Sprinkle surface evenly with fruit filling mixture. Working from a longer side, tightly roll up dough to form a log. Gently stretch out dough to form an evenly thick 24-inch-long log. Mark, then cut, dough into seventeen to eighteen uniformly thick pinwheel slices. Place pinwheels cut side up in muffin tins (they will fill the cups). Set aside, uncovered, in a very warm spot (80° to 90°) for 20 minutes. Preheat oven to 375°.

Bake pinwheels for 17 to 20 minutes, or until slightly springy to the touch and tinged with brown. Meanwhile, prepare honey glaze as follows: Stir together confectioners' sugar, ⅓ cup honey, 1½ tablespoons butter and orange rind until well blended and smooth. Set aside. Remove tins from oven and immediately run a knife around cups to loosen buns. Place buns on racks over sheets of wax paper. Let buns cool for 5 minutes; then spread glaze over tops, using a knife. Allow excess glaze to drip onto wax paper for 2 to 3 minutes; serve immediately. Completely prepared buns may also be frozen for later use and then reheated, if desired. Makes about 18 very large sweet buns.

Approximate Preparation Time: 40 minutes
Rising/Baking Time: 1 hour 3 minutes

◆ *Almond-Honey Tea Twist Loaves* ◆

Start to Finish: About 1 hour 40 minutes

Tender and delicious as well as very attractive, these make a special addition to any tea or coffee table. They are surprisingly easy to prepare.

4 to 5 cups all-purpose white or unbleached flour
2 packets fast-rising dry yeast
⅓ cup instant nonfat dry milk
1 teaspoon salt
1 cup water
⅓ cup honey
¼ cup butter or margarine
1 egg, at room temperature
⅓ cup ground blanched almonds (prepared in blender or food pro-
  cessor)
HONEY GLAZE AND GARNISH
1¼ cups confectioners' sugar
2 tablespoons butter or margarine, softened
¼ cup honey
½ cup unblanched sliced almonds

Combine 1¼ cups flour, the yeast, milk powder and salt in a large mixer bowl. Combine water, ⅓ cup honey and ¼ cup butter in small saucepan. Stirring until honey dissolves, heat mixture to 125° to 130°. With mixer on low speed, beat liquid into dry ingredients until blended. Raise speed to high and beat for 2½ minutes. Add egg, ground almonds and ¼ cup more flour, and beat for 1 minute longer. Stir in 2½ cups flour, or enough more to yield a kneadable dough. Turn dough out on a clean, lightly floured surface. Gradually knead in enough more flour to yield a smooth and manageable but still slightly moist dough. Shape dough into a ball and transfer to a large, well-greased bowl. Grease dough top. Cover bowl with plastic wrap and set aside in a very warm spot (80° to 90°) for 20 minutes. Meanwhile, grease a 17½ × 15-inch (or similar very large) baking sheet.

Punch down dough and knead in bowl for 1 minute. Divide dough in half. Divide first half into two equal portions. With lightly greased hands shape portions into 7-inch logs. Gently stretch out and roll logs back and forth on a clean work surface to form 12-inch-long ropes. Transfer ropes to baking sheet and intertwine to form a smooth, well-shaped twist. Compress twist slightly and tuck ends under to form a neat, slightly tapered loaf. Repeat process with second dough half to form second twist. Cover twists with plastic wrap and set aside in a very warm place (80° to 90°) for 25 minutes. Preheat oven to 350°.

Bake twists for 24 to 29 minutes, or until they are nicely browned and tops sound hollow when tapped. Immediately transfer twists to racks to cool. Meanwhile, prepare honey glaze as follows: Stir together confectioners' sugar, 2 tablespoons butter and ¼ cup honey in a small bowl until smooth and well blended. Set aside. With a kitchen knife, spread glaze over twists while still warm, but not hot. Immediately top glaze with sliced almonds. Serve while still warm. If desired, twists may be made ahead and frozen for later use. In this case, add icing and almonds after twists have been thawed and reheated. Makes 2 medium-sized loaves.

Approximate Preparation Time: 25 minutes
Rising/Baking Time: 1 hour 12 minutes

• Sally's Iced Easter Bread •

Start to Finish: About 1 hour 45 minutes

This is a delectable and festive iced coffee ring enlivened with anise seed. My sister serves it on Easter morning.

3½ to 4 cups all-purpose white or unbleached flour
1 packet fast-rising dry yeast
⅓ cup granulated sugar
⅓ cup instant nonfat dry milk
¾ teaspoon salt
Generous ¼ teaspoon anise seed
¾ cup water
3 tablespoons vegetable oil
2 eggs, at room temperature
½ cup diced mixed candied cherries, pineapple and citrus peel
BUTTERCREAM GLAZE
1 cup confectioners' sugar (sifted if lumpy)
1 tablespoon butter or margarine, softened
1 teaspoon vanilla extract
2½ to 3½ teaspoons hot water, approximately
2 tablespoons diced mixed candied fruit

Stir together 1 cup flour, the yeast, granulated sugar, milk powder, salt and anise seed in a large mixer bowl. Combine water and oil in small saucepan and heat to 125° to 130°. With mixer on low speed, beat liquid into dry ingredients until blended. Raise speed to high and beat for 2½ minutes. Add eggs and ½ cup more flour, and beat on medium speed for 1 minute longer. Stir in about 1½ cups additional flour, or enough to yield a kneadable dough. Working in the bowl or on a clean, lightly floured surface, quickly and vigorously knead in enough more flour to yield a smooth and manageable but still slightly moist dough. Cover with plastic wrap. Set aside in a very warm spot (80° to 90°) for 25 minutes. Meanwhile, grease a 12-inch-diameter pizza pan or a baking sheet at least 12 inches wide and long.
    Punch down dough. A tablespoon or two at a time, gently knead ½ cup candied fruit into dough; distribute as evenly as possible.

294

Divide dough in half with well-greased hands. On a lightly greased work surface alternately roll back and forth and gently stretch out each dough half to a 22-inch, evenly thick rope. Entwine the two ropes and form into a circle on pizza pan. Gently twist ropes together; then join ends and press together into a seam. Adjust dough to make ring as round and evenly shaped as possible. Cover ring with plastic wrap. Set aside in very warm spot (80° to 90°) for 20 minutes. Preheat oven to 375°.

Bake bread for 25 to 30 minutes, or until ring is nicely browned and sounds hollow when tapped on top. Transfer ring to rack with a spatula. Let cool for 10 minutes. Meanwhile, prepare Buttercream Glaze as follows: Stir together confectioners' sugar, butter, vanilla and enough hot water to yield a smooth, fairly thick glaze. While ring is still warm, but not hot, drizzle with glaze. Immediately sprinkle 2 tablespoons diced fruit over glaze. Let bread stand for 5 minutes before serving. Alternatively, let unglazed ring stand until cold; then wrap and freeze until needed. Warm ring and add glaze and diced fruit a few minutes before serving. Makes 1 large ring.

Approximate Preparation Time: 30 minutes   *Rising/Baking Time:* 73 minutes

Iced Cranberry-Currant Coffee Rings

Start to Finish: About 1 hour 50 minutes

These are fragrant, buttery rings filled with a colorful and zesty cranberry mixture and drizzled with an easy confectioners'-sugar glaze. They make a beautiful and delicious Christmas gift.

FRUIT FILLING
Generous ½ cup light brown sugar, packed
⅓ cup granulated sugar
3½ tablespoons cornstarch
⅛ teaspoon ground cinnamon
½ teaspoon freshly grated orange rind
2 cups fresh (or frozen, thawed) cranberries, coarsely chopped
1⅓ cups dried currants
¾ cup golden raisins
DOUGH
5½ to 6 cups all-purpose white or unbleached flour
3 packets fast-rising dry yeast
¾ cup granulated sugar
⅓ cup instant nonfat dry milk
¼ teaspoon freshly grated orange rind
⅓ cup orange juice
Scant 1 cup water
⅔ cup butter or margarine, cut into 5 or 6 pieces
2 eggs, at room temperature
GLAZE
1 cup confectioners' sugar (sifted if lumpy)
¼ teaspoon vanilla
1½ to 2 tablespoons orange juice, approximately

To prepare filling, stir together brown and granulated sugars, cornstarch, cinnamon and ½ teaspoon orange rind in a medium-sized saucepan until well blended. Stir in chopped cranberries, currants and raisins. Bring mixture to a simmer over high heat, stirring. Reduce heat to medium and continue to cook, stirring, 3 to 4 minutes, or until mixture is thickened and clear. Remove from heat and set aside to cool to room temperature.

To prepare dough, stir together 2 cups flour, the yeast, ¾ cup granulated sugar, milk powder and ¼ teaspoon orange rind in a large mixer bowl until well blended; set aside. Combine ⅓ cup orange juice, water and butter in a small saucepan, and heat until butter melts and mixture reaches 125° to 130°. With mixer on low speed, beat liquid into dry ingredients until blended. Raise speed to high and beat for 2 minutes. Add eggs and 1 cup more flour, and beat for 30 seconds longer. Vigorously stir in 2¼ cups more flour, or enough to yield a kneadable dough. Kneading in the bowl or on a clean, lightly floured surface, quickly work in enough more flour to yield a soft but not sticky dough. Transfer dough to a large, lightly greased bowl. Grease dough top and cover bowl with plastic wrap. Set aside in a very warm spot (80° to 90°) for 25 minutes. Meanwhile, lightly grease and set aside two 15 × 11½-inch (or similar) baking sheets.

Punch down dough and divide in half. On a large, lightly floured

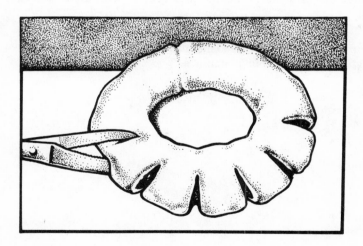

work surface, roll out one half into a 22 × 12-inch rectangle. Thinly spread half the cooled fruit filling over dough to within ½ inch of edge on longer sides and out to edge on shorter sides. Working from a longer side, roll up dough jelly-roll style. Transfer log, seam side down, to baking sheet. Form into a circle; then smooth and press together seam where ends join. Gently stretch dough away from center of each ring to enlarge hole slightly; adjust position to make ring as round and evenly shaped as possible. Using kitchen shears or a sharp knife, produce a scalloped effect by making 1-inch-deep cuts about 2 inches apart into outer edge of ring (as shown in illustration on page 297). Repeat process with second ring. Lightly brush rings with butter. Loosely cover with a damp cloth. Set aside in a very warm spot (80° to 90°) for 20 minutes. Preheat oven to 350°.

Bake rings for 26 minutes. Remove baking sheets to racks. Let rings stand for 5 to 8 minutes before removing from baking sheets to racks. Meanwhile, prepare glaze. (If rings are to be frozen for later use, prepare glaze and add shortly before serving.) Stir together confectioners' sugar, vanilla and enough orange juice to yield a smooth, liquefied glaze. Drizzle over still warm, but not hot, rings. Let rings stand on racks for 5 minutes before serving. Rings may also be frozen for later use and then reheated and glazed, if desired. Makes 2 large rings.

Approximate Preparation Time: 45 minutes
Rising/Baking Time: 1 hour 10 minutes

• *Strawberry Shortcakes* •

Start to Finish: About 1 hour 45 minutes

This makes two large, beautiful shortcakes, each of which yields six or eight servings. Unlike most shortcakes, these can be made and assembled ahead; the "cake" portion absorbs some of the juices from the berries but does not become soggy. Just prior to serving, the cakes are garnished with additional berries and whipped cream.

The following recipe is my slightly modified version of one created by a fine cook and good friend of mine, Chris Tischer.

4½ to 5 cups all-purpose white or unbleached flour
2 packets fast-rising dry yeast
2 tablespoons granulated sugar
2 tablespoons instant nonfat dry milk
1 teaspoon salt
½ cup water
½ cup butter (or margarine), cut into 5 to 6 pieces
4 eggs, at room temperature
BERRIES AND GARNISH
¼ cup water
½ cup granulated sugar
6 cups fresh strawberries, hulled and sliced
2 tablespoons orange-based liqueur (or orange juice)
About 1½ to 1¾ cups lightly sweetened whipped cream for garnish
About 1 cup small whole strawberries for garnish

Stir together 1 cup flour, the yeast, 2 tablespoons sugar, milk powder and salt in a large mixer bowl. Combine water and butter in a small saucepan and heat until butter melts and mixture reaches 125° to 130°. With mixer on low speed, beat liquid mixture into dry ingredients until blended. Raise speed to high and beat for 2½ minutes. Add eggs and ½ cup more flour, and beat for 2 minutes longer. Stir in about 2¼ cups flour, or enough to yield a kneadable dough. Turn dough out onto a lightly floured board and gradually knead in enough more flour to yield a smooth and malleable but not dry dough; kneading should take 6 to 7 minutes. Transfer dough to a clean, well-greased bowl and cover with a damp cloth. Set aside in a

299

very warm place (80° to 90°) for 25 minutes. Meanwhile, thoroughly grease two 8-inch-diameter (or similar) cake pans and set aside.

Punch dough down. With well-greased hands, divide dough in half. Shape each half into a round; flatten slightly and place in greased pans. Gently press dough out almost to pan edges. Cover pans lightly with wax paper and set aside in a very warm spot (80° to 90°) for 25 minutes. Preheat oven to 375°.

Bake shortcakes for 30 to 35 minutes, or until they are golden brown and tops sound hollow when lightly tapped. Remove cakes from pans and transfer to racks to cool. Shortcakes may be cooled and then assembled, or frozen for later use.

Up to several hours before serving time, complete assembly of

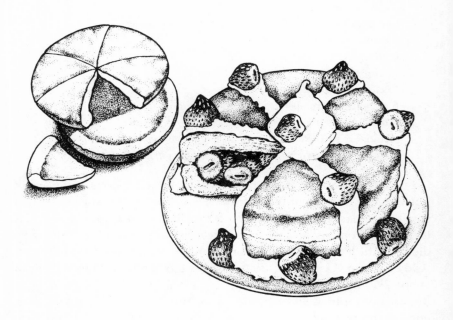

shortcakes as follows: Combine ¼ cup water and ½ cup sugar in a small saucepan over medium heat. Bring to a boil, stirring until sugar dissolves; boil for 1 minute. Remove this simple syrup from heat and cool to room temperature. Stir together 5 cups berries, the simple syrup and liqueur and set aside. Slice cakes in half horizontally. Form a "bowl" of bottom half of each cake by carefully cutting away interior to within ¾ inch of edge and bottom. Form a "lid" of top by cutting away interior to leave a 1-inch-thick shell. Cut lids into six or eight equal wedges. Spoon berry-syrup mixture into shortcake bowls. Top with lids by reassembling wedges over bottom layers. At this point, you may cover shortcakes and set aside for up to 2½ hours. Shortly before serving, garnish as follows: Generously pipe whipped-cream rosettes over center top and along "seams" between wedges. Pipe an additional ring of whipped cream around bases of shortcakes. Garnish shortcakes with whole berries and serve. Makes 2 shortcakes, 6 or 8 servings each.

Approximate Preparation Time: 23 minutes
Rising/Baking Time: 1 hour 21 minutes

• *Raisin and Cherry Stollen* •

Start to Finish: About 2 hours

Stollen is a traditional German yeast bread prepared at Christmas time. It is rich and buttery, laden with fruits and nuts, and dusted with confectioners' sugar. The loaves are always formed into an elongated oval, said to symbolize the Christ child in swaddling clothes.

> 1 cup brown raisins
> 1 cup golden raisins
> 1 cup quartered candied red and green cherries (about 8 ounces)
> ½ cup chopped blanched almonds
> ⅓ cup light rum
> 6¼ to 6¾ cups all-purpose white or unbleached flour
> 3 packets fast-rising dry yeast
> ⅔ cup granulated sugar
> ¼ cup instant nonfat dry milk
> ½ teaspoon salt
> 1 cup water
> 1 cup butter, cut into 11 or 12 pieces
> 2 eggs plus 2 egg yolks, at room temperature
> ¾ teaspoon almond extract
> ¾ teaspoon freshly grated lemon rind
> About 3 to 4 tablespoons sifted confectioners' sugar for sprinkling over
>   finished loaves

Combine all fruit, almonds and rum in a medium-sized, corrosion-proof bowl. Stir until mixture is well moistened with rum; cover bowl with plastic wrap and set aside.

Stir together 1¾ cups flour, the yeast, granulated sugar, milk powder and salt in a large mixer bowl. Heat water and butter in a small saucepan until butter melts and mixture reaches 125° to 130°. With mixer on low speed, beat liquid into dry ingredients until blended. Raise speed to high and beat for 2 minutes. Add eggs and yolks, almond extract, lemon rind and ½ cup more flour, and beat for 2 minutes longer. Vigorously stir in about 3 cups more flour, or enough to yield a kneadable dough. Working in the bowl or on a clean lightly floured surface, slowly yet vigorously knead in enough

302

more flour to yield a very smooth and malleable yet still soft and moist dough; kneading should take about 5 minutes. Form dough into a ball and transfer to a large, well-greased bowl. Cover bowl with a damp cloth. Set aside in a very warm spot (80° to 90°) for 25 minutes. Meanwhile, thoroughly grease a 17½ × 15-inch (or similar very large) baking sheet, or two small baking sheets.

Punch down dough and transfer to a clean, lightly floured surface. Turn out reserved fruit-and-nut mixture into a colander and drain well; pat mixture dry with paper towels. With well-greased hands, slowly and gently knead in reserved fruit-and-nut mixture until evenly distributed throughout dough. Divide dough in half. Roll or press out each half to form a 12 × 10½-inch rectangle. Then fold each rectangle as follows: First fold a longer side in toward center; fold other long side so it overlaps the first about 1 inch. Gently press down seam to hold in place. Transfer loaves to baking sheet with spatula. Taper ends of loaves slightly to form smooth, elongated ovals (as shown in illustration). Cover loaves with slightly damp towels and set aside in a very warm spot (80° to 90°) for 30 minutes. Preheat oven to 350°.

Bake stollen for 42 to 49 minutes, or until well browned and slightly crusty. If loaves begin to brown too rapidly, reduce heat to 325° for last 15 minutes of baking. Transfer stollen to racks and let cool for 10 minutes. Dust loaves with sifted confectioners' sugar, then slice and serve. Stollen may also be frozen and gently reheated in a warm oven, if desired. Makes 2 large loaves.

Approximate Preparation Time: 30 minutes
Rising/Baking Time: 1 hour 40 minutes

• *Swaddling Bread* •

Start to Finish: About 1 hour 20 minutes

Prepare this traditional cherry-filled Christmas pastry using a batch of Refrigerator-Rise All-Purpose Sweet Dough.

Swaddling Bread is shaped much like a latticework Danish pastry. It is perfect for the holiday coffee table and also makes an appealing gift.

> *1 recipe Refrigerator-Rise All-Purpose Sweet Dough (see page 280)*
> CHERRY FILLING
> *½ cup granulated sugar*
> *¼ cup cornstarch*
> *¼ teaspoon ground cinnamon*
> *1 16-ounce can pitted tart red cherries (unsweetened), including juice*
> *2 teaspoons lemon juice*
> *1 tablespoon brandy (or orange juice, if preferred)*
> *1 teaspoon vanilla extract*
> *1 egg beaten with 1 tablespoon water for brushing over pastries*
> CREAM CHEESE GLAZE
> *½ cup confectioners' sugar (sifted if lumpy)*
> *1½ ounces cream cheese, softened (half a 3-ounce package)*
> *¼ teaspoon vanilla extract*
> *¼ teaspoon lemon juice*
> *1 tablespoon warm water, approximately*

Remove dough from refrigerator and let stand, covered, in a warm spot (70° to 80°) while Cherry Filling is prepared. Prepare Cherry Filling as follows: Stir together granulated sugar, cornstarch and cinnamon in a medium-sized saucepan until well blended. Gradually add juice drained from cherries; stir until mixture is smooth. Stirring constantly, bring mixture to a boil over medium-high heat and simmer for 3 to 4 minutes, or until thickened and clear. Remove from heat and stir in cherries, 2 teaspoons lemon juice, brandy and 1 teaspoon vanilla. Set aside to cool to room temperature.

Punch down dough; knead in bowl for 1 minute. With lightly greased hands, divide dough in half. One at a time, on a clean, lightly-floured surface, roll or press each half of dough out to a 15 × 12-inch rectangle. Transfer dough rectangles to one well-greased 17½ × 11-inch baking sheet or two 15½ × 10½-inch baking sheets. (Dough will overlap baking-sheet sides at this point.)

Complete each pastry by cutting 3½-inch slashes (from the edge of the pastry toward the center) at 1-inch intervals all the way around each rectangle. Spread half of cherry filling lengthwise down center of each rectangle to within ¾ inch of cuts. Alternating from side to side, lap cut strips over filling to form an elongated latticework oval (see illustration); tuck end strips neatly under side strips. Cover pastries lightly with plastic wrap. Set aside in a very warm place (80° to 90°) for 25 minutes. Preheat oven to 350°.

Carefully brush pastry tops and sides with egg-water mixture, using a pastry brush or paper towel. Bake pastries for 25 to 30 minutes, or until tops are nicely browned and sound hollow when tapped. Immediately remove pastries from pans and carefully transfer to racks to cool. Meanwhile, prepare Cream Cheese Glaze as follows: Stir together confectioners' sugar, cream cheese, ¼ teaspoon

Forming Swaddling Bread

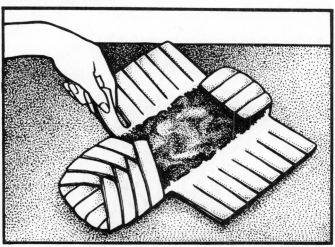

vanilla and ¼ teaspoon lemon juice. Gradually stir in enough warm water to yield a smooth, fairly thick glaze. Drizzle glaze over pastries while still warm, but not hot. Allow glaze to set for 2 to 3 minutes before serving pastries. Pastries are best served warm. They may be frozen and gently reheated for later use, if desired. In this case, add glaze just before serving. Makes 2 medium-sized pastries.

Approximate Preparation Time: 25 minutes   *Rising/Baking Time:* 52 minutes

NOTE: Time does not include preparation of basic make-ahead dough. See Refrigerator-Rise All-Purpose Sweet Dough for total time required.

• *Pineapple "Jelly Rolls"* •

Start to Finish: About 2 hours

Served with a dollop of whipped cream, these make a luscious and festive dessert. The pineapple filling and the tender dough complement one another perfectly.

5¼ to 5½ cups all-purpose white or unbleached flour
2 packets fast-rising dry yeast
⅔ cup light brown sugar, packed
⅓ cup wheat germ
Generous ¼ teaspoon ground mace
½ cup pineapple juice (drained from crushed pineapple, see below)
½ cup water
½ cup vegetable oil
2 eggs, at room temperature
PINEAPPLE FILLING
½ cup granulated sugar
2½ tablespoons cornstarch
⅔ cup orange juice
1-pound, 4-ounce can crushed pineapple, well drained (reserve juice)
GLAZE AND GARNISH
¾ cup confectioners' sugar (sifted if lumpy)
1 tablespoon butter or margarine, softened
¼ teaspoon vanilla extract
2½ to 3½ teaspoons orange juice
2 to 3 tablespoons diced candied pineapple or dried pineapple rings
   (optional)

Stir together 1¼ cups flour, the yeast, brown sugar, wheat germ and mace in a large mixer bowl. Heat pineapple juice, water and oil in a small saucepan to 125° to 130°. With mixer on low speed, beat liquid into dry ingredients until blended. Raise speed to high and beat for 2½ minutes. Add eggs and beat 30 seconds longer. Vigorously stir in 3 cups more flour, or enough to yield a kneadable dough. Working in the bowl or on a clean, lightly floured surface, quickly and vigorously knead in enough more flour to yield a smooth, fairly stiff yet not dry dough. Form dough into a ball and transfer to a large, well-greased bowl. Cover bowl with plastic wrap. Set aside in a very warm spot (80° to 90°) for 20 minutes.

Meanwhile, prepare Pineapple Filling as follows: Stir granulated sugar and cornstarch together in a medium-sized saucepan until thoroughly blended. Stir in ⅔ cup orange juice and crushed pineapple. Bring mixture to a boil over medium heat, stirring. Reduce heat and simmer, stirring, for 1½ to 2 minutes, or until mixture is thickened and almost clear. Remove from heat and set aside; cool to lukewarm. Grease a 17½ × 15-inch (or similar very large) baking sheet.

Punch down dough and divide in half. On a lightly floured surface, roll out each half to form a 14 × 11-inch rectangle. Spread half the Pineapple Filling over each rectangle. Working from a longer side, roll up jelly-roll style. Tuck ends in and lay rolls seam side down on baking sheet. Cover rolls with plastic wrap and set aside in a very warm spot (80° to 90°) for 20 minutes. Preheat oven to 375°.

Remove plastic wrap and place pastries in oven; immediately reduce thermostat to 350°. Bake for 32 to 37 minutes, or until tops are tinged with brown and springy to the touch. Transfer rolls from oven to racks and let cool for 12 to 15 minutes. Meanwhile, prepare glaze as follows: Stir together confectioners' sugar, softened butter, vanilla and 2 teaspoons orange juice until well blended. Gradually add enough more orange juice to yield a fairly stiff yet spreadable glaze. Spread glaze evenly over tops of pastries with a knife and immediately garnish with pineapple, if desired. Pineapple "Jelly Rolls" are best served warm from the oven. However, they may be frozen, reheated in a warm oven and then glazed, if desired. Makes 2 large pastries.

Approximate Preparation Time: 45 minutes
Rising/Baking Time: 1 hour 15 minutes

◆ King's Crown Coffee Ring ◆

Start to Finish: About 2 hours

This glazed and nut-studded coffee cake looks stunning and tastes even better than it looks. Either black walnuts or pecans may be used in the recipe; each variety of nut lends its own distinctively different and delicious appeal.

> 3¾ to 4¼ cups all-purpose white or unbleached flour
> 2 packets fast-rising dry yeast
> ¼ cup light brown sugar, packed
> ¼ cup instant nonfat dry milk
> ½ teaspoon salt
> 1 cup water
> ¼ cup vegetable oil
> 1 egg, at room temperature
> FILLING AND GLAZE
> 1 cup coarsely chopped black walnuts or pecans
> ½ cup dark corn syrup
> ⅓ cup light brown sugar, packed
> ½ teaspoon vanilla
> 2 tablespoons butter or margarine, softened
> 2 tablespoons water

Stir together 1 cup flour, the yeast, ¼ cup brown sugar, milk powder and salt in a large mixer bowl. Heat water and oil in a small saucepan until mixture reaches 125° to 130°. With mixer on low speed, beat liquid into dry ingredients until blended. Raise speed to high and beat for 2½ minutes. Add egg and beat 30 seconds longer. With a large spoon, vigorously beat in about 2 cups more flour, or enough to yield a kneadable dough. Working in the bowl, quickly and vigorously knead in enough more flour to yield a very smooth and malleable dough. Cover bowl with a damp cloth. Set aside in a very warm spot (80° to 90°) for 25 minutes. Meanwhile, thoroughly grease a 12-cup Bundt pan. Sprinkle interior with ¼ cup nut pieces. Stir together syrup, ⅓ cup brown sugar and vanilla in a small bowl.

Punch dough down. With well-greased hands and on a very lightly floured work surface, roll or press dough into an evenly thick

16 × 12-inch rectangle. Spread butter, then all but ¼ cup of the syrup-sugar mixture, and the remaining nuts over surface of rectangle. (Reserve ¼ cup syrup-sugar mixture for glaze.) Working from a longer side, tightly roll up dough jelly-roll style. Gently but firmly stretch out dough to produce an evenly thick log about 24 inches long. Place log seam side up in Bundt pan, pressing and smoothing ends together to form unbroken ring. Cover pan with a damp cloth. Set pan aside in a very warm spot (80° to 90°) for 20 minutes. Preheat oven to 350°.

Bake coffee cake for 42 to 47 minutes, or until lightly browned on top and slightly springy to the touch. Meanwhile, prepare glaze by combining reserved ¼ cup syrup-sugar mixture with 2 tablespoons water. Bring to a boil in a small saucepan over medium heat. Stirring occasionally, boil for 2 minutes. Set aside to cool.

Remove pan from oven and let stand on rack for 8 to 10 minutes. Carefully run a knife around pan edge to loosen ring. Invert pan over a serving plate and slide ring out (so that the bottom now becomes the top of finished coffee cake). While coffee cake is still warm, drizzle syrup–brown sugar glaze over top. Serve coffee cake immediately or freeze for later use. Makes 1 very large coffee ring.

Approximate Preparation Time: 30 minutes
Rising/Baking Time: 1 hour 30 minutes

Austrian Poppy Seed
◆ Swirled Rings ◆

Start to Finish: About 2 hours

Cakes and breads filled with poppy seeds are extremely popular throughout Europe, and the following very dramatic swirled bread is one such creation from Austria. Traditionally, decorative slashes are made in the top of the finished ring to let the dark filling peek through. When the bread is sliced into servings, the beautiful spiral pattern inside is also revealed.

Since it may be inconvenient or expensive to purchase the large quantity of poppy seeds required for this ring, and because not all Americans are accustomed to the flavor, an alternate raisin filling is suggested as well. This variation is equally delicious and festive looking, though admittedly not quite as authentic.

4½ to 5 cups all-purpose white or unbleached flour
2 packets fast-rising dry yeast
½ cup granulated sugar
⅓ cup instant nonfat dry milk
¾ cup water (125° to 130°)
3 eggs, at room temperature
½ cup butter, at room temperature
Grated rind of half a large, well-washed lemon
FILLING
1 cup poppy seeds
¼ cup granulated sugar
3 tablespoons brown raisins
Grated rind of half a large lemon
½ cup evaporated milk
¼ teaspoon ground cinnamon
1 egg, lightly beaten
2 tablespoons rum

1 egg beaten with 1 tablespoon water for brushing over rings

GLAZE
⅔ cup confectioners' sugar (sifted if lumpy)
1½ to 2 tablespoons lemon juice, approximately

311

Stir together 1 cup flour, the yeast, ½ cup granulated sugar and milk powder in a large mixer bowl. With mixer on low speed, beat water into dry ingredients until blended. Raise speed to high and beat for 2½ minutes. Add eggs, butter and lemon rind, and beat for 1 minute longer. Vigorously stir in about 2 cups more flour, or enough to yield a kneadable dough. Working in the bowl, slowly yet vigorously knead in enough more flour to yield a very smooth and malleable dough; kneading should take about 5 minutes. Cover bowl with a damp cloth. Set aside in a very warm spot (80° to 90°) for 20 minutes.

Meanwhile, prepare filling as follows: Combine poppy seeds and ¼ cup granulated sugar in blender container. Blend on medium speed for 1½ to 2 minutes, or until poppy seeds are thoroughly ground; if necessary, stop blender several times and stir to redistribute contents. Put ground poppy seeds in a small saucepan. Combine all remaining filling ingredients, except rum, in blender container. Blend on medium speed for 1 minute, or until completely smooth. Add liquid mixture to saucepan and stir to blend. Bring mixture to a simmer over medium heat, stirring. Simmer for 3 to 4 minutes, or until filling is well blended and thick. Remove from heat and stir in rum. Set aside to cool to lukewarm. Thoroughly grease two 15 × 11½-inch (or similar) baking sheets or one 17½ × 15-inch sheet.

Punch dough down and divide in half. With lightly greased hands, press or roll one half out on a lightly floured work surface to form an evenly thick 15 × 10-inch rectangle. Spread half the filling over dough surface. Working from a longer side, tightly roll up jelly-roll style. Gently but firmly, stretch out dough to form an evenly thick, 18-inch log. Transfer log to baking sheet. Form a ring by pressing and smoothing ends neatly together. Repeat process with second half of dough. Cover rings with a damp cloth. Set pans aside in a very warm spot (80° to 90°) for 30 minutes. Preheat oven to 350°.

Brush tops and sides of rings with egg-water mixture. Cut 2-inch-long vents crosswise at 2½-inch intervals in top of rings; be sure cuts are deep enough so that filling shows through. Bake rings for 35 to 40 minutes, or until golden brown on top and slightly springy to the touch. Meanwhile, prepare glaze by stirring together confectioners' sugar and 1 tablespoon lemon juice. Add enough more juice to yield a smooth, very thin glaze. Transfer rings to racks and let stand 5 minutes. Brush a thin layer of glaze over rings. Serve rings immediately or freeze for later use. Makes 2 medium-sized rings.

VARIATION: Raisin Filling—Omit poppy seeds and increase raisins to 1¼ cups. Add 1 teaspoon grated orange rind to filling. Combine granulated sugar, raisins, lemon and orange rind and all remaining filling ingredients, except rum, in blender container. Blend on medium speed until mixture is pureed. Transfer puree to saucepan and proceed as for basic recipe.

Approximate Preparation Time: 40 minutes
Rising/Baking Time: 1 hour 27 minutes

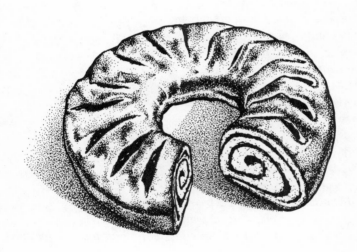

Alsatian Holiday Prune and Fig Log (Oegi)

Start to Finish: About 2 hours (plus overnight maceration of filling)

This handsome fruit-filled pastry is traditionally served in Alsace during Christmas.

FILLING
1¾ *cups finely chopped, pitted dried prunes*
1 *cup finely chopped dried figs*
1 *cup golden raisins*
½ *cup finely chopped walnuts*
¼ *teaspoon ground cinnamon*
¼ *teaspoon freshly grated orange rind*
⅓ *cup granulated sugar*
⅔ *cup boiling water*
⅓ *cup brandy*
DOUGH
4 to 4¼ *cups all-purpose white or unbleached flour*
2 *packets fast-rising dry yeast*
½ *teaspoon salt*
⅓ *cup granulated sugar*
¼ *cup instant nonfat dry milk*
1 *cup water*
⅓ *cup butter, cut into 4 or 5 pieces*
1 *egg plus 1 egg yolk, at room temperature*
1 *egg yolk beaten with 1 tablespoon water for brushing over pastries*
GLAZE
¾ *cup confectioners' sugar (sifted if lumpy)*
⅛ *teaspoon vanilla*
1 *tablespoon water, approximately*

To prepare filling, combine all dried fruits, nuts, cinnamon, orange rind and granulated sugar in a medium-sized, corrosion-proof bowl. Add boiling water, stirring well. Set mixture aside for 10 minutes. Add brandy and stir again. Cover bowl with plastic wrap. Set

314

aside at room temperature for at least 12 hours and up to 24 hours. Stir filling several times during maceration period.

To prepare dough, stir together 1 cup flour, the yeast, salt, granulated sugar and milk powder in a large mixer bowl. Heat water and butter in a small saucepan until mixture reaches 125° to 130°. With mixer on low speed, beat liquid into dry ingredients until blended. Raise speed to high and beat for 2½ minutes. Add egg and yolk, and beat for 30 seconds longer. Vigorously stir in about 2 cups more flour, or enough to yield a kneadable dough. Working in the bowl or on a clean, lightly floured surface, slowly yet vigorously knead in enough more flour to yield a very smooth and malleable dough; kneading should take about 5 minutes. Cover bowl with a damp cloth. Set aside in a very warm spot (80° to 90°) for 20 minutes. Meanwhile, thoroughly grease a 17½ × 15-inch (or similar very large) baking sheet, or two smaller baking sheets.

Punch dough down and divide in half. With well-greased hands

and on a clean, lightly greased work surface, slowly and gently roll or press one half of dough out into a thin 14 × 11-inch rectangle. (Be careful not to tear dough.) Spread half the fruit filling mixture over dough surface. Working from a longer side, tightly roll up dough jelly-roll style. Gently but firmly stretch out dough slightly to produce an evenly thick 15-inch-long log. Seam side down, transfer log to baking sheet. Repeat process with second half of dough. Cover logs with a damp cloth. Place pan in a very warm spot (80° to 90°) for 25 minutes. Preheat oven to 350°.

Neatly brush tops and sides of logs with egg yolk-water mixture; be careful not to let mixture drip onto baking sheet. Bake logs for 28 to 33 minutes, or until a rich golden brown. Remove pan to rack and let logs cool for 10 minutes. Meanwhile, prepare glaze by stirring together confectioners' sugar, vanilla and enough water to make a smooth, slightly thick glaze. Drizzle glaze back and forth across logs to form a simple diagonal pattern (as shown in illustration on page 315). Serve logs warm. Logs may also be frozen for later use. In this case, add glaze after thawing and reheating. Makes 2 large pastries.

Approximate Preparation Time: 40 minutes
Rising/Baking Time: 1 hour 17 minutes

German Cheese and Apple Tart
• (Fränkischer Käsekuchen) •

Start to Finish: About 2 hours

An impressive-looking, not-too-sweet dessert with a light and creamy cheesecakelike filling. This is a German regional specialty traditionally presented at the afternoon coffee table.

2¾ to 3 cups all-purpose white or unbleached flour
1 packet fast-rising dry yeast
⅓ cup granulated sugar
¼ cup instant nonfat dry milk
¼ teaspoon salt
¾ cup water
½ cup butter or margarine, cut into 5 to 6 pieces
1 teaspoon freshly grated lemon rind
FILLING
2 cups dry-curd cottage cheese
⅓ cup buttermilk
3 eggs
½ cup granulated sugar
1 teaspoon vanilla extract
½ teaspoon freshly grated lemon rind
3 large, cooking apples, peeled, cored and cut into ¼-inch-thick slices
1½ teaspoons lemon juice

Stir together 1 cup flour, the yeast, ⅓ cup sugar, milk powder and salt in a large mixer bowl. Combine water, butter and 1 teaspoon lemon rind in a small saucepan and heat until butter melts and mixture reaches 125° to 130°. With mixer on low speed, beat liquid into dry ingredients until blended. Raise mixer speed to high and beat for 2½ minutes. Stir in 1½ cups more flour to make a soft dough. Turn dough out onto a lightly floured board and quickly and vigorously knead in enough more flour to yield a smooth and malleable but still moist dough. Transfer dough to a clean, well-greased bowl and cover with a damp cloth. Set aside in a very warm spot (80° to 90°) for 20 minutes. Meanwhile, lightly grease a 10- to 11½-inch diameter

317

springform pan and set aside. Prepare filling by combining all ingredients except apples and lemon juice in a blender container. Whirl mixture on high speed for 1½ to 2 minutes, or until completely smooth and well blended; if necessary, stop motor several times to scrape down sides of container and redistribute contents with rubber spatula. Set aside. Toss apple slices with lemon juice and set aside. Preheat oven to 375°.

Punch down dough. Put in springform pan, evenly pressing dough out to edges and 1¾ inches up sides to form a smooth bottom "crust" and rim. Pour blended filling mixture into dough crust. Beginning at outer edge of pan, neatly lay apple slices, just barely touching one another, in concentric circles on filling. (The slices will stay afloat and form a decorative pattern in the finished tart.)

Immediately transfer tart to oven and bake for 1 hour and 15 to 18 minutes, or until apples are nicely browned and center of filling appears set when pan is jiggled slightly. Transfer pan to rack and let cool thoroughly. Refrigerate tart at least 2 hours and preferably overnight before serving. Best served slightly chilled. Makes 1 large tart.

Approximate Preparation Time: 30 minutes
Rising/Baking Time: 1 hour 36 minutes

NOTE: If dry-curd cottage cheese is unavailable, substitute regular lowfat cottage cheese. Remove excess liquid by placing cottage cheese in a colander and pressing it down with the bottom of a glass until most of the moisture is squeezed out. Add 2 teaspoons flour to blender along with cottage cheese.

• *Scandinavian Coffee Rings* •

Start to Finish: About 1 hour 20 minutes

Prepare Refrigerator-Rise All-Purpose Sweet Dough as directed on page 280. Refrigerate for 3 to 36 hours. Then complete Scandinavian Coffee Rings as directed below.

These pretty, fruit-filled rings are enlivened with cardamom, a very popular spice in Scandinavian baked goods.

1 recipe Refrigerator-Rise All-Purpose Sweet Dough
FILLING
1 cup finely chopped dried apricots
1 cup golden raisins
1 cup finely chopped pitted dates
Generous ¼ teaspoon ground cardamom
3 tablespoons honey
⅓ cup light brown sugar, packed
½ cup chopped walnuts
GLAZE AND GARNISH
1 cup confectioners' sugar (sifted if lumpy)
⅛ teaspoon ground cardamom
4 to 5 teaspoons orange juice, approximately
1 tablespoon finely chopped dried apricots for garnish
1 tablespoon finely chopped walnuts for garnish

Remove dough from refrigerator and let stand, covered, in a warm spot (70° to 80°) for 15 minutes. Meanwhile, prepare filling as follows: Stir together fruit, ¼ teaspoon cardamom and honey until well blended. Ready brown sugar and walnuts and set aside. Generously grease a 17½ × 15-inch (or similar very large) baking sheet, or two smaller baking sheets.

Punch down dough and divide in half. On a large, lightly floured work surface, roll out one half to an 18 × 9-inch rectangle. Spread half the fruit filling over dough. Sprinkle fruit filling with half the brown sugar and walnuts. Working from a longer side, roll up dough jelly-roll style. Transfer log, seam side down, to baking sheet. Form into a circle; then smooth and press together seam where ends join. Gently stretch dough away from center of ring to enlarge hole

319

slightly; adjust position to make ring as round and evenly shaped as possible. Using kitchen shears or a sharp knife, make 1¾-inch-deep cuts about 1½ inches apart into outer edge of ring. Then turn slices on an angle to expose interior (as shown in illustration). Repeat process to form second ring. Loosely cover rings with a damp cloth. Set aside in a very warm spot (80° to 90°) for 25 minutes. Preheat oven to 350°.

Bake rings for 23 to 28 minutes. Transfer baking sheet to racks. Let stand for 5 to 8 minutes, then transfer rings from baking sheet to racks. Meanwhile, prepare glaze. (If rings are to be frozen for later use, prepare glaze and add shortly before serving.) Stir together confectioners' sugar, ⅛ teaspoon cardamom and enough orange juice to yield a smooth, liquefied glaze. With a kitchen knife, smooth glaze over warm, but not hot, rings. Immediately sprinkle with a tablespoon each of chopped dried apricots and walnuts. Let glazed rings stand on racks for 5 minutes before serving. If desired, rings may be frozen (without glaze) and then reheated, glazed and garnished. Makes 2 medium-sized rings.

Approximate Preparation Time: 25 minutes   *Rising/Baking Time:* 65 minutes

NOTE: Time does not include preparation of basic make-ahead dough. See Refrigerator-Rise All-Purpose Sweet Dough for total time required.

Preparing Scandinavian Coffee Rings